B   215697

Marzo, Clay.

Just add water

AUG 1 0 2015

Just Add Water

JUST
ADD
WATER

A Surfing Savant's Journey with Asperger's

CLAY MARZO

AND ROBERT YEHLING

HOUGHTON MIFFLIN HARCOURT
BOSTON   NEW YORK   2015

Copyright © 2015 by Clay Marzo and Robert Yehling

For information about permission to reproduce selections
from this book, write to Permissions, Houghton Mifflin
Harcourt Publishing Company, 215 Park Avenue South,
New York, New York 10003.

www.hmhco.com

Library of Congress Cataloging-in-Publication Data
Marzo, Clay.
Just add water : a surfing savant's journey with Asperger's /
Clay Marzo, Robert Yehling.
pages cm
ISBN 978-0-544-25621-7 (hardback) — ISBN 978-0-544-25317-9 (ebook)
1. Marzo, Clay. 2. Surfers — United States — Biography. 3. Asperger's
syndrome — Patients — Biography. I. Yehling, Robert. II. Title.
GV838.M375A3 2015
797.3'2092 — dc23
[B]
2014034432

Book design by Patrick Barry

Printed in the United States of America
DOC 10 9 8 7 6 5 4 3 2 1

To my family, and to everyone who struggles when told they cannot do something. Get out there and do it — and make your world and ours greater.

CONTENTS

Just Add Water

1

In the Pocket

There's a set! Look at the set coming! Look at the first one barreling . . . here comes one — look at this one, dude! See how you go underground when you're in there, then it throws you into the shallow? Sometimes there's a little left that goes into the bay, a re-form that happens when it gets really big — but you'd rather surf somewhere else . . . you don't want to surf out here when it's bigger than five or six feet. It gets too gnarly, closes out, and throws you on that shallow reef. This is a small wave spot. It's the steepest small wave around. It's best when it's glassy, but the wind's coming from a weird direction . . . see how the wave is balling up?

That was a big set we saw earlier, so much bigger than anything else . . . that was the north influence. The south influence pushes into the total wave shape. It breaks from two directions here, sometimes at the same time. It gives me a thrill, this kind of wave.

The pristine waters off Maui's west coast convey majesty and presence befitting the ancient Polynesian Sport of Kings. They are about to be stirred by a tall, angular magician with a swimmer's build and moves that very few on earth can match. Every time Clay Marzo enters the Pacific — nearly every sunlit hour of every day he's not traveling, if the waves cooperate — he paddles out to commingle with his soul, which seems to breathe with gills. Waves come to him as if silently summoned, enabling him to turn around, drop in, and unleash rides so dynamic, outrageous, daring, and graceful that you're left grasping for superlatives. He speeds through waves like a dolphin, explodes off the top like an attacking leopard, inverts and bends into impossible positions like an Olympic gymnast . . . and always seems to land on his feet. Like a cat.

Such is the case on a warm morning charged with sea spray and crowded surf spots, which can mean only one thing: the waves are pounding. The season's first major northwest swell has arrived, bringing waves up to forty feet at infamous Pe'ahi, or Jaws, where tow-in surfers risk their lives as they tackle the monsters calved by a disturbance in the Aleutian Islands, far to the north. Meanwhile, at a break called Windmills, Clay Marzo sits with a videographer, fifteen miles and a world away from the nineteenth-century colonial seaside mystique of Lahaina and the luxury resorts on Kaanapali Beach. To the southeast, Haleakala towers two miles above the island, a conic crown and dormant volcano where Jimi Hendrix once played live, where silence surpassed only by space exists.

Silence. Nothing suits Clay better. He is entirely silent as he faces west, his hands smacking the steering wheel, his body twitching. He surveys the horizon, then the lineup, where waves peel in both directions from their breaking point. His mind works out the wave angles, where they break, how they break, and how the current and ever-present trade winds impact them. When wave faces approach fifteen feet, as they do at Windmills on this day, good choices can become life-saving choices. His focus is laserlike, absolute. Nothing can or will interrupt his concentration.

After studying the waves for forty-five minutes, Clay grabs his board and moves toward the ocean. He walks away from his life on land, a mighty and never-ending struggle between the way his brain is wired and the noise, crowds, social interactions, expectations, anxieties, and facial expressions the rest of us use to get by. He negotiates the everyday world clumsily, always a step off or to the side, it seems. If he's connected to it at all, which is often not the case. If the activity of the moment isn't about surfing, eating, basketball, music, or his girlfriend, Jade Barton, he's oblivious. Uncomfortable.

There's nothing uncomfortable about the way he approaches the ocean. His coordination while walking rocks and steep trails is superior, rhythmic, and smoother than the way most people amble down the road. His eyes scan from side to side, watching the action of every wave, calculating where to paddle out and position himself. He throws himself into the frothing shorebreak, surfaces, shakes his head a few times, yells out with excitement (or is it the relief of no longer being on land?), and sets off in the direction of the neighboring island of Lanai with paddle strokes that his videographer, Adam Klevin, calls "the best I've ever seen. He would win every paddle battle there is. Hands down."

Minutes later, a set of twelve- to fifteen-foot behemoths approaches. Clay paddles into position. He notices a bump in the wave, a subtle shift beyond the sensory range of most humans. He wheels his board around and strokes to a point he's already predetermined and anticipated through knowledge and intuition. His deep, powerful strokes are those of a champion swimmer. His instincts are beyond that. When a wave emerges and jacks up to its full two-story height, Clay sits in perfect position. With a GoPro camera mounted on the back of his board, he paddles hard, easily catches the wave, and looks down the line, his right foot forward, the direction in which he faces the wave.

Let the show begin. Clay connects in a way one would imagine Mozart diving into the wellspring of his latest symphony, Beethoven hugging the floor with his deaf ear to feel the vibration of his Fifth Symphony, or Monet immersing himself in French light. He races down the wave face as it peels behind him, seemingly at one with it. Clay leans like a motorcycle street racer into a deep bottom turn and propels himself up the face, then slots himself inside the pocket of the wave.

Just like that, he's *gone*. Disappeared. Out of view. Spectators on the rocky beach or in their cars wonder the same thing: *is he coming out?*

Seconds later he emerges, arms raised high, GoPro still in his mouth, the shot of him scorching a nasty Windmills barrel certain to be played over and over on his flat-screen later in the day. And soon, on video throughout the world. Whenever Clay Marzo hits it big, the beach buzzes and the world finds out soon enough. "Kid's off the charts," says Les Potts, a longboard surfing legend who's produced and witnessed plenty of greatness in his fifty years of surfing. "How'd he find that tube?"

This is where rides usually end, where most surfers pull out and paddle into position for another wave while story-building their ride to everyone else in the lineup.

Clay is warming up for round two. His fans on the beach wonder, *what the hell is he going to do next?* They cannot guess, but they know they may see something no other surfer in the world will attempt, let alone execute successfully. Anything is possible.

Clay whips to the bottom of the wave to gain speed and propulsion, then smacks it off the top, getting a few feet of air before landing in the wave. He throws the tail of his board sideways, like a skateboarder in a half-pipe, leaving a rooster tail of displaced water, and descends onto the diminishing lip *backwards.*

Now it's time for the Merlin moment, when a wizard's instincts take over. About to be swallowed by the massive turbulence, and while lying back almost in a sleeping position, he whips the tail of the board back around. With cat-quick moves and the flexibility of a long-standing yogi, he jerks to his feet, his reverse throw-tail complete, and snaps a few more moves — *Bam! Bam! Bam!* He keeps standing until his board sinks, slowly taking him down. Call it surfing's version of the denouement, when the hero rides into the sunset.

Clay shakes his curly dark blond hair, stretches out on his board, pumps his fist in the air, and looks to the shoreline to see if his accomplices are watching. "He's putting on the show for you," his friend Johnny says over and over again. Clay rubs his hands together a dozen times, jazzed and ecstatic beyond measure, and turns toward the horizon. A few minutes later, he wheels the board into a rising peak, his last brilliant ride already deep in his prodigious cellular memory banks. He throws down a few more moves that leave people on the beach wondering: *have I ever seen that before?*

Therein lies a clue about Clay's mastery, his gift, the difference between him and his friends — many of whom, like him, are professional surfers. He tunes in to the present moment, pours forth his entire spirit and knowledge, and blocks out everything — thoughts, issues, what he ate, where he may have misplaced his car keys or wallet, his next magazine photo shoot, friends on the bluff. His last amazing ride. In this stressed-out world, he operates with a frame of mind that treats every moment like it's both the first and the last.

Isn't that what the millions who take mindfulness, yoga, or meditation classes seek?

"Clay lives in the moment," his behavioral specialist, Carolyn Jackson, says. "Isn't that what most of us want to do? Most people, when they watch Clay, they want to be that deep down inside. They want to be the one that says 'Get out of my face.' They want to be the one to flip off some social convention that they cannot stand, but they do [it] anyway. They want to excel at one particular thing, rather than spreading themselves out amongst a bunch of things. Well, that's exactly who Clay is."

Whenever anyone sees a great surfer in action — or any great athlete with superior technical skills combined with the grace of Baryshnikov — a few questions may pop to mind: How can that person maintain such control and poise? How does he or she develop the courage to ride large, snarling swells that may have originated from typhoons or winter storms thousands of miles away? How can that person look so masterful in everything from sloppy two-foot shorebreak to twenty-foot giants that could crush and kill in one fell swoop (and have)?

That perception increases noticeably when onlookers watch this twenty-six-year-old son of lifelong surfers Gino and Jill Marzo. Eyes burst open like cartoon characters. Heads shake, followed by "Holy shit!" or "What the f—?" and other expletives, all compliments of the highest order. Wave warriors try to figure out how he surfs with the nimbleness of a cheetah, the power of a bull, the balance of a gymnast, the acrobatic prowess of a Cirque du Soleil star, the aerial daring of Shaun White and Tony Hawk, the staying power of ultramarathon legend Scott Jurek, and the inventiveness of . . . well, that's where the comparisons end. The prevailing global opinion was best summed up by a few words in the 2008 Quiksilver documentary *Just Add Water,* which introduced the world at large to Clay's riveting story:

"Clay surfs amazing," Tom Curren, the sport's dominant figure in the 1980s, said. "I don't know how he does what he does."

The greatest competitive surfer of them all, eleven-time world titlist Kelly Slater, minces no words either. "There's probably no one in the world who does the stuff he does. If he's not sleeping, he's getting barreled. When I first saw him surf, I'm like, 'He knows things I don't know. He knows things the guys I surf with don't know.'"

Maybe that's why the surfing version of *Young Guns II*, the first movie in which Clay appeared, at age fifteen, drew millions of viewers. Or why Clay won "Best Maneuver" in the prestigious Surfer Poll Movie Awards at age seventeen. Maybe that's why *Just Add Water*, the documentary, sold 500,000 copies and was seen by millions. Through these films, the unbelievable could be carried into the realm of the believable via visual documentation. *See it to believe it.*

Clay is a hero to millions of surfers and others of his generation who appreciate great wave riding and pushing the limits of athletic potential. Those twice his age, or even older, revere him almost equally. "Clay Marzo? Mate, he's in another world," says professional surfing's first world champion, Peter Townend, now in his early sixties.

New questions emerge for anyone watching Clay work his artistry on waves. Even people who have surfed for fifty years, like Potts and Townend, scratch their heads and ask, *Did I just see that?* Some observers even resort to the absurd: Is he part dolphin? Are his neurons hard-wired to the primordial depths of his brain stem, linking him somehow to the gilled creatures that came ashore, grew lungs, and became amphibians? Does he glue his feet to the board? Do his instincts enable him to anticipate what's coming long before the wave fully forms? Is he so deeply immersed in his relationship with the ocean that he and the waves sense each other, breathe through each other, commingle for precious moments, and enjoy a level of being neither can experience on land?

The fascination with Clay Marzo stretches worldwide, beyond surfing, even beyond sports. He's a hero to an entirely different group of people whose life challenges are tougher than choosing where to paddle out the next day.

Soul surfer . . . the term is not often associated with youth. Surfers find a thousand different ways to describe the soul-surfing experience, an inner and outer life that revolves around the next dawn patrol, the next road junket to a "secret spot," the next swell. Some descriptions stand forever through the sport's most cherished movies: *The Endless Summer. Five Summer Stories. Free Ride. Step into Liquid. Thicker Than Water. Big Wednesday. Riding Giants.* Other monikers describe this communion: Free surfing. Expression sessions. Dawn patrols. Pure stoke. Not only is surfing a graceful sport, but it also possesses a sweet language filled with captivating imagery.

Since the late 1970s, when professional surfing began, thousands of riders Clay's age and younger have scanned the sea through lenses a little less rose-colored. They've traveled the world in search not of the perfect wave, like Robert August and Mike Hynson did in the classic 1965 film *The Endless Summer,* but for contest winnings, career opportunities, large endorsement contracts, and world championships. For most of them, soul-surfing terminology often falls by the wayside. You rarely hear of someone under thirty described as a soul surfer, even though most of his or her time is spent surfing for the pure pleasure and stoke of riding waves. "Most kids in Clay's age group have already gone through clinics with publicists, so they know just what to say to the media — and they say the same thing," says Jamie Tierney, a good friend of Clay's and the director of the *Just Add Water* documentary. "That's one thing that makes Clay so special: he doesn't fit into anyone's mold. It's refreshing."

Jill Marzo describes her son's connection to the sea — how he dials himself into its rhythm, how he watches surf videos over and over, "and over and over," she says, her rolling eyes speaking of the obsession she's dealt with his entire life. When she finishes, one wonders if Clay Marzo is one of the purest soul surfers on earth. "He lives very much in the present, that place where most of us want to be," she says. "When the ocean's going off and he's not in it, he becomes uncomfortable in his skin. He has to feel it. He's living, keeping it simple, and everyone's trying to figure him out. Clay does not live in his ego. Clay is pure, raw."

Her words reveal a deeper, fundamental reason why Clay will spend eight to ten hours in the ocean without food or water, risking dehydration and exhaustion. Her words allude to why he teeters at the intersection of ocean and earth, comfort and discomfort, aquatic graciousness and social awkwardness, attunement to the music of the sea and disdain for the noise on land, superhuman capabilities in water and clumsiness in normal living skills: Clay lives with Asperger's syndrome, which is at the highest-functioning end of the autism spectrum. Some, his mother included, think he's on the line between Asperger's and full-blown autism. In his differently wired mind, Clay *has* to surf the way he does. It's his gift. Nothing else matters as much. Nor will it. Nor can it. For Clay, riding waves is more than a passion, pastime, or lifestyle.

It is the sustaining source of his life.

2

The Shorebreak Toddler

I don't remember anyone teaching me how to surf. I only remember surfing.
Ever since I was a baby, I've lived by the ocean. It was always home.
I've always had trouble being comfortable unless I was in water.

Every day we would go to the beach, and Dad would help me stand up and ride,
then go surfing with Cheyne. Mom would film every wave he rode. He was already
surfing in contests. Cheyne wanted to be the best — he was always stoked on
contests. He won a lot. I'd play on the beach, but watch every wave he caught.
I wanted to be out there with him. At night we would all watch his videos together.
Mom and Dad say that by watching Cheyne so much I was already in training.

Jill Marzo knew something was wrong — very wrong. She looked and felt pregnant enough to burst, but two weeks had passed since her second child was due, with no sign the baby would come anytime soon. Except for one thing: she was losing water. The doctor affirmed that everything was okay, but Jill wasn't convinced.

"I went three weeks overdue with him," she says. "They don't allow you to do that anymore. I worried that he didn't have enough oxygen; it's something I've always thought since."

When she returned to the hospital, her obstetrician put a stethoscope on her stomach and also hooked her up to a fetal heart monitor. What he saw and heard confirmed Jill's fears — a barely detectable heartbeat. She was rushed into surgery, where they performed an emergency C-section. Soon, she held her second son, Clayton Marzo, who weighed six and a half pounds — a full pound less than on his due date, by the attending obstetrician's estimate.

Jill looked down at her baby and noticed a couple of other features uncommon in newborns. "He had long fingernails, a lot of hair. His APGAR (Appearance, Pulse, Grimace, Activity, Respiration) score was low. It worried me, but the doctor said he was fine. But I wondered if he'd lost oxygen."

Twenty-six years later, it's hard for Jill not to see the symbolism in Clay's birth experience when she recollects that July 24, 1989, day in San Diego. *She lost water. The baby may have lost oxygen — oxygen he drew from her umbilical cord, while floating inside the water of her womb.* "Of course I think about it," she says with a smile. "It makes sense in a lot of ways when you think about who he is today. I mean, he was already in the water by the time he was two weeks old."

That makes sense too. Gino and Jill Marzo were steeped in the Southern California surfing lifestyle. Jill's older son, Cheyne Magnusson, was the six-year-old progeny of Tony Magnusson, a professional skateboard legend in California during the late 1970s and 1980s. Gino Marzo grew up in Arcadia, thirty miles east of Los Angeles, but moved into a life of construction and surfing when he realized he would never reach the major leagues in baseball, in which he excelled through junior college. On the other hand, Jill belonged to a surfing family of some renown. Her mother, Joanne, was a champion surfer in the 1950s and early 1960s, when women surfers weren't always welcomed in the water. In Jill's Maui home, a picture hangs on the wall showing Joanne in 1959 with Rabbit Kekai, the well-known "beach boy of Waikiki" who, at age ninety-four, continues to show up at various Oahu surf spots and the Association of Surfing Professionals' climactic series, the Triple Crown of Surfing. Jill's aunt and sister were also top competitive surfers, while her father, Clay Darrow, retired from his years as a bank executive and investment banker to sail, surf, and fish in San Diego and Maui.

So Jill thought nothing of taking Clay to his first swim lesson when he was two weeks old. They enrolled at the prestigious Murray Callan Swim School in Pacific Beach, which has offered swimming to infants, toddlers, kids, and adults since the early 1950s. The instructors at Murray Callan emphasize a gentle introduction to water that's as close to the experience of being in the womb as possible. The idea is to create instant comfort, to give infants and small kids immediate recognition that a water environment is just as natural to them as land — or, for some, more natural.

To no one's surprise, Clay found himself at home — as had Cheyne when Jill brought him into the program. "Both Clay and Cheyne were swimming underwater at two and a half weeks," she says. "I believe that's a huge reason why both my boys are so into water. All three of my kids (Gina, the youngest sibling, was born eight years after Clay) could swim the length of the pool before they were eight months old."

Jill and Gino were thrilled with the way Clay embraced the water, just as Jill had welcomed Cheyne's immediate comfort level. With both of their sons swimming as infants, they could proceed with their dream lifestyle — raising a family near the beach, with surfing as the central activity. They already had their sights on a location far beyond the shoreline of Mission Beach, where Sea World meets the sea — Maui.

However, home life in those first months was a different story. From the outset, Clay was irritable to the point of distraction and exhaustion. At first, both Jill and her pediatrician thought it was a typical case of colic, and Jill went with that diagnosis, but deep inside she thought Clay's irritability had something to do with his delayed arrival. Or a possible lack of oxygen to his brain. She tried everything to calm Clay, but only one thing seemed to work on a regular basis: baths. Constant baths. As soon as she submerged him in water his irritability and crying stopped and a contented calmness ensued.

"Mom gave me a lot of baths. She says it was the only way I would calm down or not be cranky," Clay says. "A lot of different things made me cranky. I don't remember what they were, but Mom says that loud noises always freaked me out. They still do. I don't like surprise noises."

"I would be in the tub and nurse the kids, three to five times a day, always in the tub," Jill says. "When Clay was cranky, I would take him into the tub, put my hand under his back, and he would float. The water would be going really slowly (from the spigot), and he would reach up and feel the water . . . weightless almost. Just with his fingertips. And he would hum."

Years later, just after Jill received an accurate diagnosis after twelve years of trying to understand Clay's social and behavioral challenges,

Gina, then eleven and already a gifted writer, composed a touching Mother's Day letter about the baths:

> *I remember you holding me in the bathtub singing "Silent Night,"*
> *rushing soft water falling through my little black ringlet baby hair,*
> *your melodic voice swaying me to sleep, the calming touch of your*
> *skin holding me like I was the most fragile, delicate thing in the*
> *world.*

"That probably describes how it was for me too," Clay says. "I love music. I guess I started loving it early on. I took baths, went swimming, and Mom told me that I hummed while the water ran over me."

While the baby's early tantrums and regular crankiness gave Jill and Gino some cause for concern, Clay's motor skills development was another story. Both parents were athletic — Gino was a perennial youth baseball star — and those genes made it down the line without any interruption. Not only did Clay exhibit strong motor skills and coordination, but he shot right out of the gate, going straight from rolling on the floor to walking. Crawling? It never entered his mind. "I did the spider crawl, where you put your hands on the ground, but then I stood up, like walking on all fours," Clay says.

Jill couldn't believe her eyes at first, but eventually decided that her early anxieties about lack of oxygen in the womb might have been exaggerated. After all, who can go from oxygen deprivation to walking in the first seven months? When she wrote about it in Clay's baby book, she revealed another area of her baby's development that impressed her — his determination to get on with life:

> *You are seven months old and think you can do everything. You are*
> *very, very determined with a bit of your mommy's temper. You love*
> *the water and love to pull and eat on your mommy's hair! You are so*
> *cute and full of love. And you spider crawl so fast!*

Not only was Clay walking, but his independent, determined streak appeared in another way, one that saddened Jill at the time, but she now reflects upon it as an early revelation of autism and

Asperger's: he weaned himself. He began to pull away from the intense love he'd known from his mother since he was conceived. "My other kids were well over one, but Clay was done breast-feeding at seven months," Jill remembers. "It made me really sad, but that's how he was. Already, he was showing that he would be in his own world, not be the cuddly little baby.

"He was always super-coordinated, though, so I stopped worrying about the things that happened when he was born and when he was a baby."

Two months later, in early 1990, the Marzos moved from San Diego to Lahaina, Maui, where Jill's parents owned an oceanfront home in the Puamana community. Lahaina was the capital of the Hawaiian island chain when royalty dating back to the ancient Polynesian explorers of a millennium ago ruled the archipelago of more than one hundred islands (seven of which are inhabited today). It was idyllic, the family home sitting empty at Puamana, and Jill and Gino realized that their family and lifestyle dream was coming true — a dream they were very proactive in realizing.

"I came back over here to check the place out and check on employment," Gino remembers. "I had a family to support, and came over on a trip by myself in December of 1989 to see whether this move financially was going to work or not. I got really positive feedback from the places I went, but there was something else. I'm standing in Lahaina, which is a south shore break, and there was a freak summer swell in December. I surfed every day when I wasn't out looking for a job. I thought to myself, *Gino, this is a sign, Maui is calling you and your family. This is a south swell in December that never happens, right in your (future) front yard.*"

Their small new home sat less than a hundred feet from the shoreline, with a perfect view of the waves. They lived directly behind the Pools, three side-by-side swimming pools that filled with parents and children on warm, sunny days — which is to say, year-round. When the residents weren't swimming, they were cheering on the kids and adults who surfed regularly in the sharp waves that peeled to their left (the surfer's right).

Puamana itself was every parent's dream — a throwback to the

Leave It to Beaver atmosphere of the 1950s and 1960s when kids ran around on the streets, invaded each other's backyards, grabbed snacks from whichever parent was shelling them out that afternoon, and returned to their houses only for meals, homework, and bedtime. The development was a mixture of newly constructed units built by East and West Coast vacationers, whose pockets had been fattened by Reaganomics, and older houses, some dating back to the 1930s and 1940s, when they were occupied by field workers from the pineapple and sugar cane plantations on which Maui's economy was based. Most of those homes had been refurbished, remodeled, or rebuilt by their sons and daughters. (Today some of those field workers' homes go for $2 million to $3 million.) About half the people lived in the gated community year-round, while the other half were vacation-home owners. Gino, who strongly espouses traditional customs and roles, sometimes to a fault, was convinced his life was complete.

So was Jill. "My boys skated and rode their bikes here, boogie-boarded down the Kauaula Creek right by the house after typically hard rains in the neighboring West Maui Mountains, hung out on the beach, and even did a lot of silly stuff, like Clay popping wheelies on a bike while stark naked or racing his little Matchbox cars on the street," she recalls.

When Clay thinks about Puamana, or goes surfing there — infrequently now — his feeling never wavers. "I loved Puamana. Of all the places I lived, Puamana made me the happiest."

The entire family loved Puamana, with good reason, one that motivated Jill and Gino to take the huge risk of uprooting their established lives in San Diego: few places in the world can match Maui's native beauty. "I've been to a lot of places in the world, and Maui is one of the most beautiful," Clay says. "Why would you leave Maui? When I was little, it wasn't crowded, and there weren't so many randoms surfing in the lineup. Not as many tourists. When you come here, just look in front of you: mountains, the greenest hills, fruit trees, great plate lunches and resort restaurants that serve some of my favorite food. Every beach is different; all the surf breaks are different. If you like jungles and rain, you can drive to the east side, to

Hana. Where I live, on the west side, it doesn't rain very much. The air is always warm. So is the water.

"When I took media boat trips and surfed in contests all over the world, I heard dudes talk about where they lived, how they wished they lived in Maui. Mom and Dad moved us to a great place."

It didn't take long for nine-month-old Clay to follow Cheyne and Gino into the water. A day or two, to be exact. "I saw water, and I wanted to play in it," Clay says. "Cheyne always went surfing with my dad, and pretty soon, Dad started putting me on his board."

When Gino realized that Clay's love of the swimming pool at Murray Callan and baths at home would transfer directly to the ocean, he didn't hesitate in introducing him to the ocean — or to riding waves on it. "He was such a water baby," Gino recalls. "People would freak out. He was pretty good in the water not long after he could walk. He was ahead of the game. Of course, he wanted to jump off the front of my board on his own when I would put him on there, but I wouldn't let that happen. At first."

It didn't take long. Jill and Gino, who are now divorced, differ a bit on the timeline, but family videos and photos show Clay riding waves on the front of Gino's board, or jumping off it, when he was one, and riding alone on a boogie board when he was two. And don't be fooled by the photos and the initial video images, which any parent could have taken — pictures of a toddler pushing off in a calm, serene body of water. Sometimes Clay got thumped by the Puamana shorebreak, which could snap quickly and decisively whenever a swell brought in stronger waves.

"Once we got to the beach, I can't remember when Clay didn't go into the water with a bodyboard or surfboard . . . something," Jill says. "Before he was one, he had water wings, he was on the front of Gino's board and jumping into the water. People would be on the beach going, 'Is that safe?' He was in the water, in the shorebreak. Gino was pretty brave with him, letting him go farther into the water than I would have, mainly because of the shorebreak at Puamana. But Clay would go into the ocean in the morning, nap, and go again later."

As Jill watched Clay — her mind and heart split between admiration for her baby's fearlessness and sheer terror because of that same fearlessness — she noticed something that struck her as truly odd: his attunement to the rhythm of the water. While Cheyne, now eight, was already showing signs of the talent that would make him a champion amateur surfer and lead to a solid professional career, she didn't recall him exhibiting such innate awareness of the ocean.

"Clay was always in tune with where that wave was breaking. This is before he was two. He'd be going under the water in the shorebreak, at the right place almost every time. Others on the beach would say, 'You'd better get your kid!' He was so in tune at such a young age, with the shorebreak and the barrel," she says.

Not only was he attuned to waves, but he also quickly became obsessed with anything in the cylindrical shape of a hollow, peeling wave (the middle of which is the tube, or barrel). He also focused intently on objects with a triangle shape, which is approximately the shape of a strong wave when it pitches out and breaks — the tip of the triangle forming the pitching lip. "If it was Legos, he would make something in one of those two shapes, either triangular or cylindrical. Or both," Jill says. "It was cute at first, but then I thought I might be seeing the earliest signs of obsessive-compulsive disorder. Little kids normally grab Lego blocks and make all kinds of things. They're trying out everything. My kid? Triangles and cylinders.

"When he got a little older, he'd be at the water fountain, at school or a beach park or a soccer or baseball game, and run it so that it projected outward like a breaking wave. He'd tell everyone how stoked he was about it."

When Clay is asked about it, he smiles slyly, broadly, as though someone has finally discovered one of his inner mysteries. Then he chuckles. "Breaking waves . . . barrels . . . slabs. My favorite things," he says.

Clay's obsession with certain shapes and objects quickly evolved into collecting things. By the time he was five, he owned the kinds of collections one might find buried behind the dirty socks and piles of clothes in any young boy's messy bedroom, a couple of which would be exclusive to the ocean lifestyle — baseball cards, Matchbox cars, seashells, sea animals, and Pokémon cards. Unusual? Not in the types of collections, but when it came to growing and maintaining those collections, Clay took on an entirely different persona, one of obsession and possessiveness. "If I collected it, I was *totally* into it," he says emphatically. As with riding waves, or modeling them with Legos, the entire world could have ceased to exist and he would not have realized it.

"What I remember as a little kid is Clay always collecting seashells," Cheyne says. "We'd be at the beach, I'd be surfing with Gino, and Mom would be trying to keep Clay out of the shorebreak when it got rough. Clay would get pissed at first. Then he'd find a seashell, and that would be it. Always collecting seashells."

"Yeah, I liked seashells." Clay nods, his poker face giving away no emotion whatsoever, the tip-off that he has long since moved on from that obsession. "I used to think about the life they had in the ocean, the way they moved in the water. I'd collect as many as I could, all the different sizes and shapes . . ." His voice rises, and he grins ever so slightly. "I can feel how much I loved it just by talking about it! I'd line up all my shells and sell them to tourists. I was so into shells. I had the best collection, especially after Hurricane Iniki."

Hurricane Iniki churned west from the Mexican mainland and hammered Hawaii in September 1992. It was the most powerful hurricane in the state's history, going back sixty years before statehood. The Category 4 storm decimated low-lying parts of Kauai with winds of up to 145 miles per hour and 30-foot seas accentuated by full moon tides. Maui was separated from Kauai by three bodies of land — Oahu, Lanai, and Molokai — but they provided virtually no protection. Iniki wiped out half the Mala Wharf, which sits at the north end of Lahaina and whose ruins now function as an artificial reef that provides plenty of snorkeling and scuba diving for locals and visitors seeking out sea turtles or fish of a hundred different shapes and colors.

"I barely remember it," Clay says, "but I do have this little memory of being into the wind and storm waves . . . just the movement, the way the waves got angry. It didn't scare me, but I couldn't believe the ocean could get so angry."

After Iniki finished taking out the few sandy beaches on Maui's lava reef–covered western shore, including the beach in front of Puamana, the Marzos walked out to assess the damage. Three-year-old Clay discovered a stripped shoreline loaded with exotic whelks, snails, cowries, conches, and other shells that normally lay on the bottom of the ocean between Maui and Lanai. He gathered them up and then did something that astonished Gino and Jill — he convinced them to set up a stand like a lemonade stand so he could sell them to tourists. Once they set it up, the fledgling entrepreneur fetched as much as $16 for individual shells, some of which are undoubtedly collectors' items in the homes of those tourists.

As Clay moved into his school years, Jill didn't know where to go with his single-minded focus when he locked in on certain items. "He loved Barney the purple dinosaur — he was obsessed with Barney," she says. "He could mimic the songs, so he would have me film him, and he was Barney. *To the tee.* He could totally model episodes of Barney, and he would do it over and over. Even then, he was already modeling things and repeating them to the point of mastering them.

"He would also collect sea animals, lots of sea animals — sharks, whales, walruses, fish, turtles. He was obsessed with them. He'd have boxes of them, and when I got up in the morning, he'd have them lined up all over the house. We'd call them setups. What was interesting is that they wouldn't be interacting, they'd just be in a line. I don't think he knew how to show anything interacting. He just didn't know how to make that work."

Cheyne was the other household member finding it difficult to deal with Clay's collections. His issue was considerably different than Jill's: it was more along the lines of, *What's up with my kid brother and his stupid collections?* Cheyne took matters into his own hands, often knocking over Clay's sea animal setups or hiding his shells.

That's when Clay lost it. Since Cheyne was six years older, Clay couldn't retaliate physically, so he responded in the way every bullied kid eventually acts out — by throwing temper tantrums. "He did have tantrums, meltdowns, as a kid," Jill says. "Pretty big ones, usually instigated by Cheyne taking something of his. Cheyne played on Clay's innocence."

While Cheyne regularly gave Clay reasons to burst out — and vice versa — Clay's focus on his older brother started turning more and more to surfing. "Every day we would go to the beach, and Dad would help me stand up and ride, then go surfing with Cheyne," Clay recalls. "Mom would film every wave he rode. He was already surfing in contests. Cheyne wanted to be the best — he was always stoked on contests. He won a lot. I'd play on the beach, but watch every wave he caught. At night we would all watch his videos together. Mom and Dad say that by watching Cheyne so much I was already in training."

Since Jill suspected any number of possible issues with Clay, ranging from attention deficit disorder to obsessive-compulsive disorder (OCD), she'd developed observation habits that spanned the attention spectrum somewhere between micromanaging and microscopic. She opened one entry in his baby book by writing about how much he embraced the *aloha* spirit of the languid Hawaii lifestyle, but then moved right into comments that revealed certain telltale signs of the years to follow:

> *He is very meticulous; he has to have a napkin when he eats. He won't look at the food until it's in front of him . . . it's funny. At Holy Innocence, where he goes to pre-school, they say he is always the last one at the table because he's putting everything together exactly right in his lunchbox. He loves to sing. He also loves animals, plastic ones, and he plays make-believe. He snorkels with [Grandma Joanna] on the boat. He insists on doing EVERYTHING by himself.*

Clay's love of singing has developed into a song list typical of the tastes of twenty-something men today but somewhat more varied, with classic rock, hip-hop, and a spacy hybrid of psychedelia, electronic, and surf music topping the list. Friends and onlookers know when Clay shows up at the beach by the way he screeches into the parking lot, his Toyota Celica thumping in a thunderous backbeat. "I love my beats — I'm always listening to music in my car, my iPod, my videos, in my head. When I drive down the street, I'm always tapping my hands to music. Both Mom and Dad say my love of music started in the bathtub. I used to sing all the time when I was little."

"He was really in tune with music," Jill remembers. "I always thought that would be a profession for him. When we would drive to the other side of the island, we would sing the same song over and over and over — *and over and over.* It was repetition like you can't believe. Mind-numbing after a while. It's just like, *ohhhhh* . . . it's common in the [autism] spectrum. It's because he knows what's coming next, and he knows because he's played it over and over so many times."

What came next was something Clay didn't know anything about: school.

3

Rough Landing in School

What bugged me about school? Not being able to focus on what the teacher says . . . kids throwing up . . . mean teachers who hated me . . . mean kids . . . new faces . . . random people . . . getting out of the car just in time to get to class . . . strange classrooms . . . no beach all day . . . getting tested . . . being looked at like I was a freak . . . Maybe I liked a few things, but then I was over it. I couldn't surf when I was in school.

The only thing I liked was the music. I had good music teachers. They were nice, and encouraged me to get into music. I liked to sing and dance. I could feel it, like I could feel waves when I surfed. The feeling of music . . . I still always rub my hands together when I hear good music. Some music, like the hip-hop I listen to and even classic rock, has the beat of the wave, like a thick slab — Ba-doom! Ba-doom! Ba-doom! Then it goes silent, the same sound when you're in the barrel, just waiting to shoot out and you hear the noise again.

When the national media descended on Maui in late 2009 and early 2010 to interview Clay, one production crew member thought to ask, "What did you like about school?"

Since Clay is generally uncomfortable with all media people (they aren't his family or friends, the only safe harbors to whom he openly expounds on what he thinks or feels), he keeps his answers short and tight, then forgets about them until he rereads or hears them. However, he remembers his answer to the school question as though he delivered it yesterday. It had taken him back to the humid Lahaina classrooms where he languished with teachers who couldn't solve the mystery that played out inside his brain:

"*Nothing*. Maybe I liked a few things, but then I was over it. I couldn't surf when I was in school.

"There were other things too," he says while staring out the car window at King Kamehameha III Elementary School, the beachfront school in Lahaina where he spent most of his elementary school years. "Not being able to focus on what the teacher says ... kids throwing up ... mean teachers who hated me ... mean kids ... new faces ... random people ... getting out of the car just in time to get to class ... strange classrooms ... no beach all day ... getting tested ... being looked at like I was a freak ..."

This combination of feelings and experiences would serve any school district well as a checklist on how *not* to handle or teach a student who is wired differently from everyone else.

His fear and trepidation started on day one. Two mornings a week Jill took Clay to Holy Innocence School in Lahaina for preschool. Jill never wanted him to attend, owing to his already obvious discomfort in new settings and groups, especially those as noisy and hyper as a roomful of preschoolers. However, with Gino working construction all day and the new job she'd taken on as a snorkeling boat tour guide so they could continue living the dream, she had no choice. Every time they arrived at the school, Clay sat in the car ... and kept sitting, petrified by the other kids running around like ants on a kicked-over hill. When the bell rang, he opened the door and walked or ran directly to the classroom.

It didn't get any better in kindergarten. Jill moved Clay to Sacred Heart School, on which she'd received many good reports from fellow parents in Puamana. Like most parochial schools, Sacred Heart combined a standard education with indoctrination into the Roman Catholic faith. While the Marzos weren't Catholic — or religious in any way — Jill and Gino felt that moving through his elementary school years with the same friends and familiar faces would give Clay the best chance to focus on academics rather than his growing trepidation over the external environment.

Sacred Heart School is attached to the back of Maria Lanakila (Our Lady of Victory) Catholic Church, a Hawaiian architectural treasure that adds to Lahaina's sweetness and historical legacy and shows any visitor a healthy dose of *kama'aina,* the "local way." The stone-built church, which has served parishioners since 1873, has a set of bells that were custom-made in France and paintings reputed to have been gifts from either King Lalakaua or his sister, Queen Lili'uokalani. Before that, it consisted of grass huts and adobe buildings that formed the faith-based hamlet of Maria Lanakila, which has long since been annexed into Lahaina's north side. Every Sunday morning locals and tourists walk into Mass beneath royal and coconut palms, the grounds scented with pikake, jasmine, and plumeria, wearing aloha shirts, shorts, and sandals. Not their parents' attire, to be sure. Locals also know the church as the Cradle of Faith.

As it turned out, Sacred Heart became a place where Jill placed all her faith when it came to Clay, and where he found his last safe cradle as a student.

Unfortunately, that safety wasn't found in kindergarten. Clay loathed the teacher, who saw him as a petulant troublemaker rather than a child slow to pick up his ABCs. Interestingly, Clay's daily apprehension about walking into class dissolved once he actually stepped inside. Then he was transformed into a socializing, talking machine more concerned with what the other kids thought of him than with completing schoolwork. That didn't sit well with the teacher, which Clay noticed. "She was mean, always made me sit down, made me feel dumb if I didn't get the right answer," he recalls. "So I never answered anything. I had to sit in the corner a lot.

"The only thing I liked was the music. I liked to sing and dance. I could feel it, like I could feel waves when I surfed. The feeling of music . . . I still always rub my hands together when I hear good music."

The best part of Clay's day, the music that filled his ears most gloriously, was the final bell. He'd jump into the car when Jill arrived, sometimes talking, sometimes not, eagerly anticipating what waited at the end of their two-mile drive — Puamana Beach. He'd grab his board, surf out front, and then walk over to the driftwood fort he'd built. Sometimes he was joined by Gino or Cheyne, sometimes by neighbor kids. Often he sat in the fort alone.

Kindergarten finally ended, but not without a report card comment that spelled out a behavioral cycle most parents of five-year-olds would rather not see right out of the academic gate:

*Needs improvement in all work habits — turning in work on time,
using time wisely, keeping things in order, and working without dis-
turbing others. Clayton is very social. We need to learn to focus on
tasks and complete work. I don't want to see Clayton get frustrated
with school, but without basic skills, he will have a tough time.*

Jill and Gino had an equally tough time stomaching the way Clay
was often singled out for disrupting the class. When several meetings failed to produce suitable answers, Jill decided to transfer Clay
a half-mile away to King Kamehameha III Elementary School. It sat
on Lahaina's beachfront, a block away from the world's largest ban-
yan tree, which provided that same cradling sense Jill had noticed
about Sacred Heart. She thought the presence of more kids in a public school setting would relax Clay and enable him to focus more on
learning.

Kam III looks like most other elementary and middle schools built
in sunny, warm climates in the 1950s and 1960s — a combination of
one-floor buildings tied together by sidewalks and hallways. Eaves
provide the only protection from rain. Kids walk outdoors to and
from classrooms, taking fresh breaths of the humid, scented Maui air,
glancing at the recess grounds, the chain-link fence, and, just on the
other side of it, the boats, docks, and waves of Lahaina Harbor.

The waves of Lahaina Harbor. Jill and Gino transferred Clay from
Sacred Heart so he would focus more on academics. How was that
going to happen when the view from the window of Clay's classroom
and from the playground was Lahaina Harbor? "I saw boat docks and
the harbor mouth," he says. "Just past that, the waves broke. Why
study when you see waves all the time? I closed my eyes and *rode*
those waves . . . the teacher got mad because I didn't pay attention. A
few years later, I started hiding my board in the bushes outside the
school's fence."

By the time Clay was in second grade, he'd found the perfect sec-
ondary outlet for his growing obsession with waves — drawing. If he
couldn't ride them during the school day, he'd depict himself riding
them. "When I couldn't be on the waves, I drew them. All the time.
Waves are home to me. I didn't want to sit in school; I wanted to be

home. So I drew barrels, tubes, slabs," he says. "Later, when I knew how to surf barrels, I drew myself deep inside them, where I was the happiest.

"The teacher didn't like it. Mom and Dad got mad at me. 'Why are you always drawing waves?'"

He smiles, his eyes instantly summoning that sense of mischief from the past to the present, and folds out his hands, palms up. *What are you going to do?* Then he rubs his hands together.

While Clay's disinterest in academics and newfound love of drawing annoyed Jill and Gino, it cast a deeper shadow in the classroom. Clay was pulled more and more often into the principal's office, where Jill would be waiting after receiving calls from the school. "They kept wanting to meet with me, or me and Clay, and they started asking me if I'd had him tested," Jill recalls, the wear and tear of those calls still resonant in her voice. "They started telling me there was something different about Clay, that he was different from all the other kids. Or that he was 'special,' and not said in a positive way. It's not like they flat-out told me, 'There's something wrong with your kid,' but that's exactly what they meant."

A single incident inflamed the situation and exposed other, deeper issues: a kid threw up in the classroom. Normally, that would stir up the entire class, perhaps making a couple of them queasy or triggering a shout-out of "gross!" Normally. For Clay—whose brain picks up anomalies or points of specific interest and hard-wires them as situations either to indulge or avoid as if his next breath depends on it—the episode unleashed a long-standing phobia toward nausea.

"He started having phobias of throwing up," Jill says. "Throwing up was a huge, huge trigger. He would have panic attacks. Someone threw up at school one time, and it became a major phobia of his until he was about sixteen. Cheyne or Kai [Barger, a friend and fellow competitive surfer] would say, 'Hey, Clay, I'm feeling sick, I'm going to throw up,' and they would harass him about it. He'd be in sheer panic mode. He ran home from school once, a couple miles to Puamana, because someone had thrown up. He had full-on anxiety over it."

Another pattern that established itself was the "one friend" dynamic. While Clay had plenty of casual friends (actually quite a few for someone with Asperger's), he focused on one friend alone each school year—a practice that continues to some extent today. "I didn't like being around other kids every day and having to give answers to the teacher with them staring at me," he recalls. "So I started finding a friend, my one friend for the year. I still do that, I guess—I like to surf with one other person. Sometimes it's my friend Johnny, or my friend Derek, who lives on the north side of Maui. I surf with my brother when he's here, or my friend Fruit Bean, who's a little older, a legend at Windmills. I go longboarding at Launiupoku with the Schweitzer brothers, Zane and Matty, when they're around. Or I'll paddle out with Casey Brown, who's really good. One friend at a time."

As she watched this strange dynamic develop, Jill began to realize not only that school administrators were on to something about Clay's eccentricities but that she needed to watch his one-friend practice to better understand how he *created and shaped his environment*.

"Socially, he talked with others okay, but he would only have one friend per year. One. Not multiple friends," she explains. "The one friend was his to kind of control; he did everything Clay wanted to do. That became more and more the case as he got to eight years old and older. Clay wasn't a bully, but he wanted to control what his friend did. And he didn't want to share his friend. Now that I look back on it, he was already closing his environment, shrinking it down to the things he could control and feel comfortable with. He would also like to see a reaction out of people—not always a positive reaction. He would do little things and watch to see what happened."

Clay sees it another way. "I like it when I make people happy. That's why it's fun to go surfing with someone who's not used to watching me, to see what they think. When they give me shaka-brah signs, hoots, whistles, or raise their arms, I'm so stoked that my barrel ride or maneuver made them happy," he says.

This description played out as though scripted during a session at a secret Maui spot. He, his friend Johnny, and a visitor met at the top of a bluff, checked out the surf, grabbed their boards, meandered down the steep cliff-side path to the pile of rocks that passed for a beach, waxed up next to a dilapidated lean-to hut built of bamboo and driftwood, and paddled out.

A half-hour after watching another aerial and tube ride display, Johnny rode in and sat on the rocks. "You know, right now, Clay's staying out there in this shitty surf because he's putting on a show for you. He always wants people to get stoked about what he does in the water. And the things he does? Through the roof. There are a lot of days where you won't find surfing that good anywhere else in the world. I mean, this is really shitty surf today, and he looks like an Olympic gymnast. As long as I've known him, he's been about doing his thing and seeing how others would react. Especially the one person who goes out there in the water. It's all about impressing and making his friend happy to be with him."

By the time Clay was eight, he could intuit when he was in the presence of other kids who, like him, saw the world differently and were seen differently than others. "He was really attuned to handicapped kids, especially kids with Down syndrome," Jill says. "He loved them, and they loved him. I always said, 'Clay will work with those kinds of people.' There was one boy, Mickey. Clay would be like, 'Mickey, Mickey!' He would have this little connection, and Mickey would put his arms around Clay — physical touch, which Clay usually didn't like. I think he was picking up that pure, innocent, nonthreatening love that comes from Down syndrome kids.

"He was always obsessed with people that were different. He would stare at them, really stare. I would go, 'Don't stare,' and he would anyway. They were safe to him; they weren't threatening. He found them interesting, because they were wired differently."

Meanwhile, Jill began to fight a pair of battles: pitting her innate love and protectiveness toward her son against the school district's constant attempts to test him, and fighting Clay to get his work finished. Another battle on the home front was brewing as Gino focused almost entirely on work and sports while removing himself from the day-to-day of Clay's growing academic and social struggles. "He was the kind of guy where everything had to be black-and-white and simple, and none of this was black-and-white or simple," Jill says. "Gino had a hard time handling things that weren't clear-cut. He'd just tell Clay, 'Get in the classroom and listen to your teacher and do your work.'"

As Clay continued struggling to sit quietly for six straight hours, comprehend course materials and teacher's instructions, hold on to his supplies, and not break pencils, Jill began to hear the phrase "learning disability" more and more from administrators. "In first grade, his processing seemed slow," she says. "In the first quarter, I started hearing, 'He isn't really focusing, he might be ADD, he's twirling, we'll give him silly putty — let's get him tested.' We got him tested, and they said he had a learning disability. He was a C student, just getting by."

Once home, Clay always raced for his surfboard and the beach. Jill had something else in mind: using the safe, secure home environment to spend extra time helping him finish his homework and gain a greater comprehension of the subjects. She thought that by working it through at home he would be fortified to deal with the classroom environment where he was required to pay attention and sit still for longer time periods than was natural to healthy, energetic six- or seven-year-olds.

"I used to ground him if he got into trouble or came back from school with notes that his work was not completed," she says. "I tried to take away his surfing, but it backfired on me. He wouldn't do his homework or stay out of trouble *unless* he went surfing. I learned quickly that keeping him out of the water was not a punishment for him, but a prison sentence."

The bigger picture was beginning to look just as dark and foreboding. Following the first barrage of tests, sessions, and appointments, the school doctor and psychologist recommended that Clay take Ritalin. This recommendation came during the 1990s, the height of Ritalin's explosive growth, when doctors and schools were dispensing Ritalin to deal with everything from hyperactivity to attention deficit disorder (ADD) to behavioral outbursts in class — whatever it took to calm down the first generation of kids raised in the super-connected world of video games, electronic devices, and countless TV choices. During the 1990s, Ritalin usage spiked to more than 8 million children in the United States. It became not the last resort for classroom behavioral issues but the first.

"I was on Ritalin as a kid, well before it became such a designer drug for parents of supposedly hyperactive children," remembers Jill, who was diagnosed with ADHD (attention deficit hyperactivity disorder). "My mom said it was like a miracle. They kept me on it for three months; in retrospect, it probably would've helped me in school, because I continued to have trouble focusing."

She saw things differently when it came to Clay. "I just didn't see why he needed Ritalin. He wasn't hyper, and outside of talking too much in class now and then, he wasn't disrupting anyone. So I refused to give it to him."

Her other reason involved yet another pattern she was starting to notice, known in the autistic and Aspergian world as "the stare." Jill's first experience with "the stare" came one day when she asked Clay to tie his shoe. He gave her a blank look: his eyes made physical contact, but his mind was a million miles away, focused on something more familiar and comfortable and completely lacking in comprehension of the question. "I don't know what you're saying," he said.

"There was this delay, and he didn't understand," she explains. "I'd told him so many other times. It was something he knew how to do, but just didn't understand what I was saying at that moment. I remember thinking that night, it was really random how he would just go blank. It scared me a little. Then it started happening more. To this day, sometimes if you're talking to him, he just misses it. I think he's watching your mouth move and . . . sometimes there's a blank, a little skip. Then he does that staring thing."

Music remained his elixir. One teacher, Wendy Keanini, picked up on his innate attraction to music, which worked for her, since she'd been an amateur musician. "I would wait all day for music to start," Clay recalls. "That was the best part of every school day. That and the final bell ringing, so Mom could pick me up and I could surf. I liked

Mrs. Keanini. She wasn't mean like the kindergarten teacher. I would write for her and do my work, just so she would be happy. And she always gave us music."

"Mrs. Keanini taught a lot with music, and Clay has good musical timing," Jill adds. "To this day, when he's watching a movie, it's very common for him to say a line before it comes, like he's anticipating the musicality of that line. He's very tone-sensitive. When he's in his room, you sometimes hear him say, 'Hey, you guyyyys!' It's from *The Goonies,* and it sounds just like the movie."

The difference of opinion between Jill and Gino over Clay's performance and placement in Kam III threatened to open a chasm between them. Jill wanted to enroll Clay in a Waldorf school, where music and rhythmic learning were intrinsic parts of the curriculum. Another foundational teaching of Austrian cultural philosopher Rudolf Steiner, the inspiration for Waldorf, was the notion that we perceive and relate to our inner and outer environments with twelve senses rather than the standard five. Steiner believed that the senses of thought, mind, I/other, balance (equilibrium), movement, warmth, and one's relationship to the world were every bit as vital as touch, taste, smell, sight, and hearing. In a Waldorf school, learning was individualistic and teachers routinely spent one-on-one time with students, focusing on their individual strengths and talents while promoting their relationship with an entire life environment, not just the prescribed academic subjects or other students. Put more simply, Waldorf encouraged holistic, 360-degree learning. And it could explain Clay's view of the world as well as any other approach.

To Jill, Waldorf seemed a perfect fit for Clay, but Gino saw it as a cop-out. "Gino didn't see the need or point of it, but I always thought that was a better learning environment for him—even when he was five," Jill says. "If he had continued to learn like that, I think he would've done a lot better in school."

"I thought then, and I think now, it's all about paying attention," Gino explains. "No matter what kind of school it is, if you pay attention, you learn. If you don't, then you have problems. So I didn't understand why we had to look at all these alternative types of schools when, to me, it was an attention thing that was in Clay's hands to improve."

Gino's attitude also perplexed Clay, especially when it led to disputes between his parents. "My dad sometimes thought I was lazy and didn't try hard enough, and I needed to focus more and work harder," he recalls. "Then he would tell me, 'It doesn't matter that much. I barely made it through school, and look at me! We live in Maui and own a house on the beach.' He worked a lot and didn't ask much about school. He was always working. Or surfing with Cheyne and me."

When Gino talks about the discussions and battles about Clay's early schooling, both his adherence to traditional elementary education and his frustration over what he perceived as Clay's half-baked efforts rise to the surface. He may look like a laid-back, deeply tanned surfer, with leathered face and scruffy dark blond hair finally showing hints of gray in his late fifties, but deep down he's nearly as hard-nosed as his father, who grew up in Brooklyn. It's not so much about feeling a need to be "right," he says, as about a deeply rooted belief in traditional values. What can be more traditional than going to school, listening to the teacher, and doing the work? Whereas Jill believes in the power of change, Gino believes in the security and comfort of maintaining the status quo. *If it worked for our parents, it can work for us.*

"What did I think when Jill, and sometimes I, had to go into school for this disorder or that problem? *He's not paying attention in class,*" Gino says. "To me, the whole point of learning as a young kid is to pay attention to what the teacher tells you. I didn't think he was focused, or even trying to be focused. I see now that there were probably other circumstances, but then, I didn't see any real issue, like a learning disability or something more challenging. Jill took him for all this testing, but I was always in the backseat. I didn't buy a lot of it. I'm only now coming to an acceptance that Clay is wired differently and for that reason, the way he approaches everything he does, and his capabilities, are different in some ways than our own. Just now accepting it."

Jill offers up a sad smile when discussing Gino's worldview. "Gino needs everything to be in order, the old-fashioned way—he's a *Leave It to Beaver* kind of guy. If anything is out of place, or a little different, he can't deal with it. He's meat-and-potatoes. Clay was a little different, extremely sensitive. From the very beginning, Gino had problems with that."

"I feel that Jill overprotected him from the beginning," Gino says. "I thought he was fine, that he needed to bear down in class. I didn't see any problem besides his lack of focus in class. I mean, look at him once he got in the water. It was obvious my son knew how to focus—sometimes well beyond the rest of us. When you see him surf, you see what I mean. Not only does he surf at a world-class level, but he focuses better than anyone else in the water. Why couldn't he do that in class? It took me forever to understand that."

Jill, Gino, and school administrators weren't the only people battling over the best way to move forward. "I didn't get why she was having him do all this testing, even in first grade—there was nothing wrong with him," says Cheyne. "I used to really get mad at her, like, 'Can't you see he's just as normal as I am?' He was a typical little brother, except he surfed better than everyone else his age."

Disappointed with the diagnosis and prescribed course of treatment, Jill decided to take matters into her own hands—a pattern she has followed to this day, for better and sometimes for worse. She enrolled Clay in the Brain Gym program, which emphasized the relationship between the brain hemispheres, the creative right side and the logical left side, to attain intellectual, creative, and emotional balance and harmony. "You hook up one side of the body to the other, like hooking your arms together," she explains. "They call it 'crossing the midline.' They say that when babies don't crawl, they miss the midline connection, and it shows when they get older.

"I was searching for whatever it took to get Clay to focus more. So I told Clay, even when he sat in a circle in class, to do the hookup. At least it gave him something to do with his hands. And the fact of him thinking it was making him smarter when he did it . . . he did it a lot."

The family's mood and Clay's results began to improve when he was regularly practicing the "hookup." He had a teacher he liked, Amy Kennett, who openly praised his improving work and encouraged him to push further. He consistently scored "excellent" in art, "probably because she liked my wave drawings," he says. He also began to score above average in speaking, physical education, and reading, a subject that had troubled him since kindergarten. However, his old bugaboos, attention span and a sense of personal order, were popping up, as Kennett's midterm report card notes point out:

> *Clay has difficulty learning about time, calendars, and measurement. He has a hard time learning new concepts, listening to directions, and applying new concepts when his attention wanders.*

Shortly after Jill and Gino signed that report card, Clay turned in a report on the ocean and Maui. He received strong compliments for his writing, understanding and presentation of the subject, and drawings (which he was adding to his assignments more and more often). Not many second graders anywhere turn in two-media assignments, and when Jill and Gino recognized that, they began to relax a bit. Their comfort level only increased when they saw Kennett's end-of-year comments:

> *Clay continued to progress in all areas. It has been fun watching his growth. He has become more responsible and showed more initiative and interest in learning. I hope Clay feels proud of his accomplishments this year.*

It was the first truly good news of Clay's school years.

4
Contests, Barrels — and a New Sister

THE LITTLE SURFER BOY

By Clay Marzo, Age 8

Once upon a time there was a little boy who surfed. He was very good, too. He was only 8 years old, and he could do snappy cutbacks, floaters and pull into a barrel. He was just learning how to do airs. He lived on Oahu right next to Pipeline and Sunset. He surfed there all the time.

Sometimes there are contests there, and he usually does good. He goes to Sunset Elementary right by Pipeline. His favorite trick is a throw-tail off the lip of the wave. Saturday he went surfing at Pipeline and it was big, really big. He was kind of scared but he went out. It was like 8 feet back and a 10-foot face. He was getting pounded, but then he got out to the peak. A huge set came in, and it broke right on the front of his board.

Then his board broke. He got thrashed around in the water onto the reef and cut his leg. He was bleeding like heck. He got up and he caught a wave in, and went to his house and his parents took him straight to the hospital. The doctor took him in. Then the doctor took a look and said you need stitches. So he gave him a shot first, then sewed in the stitches. Then after 2 hours he was done.

He said he couldn't surf for two weeks. He was bummed. He had 15 stitches.

Then they went home and watched surf videos. At night it hurt him so bad. In the morning he woke up and his stitches felt a lot better. So then a week passed. He went back to the hospital and got his stitches taken out. So then he went to his friends' house and went out at small Pipeline and had a blast.

THE END

The Marzo family showed up at Launiupoku Beach Park one Saturday morning in 1994 to surf, picnic, visit with Puamana neighbors and other friends, and watch Cheyne compete in another contest. Like the other beach parks lining Maui's shoreline, Launiupoku offered simple charms — a couple of picnic areas, a shady canopy of ironwood trees, and a nice, rolling wave often frequented by longboarders.

After Jill and Gino unpacked the car, Cheyne and Clay grabbed their boards (Clay's was a loaner from Cheyne) and headed toward a tent canopy. It was a big day for the five-year-old Clay. No longer would he just sit on the beach and watch Cheyne. When Gino signed on the dotted line of the entry form, Clay was entered in the Hobie Hawaii Keiki Surf Jam too. The surf was a perfectly small and tame one to three feet for a competition featuring boys and girls. It was common to see two, three, or even four members of the same family compete in the Keiki Surf Jam, so Clay's entry just let the others know that another eager kid was entering the contest arena.

Amid a weekend contest scene as popular as Little League and soccer on the mainland, Clay paddled out for his first competitive heat. Given his current stature, history would suggest that Clay blew everyone out of the water. A revisionist would state that like a two-year-old Tiger Woods smacking golf balls on *The Mike Douglas Show* in the late 1970s, Clay was an unstoppable force just waiting to grow.

Reality painted a different picture: Clay finished sixth in his first heat. Nevertheless, this local menehune heat began to bring out what would become one of the most talented, tightly knit groups of surfers to ever hit the world scene together. The boy just ahead of Clay, Matty Schweitzer, became one of the world's premier stand-up paddleboarders; his father, Matt, was one of the world's top professional windsurfers in the 1980s, while his grandfather, Hoyle, invented the sailboard. Matty's grandmother, Carolyn Jackson, entered Clay's life years later as his behavioral therapist. Matty and Clay competed many times against each other in amateur events, and they still get together occasionally to ride longboards at Launiupoku.

After the contest, Jill and Gino decided Clay was ready for his own equipment, so they bought him a surfboard. He surfed more and more frequently at the Pools in front of the house, Lahaina Harbor, and Shark Pit, just up the coast from Puamana. Clay displayed more dexterity and solid backside technique (his back facing the breaking wave) at the Pools, a fast, short, and hollow right-handed break. He was also able to surf frontside (facing the wave) on the lefts, where he started trying out what would become one of his signature moves—the aerial, when body and board blast above all contact with the wave and then drop back into it. (The aerial was originally a skateboard maneuver innovated and perfected by some hard-charging 1970s teens outside LA known as the Dogtown crew. Some were inspired by Cheyne's biological father, Tony Magnusson.) Gino took note as Clay's dexterity and skill began to catch up to his fearlessness, and he started taking him to other spots where he and Cheyne always surfed. They included Breakwall (outside the Kam III school window) and a secret spot called Shitty's.

Surfing was an all-in-the-Marzo-family sport and lifestyle, so much so that Jill designed their Christmas card in 1996 around it. On the card, she and Gino are hugging each other with one arm, while she and Clay hold a longboard and Cheyne proudly poses with his surfboard. "We look like a very happy ocean family," Clay says.

Ironically, Clay's biggest first splash in sports came not from surfing but from baseball. "I played for the Athletics and hit a grand slam the first time I ever batted," Clay recalls. "I wanted to be a good baseball player like Dad, who almost got drafted by a major league team."

True: Gino was an all-conference pitcher and infielder at Citrus Community College in Southern California. During his second and final year at Citrus, a number of scouts watched the hard-throwing six-foot-one right-hander. His father had been a tough, driven man who grew up near the Brooklyn Dodgers' Ebbets Field and moved with his wife to Pasadena shortly before the Dodgers headed west—and shortly before Gino was born, in 1957. Gino's dad had lived, breathed, and dreamed baseball and horse racing, for which his new environs suited him perfectly. (The racetrack at Santa Anita Park was just down the road.) Gino tried to live his father's dream of becoming a professional baseball player, but when the scouts started saying his fastball was shy of big-league velocity, Gino took a hard look at the odds, thought of surfing, packed away the glove, and moved to the coast.

Clay wanted to please Gino, who, like his own father, was a tough customer when it came to dishing out compliments. It was part of the Italian way — the "old country" way. How better to get "atta boys" than by playing Dad's favorite sport? Within two seasons, however, Clay ran into a brick wall that neither he nor Jill and Gino had anticipated: local racism. Though he'd lived in Hawaii since he was nine months old, Clay was a *haole,* a white boy, not a local. While one would have expected Hawaiian children on the playground to pick and poke at him (which they did, often), who would have thought the parents would get involved? And to top it all off, his baseball coach?

"Clay liked to pitch, and hit, and he was pretty good at both. Not one of the very best, but good enough to make it a happy time for him and Gino," Jill recalls. "But when he was nine, they started putting him on the bench and starting local kids who weren't nearly as good. At first, we just thought they wanted to be sure everyone played, but then they stopped playing Clay too. Gino said it first, and I didn't want to admit it, but yes, Clay was benched because he was white."

Years later, Gino and Jill would realize the invisible added cruelty of the benching: though most kids with Asperger's or autism are notoriously poor at activities involving keen hand-eye coordination, such as ball sports, Clay was a good youth baseball player and a very good soccer player with range and speed. However, because of the incident with the baseball coach, he grew wary and never again competed in a traditional team sport.

"When I was getting diagnosed," Clay recalls, "the doctors couldn't believe I was so good at something like surfing, or that I played baseball and soccer and I was a swimming champion. But I love sports. I always will."

Surfing strengthened its hold on Clay's desires and focus. He entered every local competition that included age group divisions. Sometimes he even bodyboarded so that he could ride waves with only a few others in the normally crowded lineup. Soon enough, results started piling up, often against competitors two, three, or even four years older — a big deal in any youth sport. When he was seven, Clay won the eleven-and-under bodyboard title in the Puamana Kids' Day competition and was a winner in other surfing and skateboarding events as well. He placed fourth in the ages-seven-and-eight surfing division in the Second Annual Honolua Surf Company Keiki Surf Contest, after taking second in the eight-and-under bodyboard division. The winners of those competitions, Dusty Payne and Granger Larsen, became two of his best friends and fellow competitors. They were part of the talented Maui crew that, years later, would dominate the world amateur scene and develop excellent professional careers.

"I liked contests," Clay recalls. "They were fun. I didn't win at first, but I got to surf with only a few guys out. That's how I like it — with no one or hardly anyone out."

"He was already ripping," Gino says. "He didn't surf smart; he still doesn't surf smart in contests, in my opinion. He would catch the most waves, because he couldn't wait to get outside; he'd just turn around when a wave came, because it was there and no one was on it. In those local events, catching the most waves usually means winning. He always wanted to catch waves, and not wait for another one to come along."

Gino and Jill both noticed that Clay lacked a killer instinct. By the time he was eight or nine, his day-to-day skill level had risen on a par with those his age and even older, like Dusty Payne. However, he often surfed hard simply for the camaraderie of sharing waves with his friends, while those same friends locked their eyes on the prize — a difference of perspective that reared its ugly side later in Clay's amateur career. The dichotomy played out along parental lines as well: Gino would exhort Clay to go for the win (though, by all accounts, he never adopted the win-at-all-costs mentality of his own father or a couple of the other Maui surf parents), while Jill contented herself with watching Clay compete and the knowledge that he loved what he was doing.

"Clay was never deadly serious about winning," Jill says. "He just wanted to surf. He just wanted to skate. He just wanted to swim. He was a natural. I don't remember him being about winning. I would sit apart from his dad during contests because his dad always wanted him to win. Someone would come to me and say how well Clay surfed, and I'd be like, 'That's good.' I was pretty humble about it. I just said, 'Have fun, and if you make the finals, great.'

"But he liked the trophies. So he liked winning in that way. If the award was something he could physically see and touch, he liked to win it. It wasn't like Cheyne. If Cheyne lost, he was a mess. Clay never took it so personally. I remember how Clay looked up to [world-class surfer] Bruce Irons. One time Bruce lost a heat he should have won in Oahu, when Bruce was *the guy,* and instead of being upset about it, he went and jumped off rocks and had a great time. I always compared Clay to that—that's how Clay took losing."

Whenever Clay made it to the finals, which happened in every local event, he'd look to the left and right in the four- to six-man heats and see his core group of friends: Dusty, Granger and Wesley Larsen, Matty Schweitzer, and later Casey Brown and Kai Barger. They began surfing together and pushing each other, both in contests and after school, forging a bond of shared excellence that held tight until they turned pro. "We were doing bigger, wilder stuff because we always had waves to play with," Clay told *Rolling Stone* magazine. "It's the Maui way: trying to top each other and look like we weren't even trying."

"Now that we're pro surfers, some competing on the World Tour and others like me sticking to soul surfing, I don't see the other guys much anymore," Clay laments. "Sometimes I'll see Granger or Wesley while driving around. And Dusty sometimes when he's home; he's my neighbor. But we're not really good friends anymore."

When Clay wasn't competing, he was dreaming about the next contest, the next heat, the next time he could paddle out. Most of his daydreams took place in the classroom. Fortunately for him and the other surf-stoked third graders at Kam III, their teacher, Patricia Akiyama, gave them journals in which to record their thoughts, stories, assignments, and personal dreams. The new assignment couldn't have come at a more opportune time for Clay, who had turned a corner in second grade and now held a sense of achievement inside the classroom. Jill noted in Clay's scrapbook as the 1997–1998 school year was to begin:

> *Clay is now eight years old and is a very serious and sensitive lil'*
> *guy. He loves to surf and he rips! He is doing good in school, he*
> *has a hard time focusing, but he's getting better. He has so much*
> *energy. He still thinks the world of his big brother. He makes the*
> *most awesome, detailed paper airplanes around. He loves Jack Pope,*
> *his very best friend. He will only wear certain clothes to school; he*
> *really cares what he looks like. I'm trying to teach him, it's what's*
> *inside that counts. He is so strong.*

The journal became an extension of Clay's world. He relished it with a ravenous appetite that any creative artist or writer can appreciate. "Almost every day, we wrote about what we did in our lives, the people we hung out with, what we wanted to be, and things like that," Clay recalls. "I also wrote stories. Years later, you look back and it helps you to remember. I drew waves on the pages . . . all the time. Writing stories and drawing barrels — best fun I ever had in school.

"It's weird how we find things we do really well when we're kids, but then we leave them behind as we get older. I don't care anymore about paper airplanes, baseball card collections, or wearing only some kinds of clothes . . . and writing. Sometimes I wish I'd continued to write more. I really liked to write, because it was a way for me to communicate without having to talk to someone. Working on this book is helping me to remember all the fun I had writing. It's really cool."

When reading through Clay's journal, what is most striking at first is the sheer volume of the journal and the passion of both the writing and the drawings. While much of the focus is on surfing and the beach lifestyle, he branches off into areas that paint a picture of a lively, active eight-year-old with plenty of friends and a well-developed sense of adventure. Not to mention empathy: his early writings show a considerable ability to sense how others feel, while also articulating how they made him feel. Not many eight-year-olds can verbalize the impact of another person on their feelings beyond "happy," "mad," or "sad." His writing demonstrates what a brilliant idea it was for Patricia Akiyama to hand out those journals and give her class a yearlong assignment that would awaken a latent creative force in Clay that he would later transfer to the way he rode waves.

In telling the larger story of his third-grade year, nearly every page of his journal is anchored by a surf or ocean environment drawing of some sort (noted in parentheses):

Sept. 8, 1997

This weekend I was in a surf contest. I made it to the finals and got 1st place.

Sept. 9, 1997

What would you do if you had 1 million dollars? I will give it to my mom and I think will go to the store, and get my mom and dad a house and a piece of paper for our plans.

When I think of yellow I see . . . a sun and a flower and a yellow house and a yellow fish and a banana and a yellow crown, clouds, sun, undersea view of octopus, fish, shark, turtle.

Sept. 29, 1997

If I were an astronaut I would want to float. I would like to take a trip to visit the Mir [space station]. I would like to visit because it would make me feel good. I would see some planets. I would like to study the planets.

Oct. 7

I don't like when people put me down because it makes me feel bad.

Nov. 4

Once mom and I walked down to the beach to go snorkeling at Puamana. We swam quite awhile. We saw a few fish. All of a sudden I spotted a big turtle. And then I went down and touched it and I came up with it and then it swam away and then we lived happily ever after.

Nov. 17

Yesterday I went to the beach with my Dad and we went surfing and my friends were there with me because he's a surfing kid like me and he is going to like me and live happily ever after. (Illustrated with a picture of Clay emerging from the barrel of a wave)

Nov. 18

My brother went to a surf contest and then he got first place in the surf contest and he was tired on the ride home but he had a fun time and my mom is sick and I hope she feels better and my brother has a big trophy. (Illustrated with a picture of a plane flying, with Cheyne in the window)

Dec. 8

On my weekend, I played with my train. We put guys on the tracks and they got smashed by the train around the Christmas tree. It's really fun.

The waves died. That's too bad but I went boogie-boarding with my friends. It was okay and I played with my friend in the hammock at night. It was fun. My brother was in the hospital. I hope he is OK. He missed a lot of school but he went today. But he's okay. We went to see a movie (Amistad). *There's supposed to be a swell coming. I hope my brother and my mom keep on talking about the kids smoking at school. But my brother doesn't like to smoke because he only thinks it is for bum people. But I'm not going to smoke when I grow up.*

During Christmas vacation, Clay's life changed again: the family added one more face. "My mom was getting ready to have a baby," he recalls. "We went to pick up my grandma, who flew in from San Diego." His journal takes it from there:

We did a few errands first and then we went to the airport and it took pretty long until Grandma got here and she is the best cook and she made pancakes for us it was good and on our way back we stopped by the doctor's office for Mom and heard the baby and they now say it's a girl and then me and Grandma waited in the waiting room. I showed her a paper airplane she thought it flew good and I did too and then in the morning we played some Nintendo.

"I looked through a window, and I saw a little baby girl lying in a blanket—Gina Marie Marzo," Clay recalls. "My baby sister was so cute, and I liked it when she smiled at me. I held her, and sometimes she spit up. It was sick, but her eyes were so pretty and cute.

"We still have a family home video shot right after Gina was born. 'She looks just like a frog!' I say in it. I was totally into her. I had my friends over, and we danced with her and I held her all the time and yelled at her, 'Gina! Gina!'"

While Gina doesn't remember those particular moments, she does recall the love Clay directed toward her—and how much she craved her brother's attention. Much of her nostalgia, she admits, is due to the relationship as it stands today—far removed, emotionally and otherwise, from those deeply loving first years of her life.

"When I watch home videos, I see that Clay was obsessed with me. He *loved* me," says Gina, a beautiful girl in her late teens with considerable talent as a poet and writer. "He loved the whole aspect of having a little sister. He always was really interested in me, interested in what girls do. He used to love to watch me eat, random stuff like that. He loves eating. When I think about it, it's really funny.

"When we lived in Launiupoko, our dog, Kalani, had a leash. I remember one time we were sitting next to each other, talking, and Kalani was out there. Clay wrapped it around my ankles, and Kalani came. I got super rope burns, and Clay thought it was the funniest thing. We used to bounce on the trampoline together, and fall backwards, because the wind was so strong. We'd just crack up and laugh."

Her smile fades, replaced by a deep, lingering sadness. "I wish we would have stayed close."

The other new girl in Clay's third-grade life was a schoolgirl, Asha, his first girlfriend. At least that's how he saw it:

All About Asha

Asha is so pretty and cool. I love her and I like her as a girlfriend.
So cute. xoxoxoxox

January 22

One day I went surfing with my older brother at Shark Pit. I got a
big barrel first the wave was about to break and I grabbed my rail
and ducked and I was in the barrel and I was happy! (At the bottom of this entry Patricia Akiyama wrote: "Maybe one day I
will see you on TV as a professional surfer.")

Feb. 5

There's this boy whose name is Kaniala. He's my best friend.
Sometimes we get into fights and then we say I'm not your friend
anymore. But then I say are we still friends Kaniala? He says yah
it's OK. Me and Kaniala like the Spice Girls and we like to skate-
board.

We love surfing and we like basketball. Me and Kaniala have a big
crush on the one girl. Her name is Asha. She is beautiful. (At the bottom, Clay rendered his best drawing to date: he and Kaniala perfectly slotted deep in the barrel, Mrs. Akiyama yelling "Help!"
because she's caught inside the wave, about to be pounded into
the reef, and an awestruck Asha onshore, saying, "Ahhhh.")

As expected in any school kid romance, things turned south with
Asha. "She was so stupid because she said that I was a loser," Clay
recalls, the stinger of that moment still stuck inside. "That hurt my
feelings. It meant she's a loser, not me. So I drew a picture of her wiping out in a barrel."

He deftly placed Asha deep in the impact zone, in a place every
committed surfer has visited at least once before suffering a nasty
wipeout. He could never have said in words how hurt and vindictive
he felt; he had neither the vocabulary for those feelings nor the ability to use it. Instead, he let his colored pencils do the talking.

Through it all, Clay's stories grew longer, becoming more detailed
and laced with emotion. His concentrated mind and wounded heart

were walking into a truth so many great, tormented writers have expressed in their best works: the truth of raw emotional turmoil.

Feb. 11

Surfing Rules

My favorite thing to do is surf because it's so cool. Skateboarding is fun, but the funnest thing to do is to get barreled on a surfboard because it just feels good inside and then you have a good life. Mrs. Akiyama always says I would take 20-footers . . . (In the anchoring drawing, he brought out the central females in his life: Mrs. Akiyama getting barreled, Asha wiping out, Jill emerging from the barrel, and baby Gina watching.)

Feb. 27

I was on a broadcast this morning it was fun but when you come back to the classroom I'm afraid that the people in my class are going to make fun of me. (Patricia Akiyama wrote, "Don't be afraid. I think they wish that they could be on morning broadcast.")

March 10

20 years from now I'm still going to surf.

March 19

If I could learn about one thing I would learn all about surfing because I love surfing because surfing's my favorite sport and I would like to learn how girls think. And that's all I have to write about. ("You probably know more about surfing than I do. As for girls, they change their minds all of the time!" Mrs. Akiyama wrote. "Watch the news; it tells you what's happening. Great picture!")

In the spring, Clay found himself on the school's performing arts stage in front of a live audience. He appeared in *The Colors,* not as an extra (though that was his original role, as a dressed-up crayon), but as the stand-in for the lead, suddenly pressed into duty when the star actor became ill. For Jill and Gino, his performance was a revelation of yet another facet of the unique and mysterious personality of their son — his ability to instantly recall facial expressions and words and play them back if he didn't understand their deeper meaning, intent, or implication.

"It was a singing and dancing performance in front of live audiences," Jill says. "Clay was never an extrovert, but he took honor in being this red crayon. He also learned the lead actor's lines, and when the kid wasn't there one day, he asked to be the lead. It was amazing; he was incredible at it, right down to the musical tone. He didn't really have his own stage expression, but he mimicked what the original lead was doing in practice. So when the kid wasn't there, he was the only one who could step in."

"When I look back at these journals, it helps me figure out how I was growing into the person I am now," Clay says. "I can see times of my life I can't remember, or don't have to remember, because I wrote them on paper. With me, it's like, I do something, and then I'm over it."

Clay had become an above-average third-grade story writer by year's end. Writing stories was the only activity requiring patience that he thoroughly enjoyed. Normally, he could never sit still because his mind kept drifting a hundred yards west, to the breaking waves of Lahaina Harbor or Breakwall.

Clay's story "The Little Surfer Boy" was the most prophetic and self-revealing piece he wrote in elementary school; while framed as fiction, it was a true story. Clay would never be able to write fiction, nor would he ever be one to exaggerate or spin yarns. Lies and untruths are as foreign to Aspies as desert heat to a penguin.

By the end of the school year, Akiyama had emerged as the unsung heroine of the Marzo household. Any teacher who could hold Clay's interest for an entire school year became a treasured friend. "I liked everything about her. She was one of the best teachers I had in school," Clay says. "I did much better when I liked the teachers and they were nice to me."

"She really loved him, put him in front of the class to be 'the teacher,'" Jill says. "Socially, it was a little weird with the other kids, but she put him there, and she was creative," she adds. "He responded to it really well. Any teacher that reached out to him, worked with him, was kind to him, he would respond to with some of his best work. But any teacher that was old-school, it was like fire and water. Extra hard on him."

The old-schoolers loomed in Clay's immediate future.

5

A Surfing Family

Roots are really important to me; it's good to know your roots. They say you take after your father's father, the second generation. Cheyne took after his dad, Tony Magnusson, who was a pro skateboarder, and I take after my dad, but I also take after both of my grandparents. They were good surfers. I also think I'm a good surfer because I always surfed with my dad and Cheyne, and I watched Cheyne a lot as he became a professional surfer himself.

I learned and tried out maneuvers Cheyne showed me, or that I saw in magazines or videos. I was getting barreled, and trying to do the things some of my favorite surfers were doing. There are photos of me when I was eight or nine at the Pools, right by my house in Puamana, getting barreled, grabbing the rail of my board while going backside, getting air. All on one page of a scrapbook.

People asked me why I kept going for barrels. They still ask me. Why? Why do you need to ask? It's the best part of surfing. It's the time I feel most away from the world, in my own world, where it's really quiet and it's just me and the ocean. If my life could be one big slab, I'd be really happy.

By the time Clay began competing regularly, Cheyne had risen up the ranks to become one of the best amateur surfers in the country. All family weekends were spent at beaches in Maui, Oahu, or Kauai, with Gino coaching Cheyne, Jill filming him, and Clay studying his moves, then trying to mimic him when he paddled out again. The Marzos seemed to be integrally involved with every aspect of each other's relationship to the wave or the contest, right down to spotting tendencies — one of which thoroughly surprised Jill and makes sense to her only now.

"I think one of the first tendencies Mom and Dad noticed about me was that I always went right," Clay says. "I surfed with my back to the wave, to my right. I didn't care — I just wanted to catch waves. Mostly, you go on your front side, facing the wave, but I went the other way."

"I think it's because he watched Cheyne all the time and modeled what he was doing," Jill explains. "Since Cheyne is a regular footer — he faces the wave when he surfs to his right — Clay became a goofy footer. A mirror image of his brother. Someone once grabbed frames from videos, showing Cheyne and Clay surfing similar waves when Cheyne was thirteen or fourteen and Clay was seven. Their styles were exactly the same — right down to foot positioning on the board and the way they held their hands. When I thought about it, I realized that the way Clay understands things sometimes is to literally model the person, gesture for gesture, and then try to figure out what it all means."

On the other hand, it also meant that a new star was rising up the star-studded Marzo family tree — at lightning speed.

"Clay didn't know how to go left," Jill recalls. "He was at the Beaches, a safer break, a little bit of a mushier break than Puamana, until you get to the inside where it's a whip-it break. He would go right, right, right. He felt awkward going left. So his strength was definitely going right. To this day, he's insane going backside. When the others said, 'Oh, bummer for Clay, the contest is being held in a right,' like at Honolua Bay, Clay would surprise them by always doing really well. And he did. When he went to South Africa with the World Amateur Team [in 2002], he did really well with the rights at Jeffreys Bay, a very famous and classic spot. It was what he learned first."

Clay's innate ability to model and emulate others turned into a great asset. And what better person to emulate than your older brother, who's knocking off the top amateur surfers in the country and getting plenty of sponsors to notice while positioning himself for a professional career? "Cheyne was really successful as an amateur, and then as a pro, so I tried to learn from him all the time," Clay recalls. "When you have a big brother who is doing the thing you want to be doing, and winning contests, then you try to learn, right?" His eyes grow big and open, his expression flat as island surf in summer, clearly spelling out his follow-up with no words necessary: *What's so hard to understand about that?*

Clay's career began hitting warp speed when he turned ten. In the period from July 1999 to July 2000, he won the thirteen-and-under division of Legends of the Bay and Puamana Surf Contest, finished second to Dusty Payne in the Shapers Keiki Surf Contest, took fourth in the Maui Surf Ohana Championship Series, and then surprised his home state by taking second in the National Scholastic Surfing Association (NSSA) Hawaiian Regional Championships, which Kekoa Cazimero won. He'd face Kekoa many more times, in much bigger events.

"I really liked surfing with my friends and doing well in contests," Clay says. "It's a lot more fun when you do good, and you're with your friends. I always got such a rush from seeing them kill it on a wave, then it was my turn, and I just went for broke and tried to kill it too, so they'd notice. So my mom and dad would notice, and say something to me about it afterward."

His runner-up finish in the NSSA Regionals qualified him for his first NSSA Nationals — and a flight to California. The brainchild of the late Chuck Allen, who brought in Australian surf stars and promotional experts Ian Cairns and Peter Townend, professional surfing's first world champion, the NSSA has been the largest and most prestigious school-age amateur surfing organization since 1978. Besides cranking out future world men's and women's champions (as of 2014, NSSA alumni have won twenty-three world titles, including eleven-time men's world champ Kelly Slater and three-time women's titlist Carissa Moore), many NSSA members excel in other career aspirations, owing in large part to the organization's emphasis on academics and character building as well as competitive surfing prowess. Matt Warshaw, the best-selling author of *The Encyclopedia of Surfing* and other books, is an alum. So is former NSSA national champion Richard Woolcott, the multimillionaire founder and CEO of Volcom. An early women's champion, Janice Aragon, now runs the NSSA. Folk music star Donovan Frankenreiter, once a national amateur surf star, bypassed the prospects of a professional surfing career to take his guitar and melodies around the world. Countless former

NSSA stars now hold major positions in the surfing and board sports industries as executives, team managers, sales reps, marketing directors, event directors, and more.

None of that entered Clay's mind when he qualified for Nationals. What did connect deeply and clearly was that he'd join his older brother on the plane ride to Southern California. Cheyne could trace the trans-Pacific flight in his sleep — he competed in seven consecutive NSSA Nationals before turning pro. "I used to draw these pictures of Cheyne flying away on the plane, wishing it was me," Clay says. "He went to California all the time and kept telling me about how good the waves could be in summer. Here the waves suck [in summer]. I wanted to go to California more than anything. That's all I would think about: California — California — California. California!" A huge smile crosses his face, as though he's right back at Lower Trestles, reliving his best waves. "So I just ripped some more in the contests to get to California."

As Clay started rising up the ranks, he ran into an unforeseen but formidable obstacle: his mother's innate fear of drowning and sea creatures. It may seem bizarre that an expert swimmer born and raised in swimming pools and waves would boil over with concern about her son's surfing, but motherhood can turn the most freewheeling adrenaline junkie into the poster child of protectiveness. When you throw in a mother's own ADHD, susceptibility to panic attacks, and sense of what could go wrong distilled from her own experiences, then you have the recipe for tight control. Quite simply, according to Cheyne, "Mom freaked out over the silliest things, like if the waves were more than three feet." Mix in a kid who showed no understanding of fear or recognition of situations that would induce fear in others, and you have a mother who became apoplectic at times. Concern over Clay grew into paranoia, then full-fledged panic in close tandem with Clay's growing skill and propensity for tackling bigger surf. Jill started to picture rogue waves, sharks, rock reefs, and any number of other potentially lethal tragedies befalling Clay. With her fears refusing to subside, she decided to impose a condition on Clay: *If you want to surf bigger waves, you're going to become an expert swimmer first.*

"I got him into competitive swimming because he was starting to surf bigger waves, and I was worried about him being held down and not able to hold his breath," Jill says. "So I told him, 'If you're gonna surf, you're gonna swim.' He didn't want to swim — he didn't want to wear the Speedos. So I let him wear surf trunks, but I made him do the sport with other kids, even though it's still an individual sport. But the relay was a team event, and Clay needed that."

Crossing Honoapi'ilani Highway from their Puamana home, Jill took Clay to where the Lahaina Swim Club met. Her condition on Clay's surfing unleashed a sleeping giant — his swimming prowess. "Clay did his first swim, and the coach came right over to me, amazed, and asked, 'How long has he been swimming?'

"'Well, he hasn't. He surfs.'"

In Clay's first-ever meet, the 1999 Coach Sakamoto Invitational, he won the 50-meter breaststroke and took home a blue ribbon. A year later, in the same meet, he racked up points in every discipline short of diving, placing second in the ten-and-under 100-meter breaststroke, second in the 200-meter freestyle (2:40.96), third in the 100-meter butterfly, third in the 100-meter freestyle, second in the 50-meter breaststroke, and second in the 200-meter individual medley. He scored fifty-seven team points, the best individual total of any boy in the seventeen-team meet.

"The feeling of competing was kind of like surf contests, only I had to wear these stupid Speedos," Clay recalls. "I did it because Mom and Dad made me, but I was kind of into the swim club thing. It was right across the street from Puamana, so that was cool."

Clay was an instant star, one of those prodigies who show up at local swim clubs and within seven to ten years are fighting it out for Olympic medals. None of the half-dozen nonfamily members who had seen Clay swim and who sat for interviews disputed that assertion. One, behavioral counselor Carolyn Jackson, says, "If it wasn't for surfing, if Clay focused only on swimming, he could have been Hawaii's best all-around swimmer since Duke Kahanamoku [a 1920 and 1924 gold medalist]. Period."

However, Clay put surfing first, just like the legendary Duke, who used his Olympic fame and celebrity to introduce modern surfing to audiences worldwide, especially Australia and California. Whenever swim meet and surf contest schedules conflicted, Clay always opted for the surf contest, a decision that frustrated his swim coaches because of his massive point-scoring capabilities. Later, when he stopped competing regularly for the Lahaina Swim Club, they would invite him into the statewide championship meets. He'd show up as an X factor, the wild card, and an ace at that. "They would put me into the relays, and the other teams would say, 'Who is that? Why didn't we see him before?' I was our team's secret weapon." When Clay relives the memory, a sly grin sweeps across his face.

"In swimming and in surf contests, he would always say, 'I'm gonna lose,' and that made him win," Jill remembers. "He'd already accepted he was going to lose, so in his mind, he had nothing to lose. Then he won, or came close to winning. Especially in swimming. He always got nervous when he stepped on the block, and said, 'I'm gonna lose.' Then he'd be the quickest one off the block. The coach, Tom Popdan, said he was the quickest young kid off the block he'd seen."

"You have to be fast to whip your board around and catch a wave," Clay explains. "You have to be *fast*. If you're not, you miss what might be the greatest ride you'll ever get. So I guess when you start fast, you can swim the greatest."

In his first all-islands championships, at age ten, Clay won the 50-meter breaststroke and 50-meter freestyle and took second in three other races. When he was eleven, he won the 200-meter freestyle in the 2001 Short Course Age Group Swimming Championships. He attained a high national ranking as a swimmer, "but the big thing was that Quiksilver sponsored it," he says, referring to the billion-dollar surf clothing behemoth. "They saw me — and right after that they saw me again."

"They did a Quiksilver camp challenge in Oahu," Jill explains. "They had surfing, swimming, and running. [Two-time world surfing champion] Tom Carroll was one of the camp leaders, and Cheyne was there as a Quiksilver team rider. Clay got first or second in the swimming portion. Everyone was blown away by his swimming. He could've been an Olympic swimmer. It looked like he floated through the water, but he was very fast.

"In one heat, he was wearing the Speedos, and didn't tie them right. They came down, but he knew that if he touched his trunks, he would be disqualified. His butt was showing the whole way . . . but he won."

Right after that, Jill and Gino decided to scratch competitive swimming from Clay's life. He wanted to do nothing but surf contests, and his career was continuing to rocket on a national level. "I guess I proved I could swim well enough to surf, because I never had to swim in a meet again," Clay says with a shy chuckle.

The contest scene became a bigger and more important part of Clay's life, as it already was with Cheyne. In the same NSSA Hawaiian Regional Championships in which Clay finished second in the Mini-Grom and Explorer Menehune Divisions, Cheyne won the Men's Open. Clay received an all-expenses-paid trip to the Nationals in Southern California. Jill and Tonya Larsen, whose son Granger was part of the emerging boy group of fledgling Maui stars, held fundraisers to help several others travel to Nationals too.

That summer, in his first NSSA National Championships, Clay reached the finals — a most significant feat, since the field comprises the best age-group surfers in the country. They surfed at Lower Trestles, near San Clemente on the northern edge of the Camp Pendleton Marine Corps Base. San Clemente is a bucolic beach town, one of nearly two dozen between LA and the Mexican border, with its own surf scene, distinct community character, and quickly growing population. In the early 1970s, it was nationally known as the location of President Nixon's Western White House — which, to surfers' chagrin, took a mile of prime waves out of play for five years.

Just south of town, surfers make the half-mile pilgrimage down a dirt path toward the beach. When embarking on dawn patrols, those refreshing sunrise surfs, they inhale the sweet smell of sycamores and castor bean plants along the path, then pass under the Amtrak train trestle that gives the spot its name. They reach Upper Trestles, a southwest-facing beach with a large rock reef and a wave machine between June and October, when swells arrive from hurricanes and other large storms off Baja California, the Southern Hemisphere, and the Mexican mainland. A hundred yards to the south of Upper Trestles is Lower Trestles, which splits the incoming waves into prime left- and right-hand breaks — take your choice. When Trestles is on, between six and eight feet, it is a sight to behold, the sweetest summer surf spot in the state.

Unfortunately, Trestles can also become the most crowded wave up and down the coast. During a swell, it is not uncommon to see two hundred surfers jostling for position, trying to outmaneuver each other for the peeling set waves. Hassles? All the time. Threats and fistfights? They happen.

That has never been Clay's path. He has never liked to surf with a crowd unless it consists entirely of his friends. However, for one of two weeks the entire year — the Hurley Pro of the Association of Surfing Professionals (ASP) World Tour is the other event — the water at Trestles is cleared of all people but the six Nationals competitors per heat, and that made competing there all the sweeter. "I met a lot of my favorite surfers and surfed with only a few other guys," says Clay. "I was lucky to surf Trestles like that, because it's crowded most of the time. I've seen a hundred people out there before. Not me. I hate that shit. I get really nervous and it's like I'm over it; I just paddle away from everyone else or get out of the water and go down the coast. What are they gonna do to me? Why are they hassling me? Why can't you catch your wave and I'll catch mine? It pisses me off. That's why I won't surf [Honolua] Bay anymore."

"Even then, even when he was with his friends, we could start to see the beginnings of his nervousness around other people," Gino says, "especially people he didn't know. What do you do? Every surfer I've ever known wants that soul session, out there all alone, but you're not going to be alone very often. I kept telling Clay to just get used to it, because he'd always have to deal with crowds, but he would sometimes give me that blank stare and go off and surf by himself ... even in contests. Yeah, that's when I started wondering about him."

When it came to throwing down the throttle and actually catching waves in heats, Clay's growing reticence in crowds didn't seem to matter. He placed second in the twelve-and-under division of the 2000 NSSA Winter Nationals behind Kai Barger. Granger Larsen was fourth. Kai, Granger, Wesley, Dusty Payne, Kekoa Cazimero, and Clay had dominated Hawaiian contests for three years; now they'd taken their game onto the national stage. They started to make every final together, then essentially take turns winning and placing. "People say now that we are one of the most talented groups of kids to ever come up together, anywhere in the world. Maybe we are. But we were having fun," Clay points out. "Contests were fun. Just me and a couple of friends. We kill our waves, then we talk about them and get shaved ice. That's how we do it in Maui."

Meanwhile, the older and more established half of the rising Marzo family surf show, Cheyne, traveled to the International Surfing Association (ISA) World Surfing Games in Brazil. He placed thirteenth in the Open Men's Division, a showing that shines more impressively considering he faced many of the world's top pros.

The following year Clay returned to the NSSA Nationals and placed third in the Open Boys' Division, then won the United States Surfing Federation National Championships — beating Dusty Payne both times. "He wants to be a pro surfer more than Cheyne did," Jill told a newspaper interviewer. "He eats, sleeps, and dreams about surfing. He talks in his sleep about waves."

By now, surf manufacturers started taking notice. One of the first to sponsor Clay was Spy Sunglasses. After watching Clay briefly, the team manager, John Oda, sent an unusual and remarkable email to Jill, remarkable in that he was talking about a thirteen-year-old kid:

> *What I really admire about Clay's surfing is his mature style. Clay doesn't surf like a grom. He already has a sense of using his rail and proper weight distribution while turning. Basically he surfs like a mature surfer. Most groms will allow their board to slide or drift from turn to turn. Groms usually figure out how to use their rail to turn in their late teens. It's visually obvious, when watching Clay surf. He's very powerful. Clay's way ahead of his peers. I feel he is underrated. But watch out, his surfing is screaming, it's all a matter of time before he gets the recognition he deserves.*

As Clay improved, Gino's old competitive fires picked up. If he could get Clay focused on winning rather than surfing every wave like it was his last—the ultimate high-risk, high-reward mentality, not always conducive to good contest strategy—he saw what the boy's enormous talent could deliver. "He wasn't a dick about it, but he preferred winning to losing," Clay remembers. "He would get upset if I caught the wrong wave, caught shitty waves, or missed a wave. Sometimes I'd get scared to paddle in, or I'd just stay out there and catch some more waves if he was angry. Or if I went for a big move and wiped out. Dad would turn his head when I went for it and missed the move and wiped out and went out to get another wave and tried to go big and wiped out again. When I catch a wave, I do everything I can. Why bother if you don't go for it?"

"The amount of heats I've sat through on the beach . . ." Gino says. "When Cheyne would go out in his heats, I didn't worry about him, because he had a pretty good strategy. He knew how to build a foundation and get a couple good rides. Clay was just so reckless, possessed with so much reckless abandon. It was a little different watching their heats. Clay's the kid that says, 'I'm just gonna go out and surf for fifteen minutes, and the judges can watch.' Cheyne's attitude was, 'Okay, I need to get a good one at the start, stay safe, do some turns.' Clay acted like every turn was his last.

"When he was a kid, Clay didn't feel the pressure," his dad says. "He didn't feel the pressure until he got older. Back then, he never saw himself as the top dog who *had* to go out there and win. If anything, he always felt a little bit of the underdog. Most of all, he saw it as fun . . . and then, a few years later, the fun aspect of competing became lost on him."

While Gino got upset when Clay lost or missed a big move on a wave, he never fell down that rabid rabbit hole that turns caring parents into win-at-all-costs adult maniacs. He often turned away, walked down the beach, kicked the sand, or cursed under his breath to Jill or himself, but he kept his wits when he was around Clay. "He never told me, 'You have to win.' He never said that," Clay recalls. "He wanted me to win, and I know I pissed him off when I did stupid things on waves, but he never yelled at me like other fathers sometimes did."

Still, Gino's intense, aggressive approach to competitive sports met its polar opposite in Clay's hypersensitive, surfing-for-the-fun-of-it mentality. As Clay's success started to grow, so did the uneasiness in the Marzo household when it came to expectations at every event. Jill wanted Clay to have fun and do well, to feel good about his performance. Gino wanted him to win; after all, winning begets more winning, which begets championships, which leads to more sponsors, which delivers major endorsement contracts — and ultimately a high professional ranking or a world title. This is the dream of countless young surfers and their families, just as it was Clay's dream. By his own admission, however, Gino focused on Clay's dream more than Clay did.

Clay found out firsthand, however, how much more mellow and restrained Gino was than some of the other parents. He and Gino island-hopped to Oahu for the Rell Sunn Makaha Invitational. The event was hosted by one of surfing's most beloved women, Rell Sunn, whose class, charm, and gracefulness earned her the title "Queen of Makaha." She wasn't a bad competitor either, having been among the top eight in the world during the first decade of the women's pro tour. Her radiant smile, the ever-present flower in her long, flowing brown hair, her engaging personality and way of making everyone feel at home on the beach, from the most informed surfing expert to a tourist just off the plane from Des Moines, reflected the love she exuded toward everyone. She embodied the *aloha* spirit in a way that made her death from cancer in 1998, at age forty-eight, a deeply saddening experience, not only for her friends but for the surfing world at large. Hundreds arrived from all over the world for her paddle-out at Makaha, a surf culture memorial service in which people paddle surfboards beyond the waves, form a massive circle, and toss flowers as a *kahuna*, a Hawaiian spiritual priest, performs a brief ceremony. Since Rell was Christian, a minister was on hand as well.

Because of her stature, Rell was a godsend of levity for young, eager, and aggressive competitive surfers, as well as for the countless number of troubled Hawaiian youths she steered toward better lives. "I felt like she got me," Clay recalls. "She just always gave me a big hug, and you look in her eyes and you know she gets you."

For that reason, among others, Clay and Gino always looked forward to their father-son visits with Rell. "All my surfer friends came and stayed in the same hotel," Clay recalls. "Every night we went down to the recreation room and played Ping-Pong or went outside to the pool and Jacuzzi. The last day we went to a water park and had a lot of fun.

"Then there were the aggro dads, the ones who only cared about their kids winning . . ."

He thuds into silence and his eyes drift toward the ground, as though a large cloud has encased his face. Even more than a dozen years later, the incident bothers him to the point where he avoids further explanation.

"All of us Maui people — the Larsen family, the Paynes, four or five Maui families in all — were staying at one of the very few places in Makaha you can rent, a little condo with a pool. It was a two-day comp [competition]," Gino says. "After we went to the comp the first day, we came back to the pool, and all the kids are running and playing Marco Polo in the pool, splashing around, being eight- and nine-year-old boys. Then one of the parents says, 'Come on, guys, let's go! We're going to the North Shore, we're going to practice.' This is at two o'clock in the afternoon, after they'd just been at the beach all day. They're tired, and they want to swim in the pool and throw water at each other. 'Come on, we're gonna go practice, we didn't come here to play in the pool, we came to win,' the dad says again.

"Clay looked over at me, confused. 'Dad? I thought we came here to have fun.'

"'Clay, you're right. We did come here to have fun,' I told him.

"That's why we were there. I mean, that's why Clay surfed comps — to have fun. It *was* fun. Though I always liked it when he won, it wasn't only about winning. For him, it was a case of 'I get to go have fun, I get to surf for fifteen minutes, hopefully the waves are good.'"

The incident calls to mind Jill's astute observation of her son. "You know how therapists and psychologists will say that it takes a positive comment or vibe about you thirty seconds or so to sink in, where it takes a negative comment only three seconds to stick? Well, with Clay, you say something negative to him, or if he's around it, then he never forgets it. *Ever.* And he thinks he's whatever the person says, because he doesn't have a filter, and those negative comments stay with even the healthiest people, at least for a bit. So when he saw this at Rell's contest, he had no way of dealing with it. So he just stayed away from those dads, never got near them."

When Gino talks about the way parents can overreact or live vicariously through their kids' athletic performances and potentials, his eyes simmer with the same anger Clay recalls seeing when his dad dealt with other parents on the beach. While Gino has his strong opinions on Clay's successes and failures, his comments are pats on the back compared to the darts he throws at parents who encase their kids' childhoods and adolescences in their own halcyon or bypassed dreams of athletic success without considering what their children want or need.

"My dad always put a lot of pressure on me to excel. It came to a point where I said to myself, *Is that what I want, or am I doing it for him?*" Gino remembers. "I think that that helped me. When I was bringing Cheyne and Clay to contests and seeing these other dads out there screaming at their kids things like, 'Paddle over, you pussy, it's a perfect wave,' it pissed me off. I might not be the most affectionate person in the world, but I knew I wasn't going to be that guy who drives his kid into the ground because he's missing something in himself and needs to relive it through the kid."

For all of the friction between Clay and Gino in later years, Clay always points out Gino's unwavering support for his amateur surfing career and his ability to take his foot off the gas pedal when some other parents were throwing it down and gunning their kids into their own expectations.

The youngest Marzo, Gina, observed her brothers' rising careers while playing in the sand or sitting next to Jill as her mother shot home videos of the boys. She, too, noticed how relatively laid-back her parents were concerning their sons' growing prowess in surfing and how they emphasized fun and fulfillment over competitive achievement.

"The thing I like most about our family, even with two great surfers in it like Clay and Cheyne, is that we do what we do because we love it. For all the other stuff we've been through, we're not this hard-core competitive surfing family, where the dad's going, 'You've got to do this perfect — you got to get out there and surf for two hours every day and catch this amount of waves — and film every single wave — and you've gotta win this contest — and if this kid cuts you off, people are going to disown them . . .' People get gnarly!

"We didn't grow up in this environment where there was so much pressure to be the best — but unfortunately, a couple of Clay's friends did. That's why I think my brothers became among the best at what they do, because they didn't get that kind of pressure. You know how a lot of kids grow to hate their sport when they're adults because of how much pressure their parents laid on them? Well, my brothers will love surfing until the day they die, because my parents did not push them like that. They promoted *passion*. They wanted us to be passionate about what we did. If I were to quit volleyball tomorrow, or my brothers quit surfing, Mom and Dad wouldn't try to push us back in.

"Both of my parents encourage us to find out what our best is. They show that they're proud of us, in their different ways. That's a lot different than pushing your kid to be the best — *or else.*"

For all great surfers, especially in Hawaii, good waves usually mean big waves, well over the rider's head — and then some. Like all other hard-charging Maui kids, Cheyne and Clay sought out bigger and better surf as they grew older. Gino and Cheyne knew that it was the best way to bring out all skill sets and become fearless in the water (while respectful of it), and they were determined to share the experience with Clay once he became old enough to ride the big stuff at Honolua Bay or Windmills, the best big-wave spots on Maui's west coast.

There was just one problem: Jill. Her deep-seated fear of big waves and ocean dangers reared up most forcefully on big-wave days.

"I remember her being so freaked out that she would always try to pull Clay out of the water. She'd even get nervous if it was three feet sometimes — and she was always worried about sharks," Cheyne says. "Clay really wasn't allowed to surf the big stuff until I got my driver's license — when he had a ride. That's when he really started charging it, when he was eight or nine."

After Clay started competing regularly, Gino took him and Cheyne on outings to Honolua Bay, a beautiful bay with a right-hand break fifteen miles up the coast from Lahaina. It was the most famous surf spot in Maui until Laird Hamilton, David Kalama, and Derrick Doerner brought tow-in surfing to Pe'ahi (Jaws) and started riding the fifty-foot monsters on the northeast side of the island for the world to see. Jill's fears would build every time Gino told her that he and the boys were off to Honolua, because she knew that Honolua doesn't show its greatest strength and beauty unless the waves are overhead.

"Whatever was big and closed out, he, Gino, and Cheyne — and Cheyne's friends — would just go out and dive-bomb," Jill says. "Straight down. I remember the first time Clay went out at Honolua with Gino and Cheyne. He was seven or eight. It was a huge day, one of those days when they're honking the horn on the cliff when a set was coming, because you have to paddle into the channel or you're going to get stuck inside. I was an anxious wreck. He was out there and did okay, but I was panicking.

"His dad would push him. His dad would give him a lot of credit for being aggro like that. Even when it closed out at Puamana, he'd go out there. I couldn't watch, I was so scared."

One of Clay's school journal entries describes his earliest big-wave experience, an entry that must have left his teacher, Patricia Akiyama, shaking her head — and smiling:

The waves were so good I got so barreled and I came out. Then I did a big snap and ate it so hard then a set came and I duck dived then I got held under for so long I thought I was going to die. Then when

I was underwater I was on rocks then I got scraped then I came up then another wave came and I got held under again, so then I was really scared so I came in then got ready for school. Then the next morning my mom said it was too big.

Part of Jill's fierce protectiveness of Clay stemmed from his difficulty both in school and in dealing with many social situations. But her fearfulness stemmed from a harrowing experience several years earlier, when Gino paddled into Honolua with Cheyne. "It was a big, big day, and you don't really wanna scare the hell out of your kid. I didn't mean to do that," Gino says. "Cheyne was maybe ten — he was definitely the youngest person out. We had to paddle from the boat ramp on the inside. You could just jump off and go. So we decided to take the longer, but safer, way out from the boat ramp and paddle all the way out. It was just Cheyne and me. Jill wasn't there at first. Then she came up later and freaked out. She was on the cliff and saw what was happening. Finally, Cheyne paddled in, and after catching a few waves, I followed him.

"When I got in, she was waiting. 'Why'd you take my kid out there and try to kill him in twelve-foot surf?'

"'You know,' I told her, 'I'm sorry, but I didn't know it was that big until we got out there.'

"Clay was different. He had no fear. He never even took half a step backwards. He even thought, *Oh wow, that's a big wave.* I don't think the size of a wave ever affected him."

Another frightening big-wave moment popped up at a 2001 HASA (Hawaiian Amateur Surfing Association) competition at Ho'okipa, best known as the world's premier big-wave windsurfing locale. Facing due north, it catches both the howling winds and thunderous surf from Gulf of Alaska winter storms. For years O'Neill Wetsuits hosted the top ocean-based windsurfing contest in the world at Ho'okipa, and Maui was home to twelve-time world champion Robby Naish, as well as Hoyle Schweitzer, the inventor of the windsurfer. Waves of up to twenty feet break at Ho'okipa when the conditions are favorable.

The conditions were favorable, though not if you were the parent of one of the competitors. Facing twenty-foot faces, the other competitors in the twelve- to fourteen-year-old age division settled for inside waves, which were still well overhead. Not Clay. He felt he had to get the best waves so he could pull off his best surfing—always his goal. "I had to get those big waves!" he remembers, rubbing his hands together, his mind and body feeling the buzz of that day all over again. "Dad was stoked that I charged it, but Mom got really worried and sick."

"In the morning, Wendell Payne [Dusty's dad and the contest director] called the contest off—it was too big. It was huge," Jill explains. "I'm thinking, *Yeah! Thank God! It's not on!* Then, just as we were about to leave, they called it back on—but the contestants were told to surf the inside section."

She shakes her head, rolls her eyes, and flashes the troubled smile that's universal among mothers of mischievous kids. "What do you know? There goes Clay—outside. Everyone's trying to follow him, but none of the other kids could get out. I was on the beach, nauseous—I couldn't see him between the waves. The lifeguard in the Jet Ski had gone to Paia [the nearby town] for gas. I went up to the tent and asked, 'Where's my son? I don't see my son!' The commentator calls out, on the mic, 'Clay, your mommy's on the beach and worried about you.'

"I was so mad. A couple of the mothers were saying, 'Don't worry, he's fine, Clay's fine in the water.' But I could see they were all nervous. Even the contest directors knew Clay wasn't supposed to be that far out."

As far as he was concerned, Clay was exactly where he was supposed to be: ready to tackle the biggest and best waves at Ho'okipa. He took off on one of those huge waves—and wiped out while going for a huge reverse throw-tail, a move in its infancy that would later become internationally identified as Clay's patented maneuver. His board leash snapped because the waves carried so much force. Then there were successive "hold-downs." He endured. When a rider plunges beneath a small wave, three or four feet, the wave and its turbulence pass by in ten seconds or so and the rider can pop back up to the surface. When it's ten feet or bigger in Hawaii, however, those little dips underwater turn into lung-burning hold-downs that can last up to a minute—or, in the case of the monster waves at Jaws or Waimea Bay, two minutes or more. Few people besides deep-water skin divers, Navy SEALs, and big-wave surfers can survive such lengthy hold-downs. Some surfers have "seen brown," technically the first stage of drowning. Others have breathed the oxygen bubbles within ocean foam, or whitewater, to sustain themselves on the way back up. Several have died.

"I got physically sick," Jill recalls. "I had to leave, and I didn't watch another surfing event for at least a year. I thought he was dead, but he was fine. The Jet Ski guy got his board, brought it back out to him, and he won the contest. Even Matt Kinoshita, who's highly respected as a surfer, told me, 'I wouldn't go out in that. It's too big, too gnarly.'"

The entire experience left a bruise on Jill's heart, which was not soothed by the troubling realization that followed. "From that point, I had to realize, the way Clay is wired, that he doesn't have any common sense when it comes to the ocean. In my opinion, I had to realize he could die out there at any point," she says. "I realized he has a primal attachment to the ocean, where it's his safest environment. No fear at all. He jumps into these blowholes where people have died. I've seen him jump off the rock at Windmills with a raft on a huge day. *Really? On a pink blow-up raft?* Even his friends—Casey Brown, Granger Larsen—are like, 'You're crazy, Marzo!' He has all this reckless abandon, but makes it look like it's good, safe, and easy.

"As a mom, it was horrible. I don't think he does it as much anymore, because he's gotten hurt a few times since then, but he still does it."

By no means is Clay oblivious to the ultimate price he could pay for his fearlessness in charging big surf. As he grows older, he seems to be gaining deeper respect for the sea and the price it extracts now and then. "I know guys who die every year surfing," he says. "The guy they made the *Chasing Mavericks* movie about, Jay Moriarty, didn't die at Mavericks, but while surface-diving in the Indian Ocean. I like to dive all the time. In the winter of 2013 a guy on the North Shore [Kirk Passmore] snapped his leash on a huge avalanche wave and they found his board but not him."

The discussion brings Clay to one of his most harrowing moments, which turned into one of his most defining experiences: a wipeout at the Tahitian break of Teahupo'o (pronounced *Cho-poo*). Accessible only by boat, Teahupo'o is a demon of a wave that rises from the bowels of Poseidon, hollows out everything beneath, and then throws itself onto a razor-sharp reef three to four feet beneath the water's surface. It doesn't break softly or gently, and it doesn't peel, feather, or in any way conjure up a Gauguin tropical image or a tourist brochure; it explodes. Surfers are left with huge barrels if they make it, and lips thick as waterfalls if they don't. Injuries are an essential part of challenging the wave. Everyone who has surfed Teahupo'o has been injured, many seriously. The ASP World Tour holds the annual Billabong Pro Tahiti at Teahupo'o, where the waves range from eight to fifteen feet.

Or bigger. The day Clay became a man in the eyes of *the man,* he completed his rise to international stardom not just with a great ride, but also with the wipeout that followed. He took off on a Teahupo'o growler that left other surfers and onlookers gasping, just like he'd left his mother and fellow competitors gasping at Ho'okipa, and he paid the price, getting thrashed on the reef. "That was such a sick wave," Clay says. "What a rush! I had to have it. Sometimes you get hurt but you have to smile, because you know you went for it and you and the wave communicated for a second and shit happens when you go for it."

When he reached the boat, there to greet him was Laird Hamilton, the most famous big-wave surfer in the world, whose ride on a Teahupo'o beast in 2005 stands in surfing lore as a true David-and-Goliath moment. Hamilton is not easily impressed. This is a man who rides fifty-foot waves routinely and who, on an early December day in 2007 when the Pacific Ocean threw a huge-wave party from Japan to California, took off on a monster that a National Weather

Service oceanographer known for his conservative estimates pegged at 110 feet on the face. What could impress him? As it turns out, the sheer guts his fellow Maui resident displayed.

"Some of the other guys were going, 'You're crazy, Marzo! You're crazy!' but Laird was there to rub lemon into all my cuts and scratches," Clay recalls. "He's *the man* at Teahupo'o and Jaws. While I'm sitting there, yelling and shit from the sting of the lemon, he's going, 'You're the man! You're the man!' for even going for it. That made me smile. *Laird* . . . yeah, it made me feel really good."

6

School Daze

A lot of kids with Asperger's and autism want to make friends. We *all* want to make friends. We all want to have friends. It is hard for me to start. Like, what do I say to you? Will you laugh or look at me funny when I say something? What can I say that will make you want to be my friend? Will you like me? Or think I'm weird because of some of the things I do? What if I surf but you don't? Or you work on cars and I don't?

It's hard for me to figure out how to be someone's friend. I always think people are looking at me like I'm this freak, because maybe I don't talk to them right away. I have to know you before I really talk to you, and then, sometimes, I still don't want to talk. But we can hang out, drive around.

You grow up used to being alone, which sucked for me, but now as I get older, it's where I want to be most of the time, even though I have friends I can call to surf, play basketball, or hang out. But when I was in school, it really sucked. The teachers thought I was retarded or something too. So that's why I always had my one friend, and then my surfing friends. I'd find my one friend, and that would be my friend for the whole year.

Clay's amateur career continued to escalate. He traveled to California, South Africa, and the other Hawaiian Islands, sometimes missing school to go on trips. He wanted to surf even more and sacrifice school to make that happen. Especially after sixth grade, the last time he liked anything about school.

Jill transferred Clay back to Sacred Heart, where he'd spent kindergarten, because his fifth-grade teacher at Kam III was an old-school traditionalist who had no idea how to deal with Clay's slower processing, different way of learning, and constant need to move around.

"They'd punish him, keep him out of PE, if he was wiggling," Jill remembers. "Clay excelled in PE, and still did well in writing and art. But I was really struggling to have him do okay in school. He had a one-on-one person who would take him out to work with him that he liked, but his actual teacher in class kept punishing him by taking away things that were comfortable for him. I talked to the principal and said, 'Look, you can't keep putting Clay in the corner like that. His self-esteem is going to go down the tubes. All he's doing is wiggling.' So they'd give him a ball of Silly Putty ... it was a matter of constantly making him fit.

"So finally, I pulled him out in the middle of the year. I was frustrated: a very academic teacher was trying to make him more academic, instead of working with him. I asked so many times for the school to put him with a teacher that would fit him."

Unfortunately, public schools don't often work that way.

All of his teachers to date had cited the same issue: an inability to pay attention in the classroom. Jill tried everything from Brain Game hookups to green algae to find the magic bullet to improve his focus and create a better mind-set for learning. Little worked. While teachers and school psychologists pointed to ADD, suggested he had learning disabilities, or came to other common conclusions, Jill worried it was something beyond that, something beyond the school's ability to recognize.

Clay saw it another way. "I sometimes had trouble paying attention because I just didn't want to be there," he says. "Give me an ocean and some waves, or something I like, and I will pay attention all the time. Mom really wanted me to fit in and tried everything to make it happen."

"I just wanted to know he was normal and could conform," Jill explains. "Now I see that was not a good way to think. I needed to dig deeper and look for more options than trying to fit a square into a round hole. I needed to appreciate the square and do what I could to figure out how to make him more comfortable. If I only knew then what I know now, it would have been so much more gentle and positive for Clay."

By fifth grade, the countless tests Clay had undergone had further diminished his interest in school and increased the negativity other students directed toward him; didn't he already stick out enough as a *haole* boy in an outer island school? Why bother showing up when you're just going to be hauled out of the classroom for more tests? "When you get pulled out of classrooms, the other kids look at you funny, like you're a freak," Clay says. "I can still see some of their looks."

The testing went on. When Clay was in fifth grade, school psychologist Ellen Kerringer diagnosed him with ADD for the second time. She also concluded that he suffered from overanxiety, which is common in "slow-processing" kids who think everyone else is aware of their every move (a perception Clay still has). Years before, Jill had taken Cheyne to Dr. Kerringer because he'd had trouble from not spending more time with his biological father, Tony Magnusson. The only time they saw each other was during Cheyne's summer vacations, when the boy flew to California. Even though Gino had assumed the father's role for Cheyne and gave him the two-parent upbringing every child craves, Cheyne's separation anxiety was strong. He'd started to think Gino preferred Clay to him, adding to a family dynamic already strained by the parents' differences of opinion on how to help Clay move forward.

During one visit, Dr. Kerringer saw Clay in the waiting room jumping around and fidgeting. She told Jill, "He's going to be in here too."

When Dr. Kerringer suggested prescription drugs, Jill went against her own instincts and revisited the idea. She approached Clay. "Clay, if you could take a pill that would help you feel better and make it easier for school, would you want to try it?"

He looked her right in the eyes. "Yes."

"He wanted to be good, and do good. He also wanted me to be happy," she says.

It didn't work. Not only that, Ritalin proved to be a disaster. "He took it, and it was awful," she recalls. "He was screaming profanities . . . he became this kid from hell. In four or five days . . . I cannot tell you how bad of an effect it had on him. It was definitely not the drug of choice."

"My friends and I were into things like surfing and video games and watching DVDs and listening to music on our MP3s and going home from school and watching reruns of movies and all these cool new fun things you could do ... a couple of them even had pagers. Then iPods. That's what I paid attention to," Clay says. "I didn't like crowded classrooms. I paid attention to the things that interested me."

Then there was the fifth-grade teacher who had little use for inattentive students. The underlying reason for Clay's difficulty became clear in the coming years, but no one at the time could identify it. Thus, the fifth-grade teacher saw him as a dumb, lazy, troublemaking surfer boy. "The fifth-grade teacher treated him like a delinquent, even though he wasn't blurting out, disrupting the class, talking to his friends in class, or hurting anyone," Jill remembers. "He just wasn't processing like the others. The school should have paid attention to how different Clay was and not put him with a strict, inflexible teacher. Finally, I took him out the middle of the year."

Another ongoing issue was Clay's difficulty in forming friendships or focusing his energy on several kids simultaneously. He couldn't do it. He would identify one friend, preferably someone whom he could influence and even control to a degree. That boy remained his social rock, his consistent go-to person, throughout the school year. During the next term, he might retain that friendship — or form another. This pattern continued through Clay's elementary and middle school years, but it had a parallel current that, as behavioral counselor Carolyn Jackson pointed out, put Clay in a better position than most of those with Asperger's or autism enjoy: his much broader cast of surfing friends.

"I had the one friend who I would always hang out with," Clay recalls. "In fifth and sixth grades, that was Jack Pope and Granger Larsen. I also had my surfing friends, and since we were all really good ([competitors], a lot of the kids in school liked us in that way. School kids always like the sports guys. I have friends that have lasted all the way until now."

Clay's sixth-grade teacher, Mary Anna Waldrop Enriquez, took it upon herself to study the way he interacted with others in what became her quest to figure out how to free Clay's mind. "He would play with other kids," she says. "He would go out to recess with them when I wasn't keeping him in to finish an assignment. He was pretty funny. The kids protected him. There were about three boys, kids like Jack Pope, that would protect him. They would make sure he was okay — especially Jack. Clay would go along with them. He never got in fights. He would never, ever volunteer to do anything. He would follow along. When it came to conversing, he was more nonverbal."

"What I knew of Clay that always worked in his benefit was that he has friends," Carolyn Jackson says. "Many Asperger's children and adults, their greatest difficulty in life is that they crave friendship but they don't know how to do friendship. Because Clay grew up with young people who loved to surf, they became their own group. He was always a part of a group. I believe that being a part of a group, even with all the psychological difficulties he has had due to his Asperger's, was one of his saving graces.

"A lot of his friends are the 'who's who' of surfing, and they have great respect for Clay, so when they would go out, he was invited. While watching him, what I was clear about was that another Asperger's child would be by themselves, but Clay would not be. People are still around him. That is the unconscious net that he has. He never has to isolate like others with Asperger's."

When Clay talks about finding it relatively easy to meet people but always difficult to build friendships from those encounters, it's clear he has put considerable thought into the matter. "A lot of kids with Asperger's and autism want to make friends. We *all* want to make friends. We all want to have friends," Clay says. "It is hard for me to start. Like, what do I say to you? Will you laugh or look at me funny? What can I say that will make you want to be my friend? Will you like me? Or think I'm weird because of some of the things I do? What if I surf but you don't? It's hard for me to figure out how to be someone's friend. I have friends I can call anytime to surf, play basketball, or hang out."

He has also developed some idiosyncrasies to compensate for or mask his discomfort in certain environments — especially ones that include loud, sudden noises. When something strongly excites Clay or makes him happy, he responds to the surge of endorphins in his brain by rubbing his hands furiously — a gesture known to everyone who has ever met him. If the waves are up, if the food is good, or if he sees himself on video shooting out of a barrel, his hands start flying together like a mad mechanic scrubbing down with pumice stone. He's been known to rub them for ten minutes at a time. Conversely, whenever he grows worried and anxious, he twirls strands of his hair and sometimes pulls it out. When he wants to get away from it all, he finds the family's dog, Kalani, and plays with her, sometimes exchanging sounds. In her language. And there's more. "When something really excites me, like a great movie scene or surf video, I might growl. If I don't get what you're saying, I'll stare at you. Or stare into space. We all have our things. Everyone who knows me is used to them, so it's no big deal."

"My grandchildren would say to me, 'You should've seen what Clay did today. You should've heard what he said!'" Carolyn Jackson says. "I was privy to that. Because Clay met these kids very young, nobody took offense to all of his idiosyncrasies. As far as they were concerned, 'That's just Clay.'"

Jill thought the latest troubles were behind them when Clay transferred back to Sacred Heart for the second half of fifth grade. Not so: he was placed in a classroom with another hard-edged teacher.

"She would joke with kids in an inappropriate way — especially for a Catholic school," Jill says. "One day Clay pushed someone who had pushed him. The teacher asked him, 'Clay, if someone told you to put a firecracker up your butt, would you do it?' Another time she said, 'Clay, are you gay?' Then, at Mass, when they got up to take communion, Clay followed along and took communion too. The only problem is that Clay is not Catholic. That fact never would have entered his mind. After he took the wafer, he turned around, chewing it, opened his mouth, and showed everyone else. The priest pulled him into the office and told him he's going to hell for that. To this day he still thinks he's going to hell for doing that. Sad that someone would say that to him.

"Well, like I said before, Clay never shakes off the bad things — they are always right with him."

The downhill streak of poor teacher-student dynamics turned around suddenly when Clay entered sixth grade, just as Jill was beginning to entertain the thought of home-schooling him. In that classroom he met the teacher who, as time now shows, would become one of the greatest benefactors of his life — just as he would become an unspoken inspiration in hers.

Mary Anna Waldrop Enriquez arrived at Sacred Heart by way of the ocean. Even though that sounds mystical even for an island chain that still has adherents to the ancient, sea-based Huna religion, her path to Maui deeply involves the sea. After growing up in New Mexico, earning her teaching and special education credentials, and then teaching in California, she sailed throughout the Pacific for seven years with her husband, visiting or living briefly in Tahiti, New Zealand, Australia, the Polynesian islands, and Mexico. Then her husband died suddenly. Unsure of how to move forward, she found Maui. She took a job teaching sixth-grade writing at Sacred Heart, which turned out to be a great gift for Lahaina as a community, for the students, and especially for the Marzo family.

Enriquez started at the elementary school in 1999, but moved in 2003 to the middle school, where she continues to teach, primarily the STEM subjects (science, technology, engineering, mathematics). She uses writing to further students' comprehension. More significantly for the Marzos, she is the most knowledgeable educator in Maui when it comes to autism.

"As life goes, the winds change," Enriquez says. "Sacred Heart School found me. Lahaina is such a tiny community; every school is its own little house on the prairie. A job was created for me."

The first time Enriquez laid eyes on Clay, she knew right away he was different from the other kids. "I thought I knew a lot about special education, but it was limited to what we knew about brain science at the time. So Clay comes in, and I just wanted to peel him back, to find out, *What are you thinking?* because I'd never had an autistic child before. And no one knew he was autistic, that he had Asperger's; that diagnosis came later. He was brand-new to me.

"In my twelve years of primary schooling, I had never had an autistic classmate. In college, it wasn't even touched upon in my special ed classes. *Never touched upon.* Now, one of the things I make a point of doing is to go to every single conference on brain research that I can get to—in Honolulu, Houston, San Francisco, or wherever. What's the latest brain research? I want to know—and I can feel Clay in the back of my mind, pushing me on."

While her basic knowledge of autism was limited in 2000–2001, she knew instinctively to tread differently with Clay if she wanted results from him in her writing class. "I knew that if I called on him in class, I'd just get an outer-space look," she says. "Even though everyone knew he was a bit different by then, I didn't want to put him on the spot. I never asked him to give an oral report or recite poetry. I did at first, but after one or two times it was like, 'Okay, we're not going to put *him* up in front, up on stage.'"

When Enriquez polled the veteran Sacred Heart teachers, she learned that there had been no previous students at the school with the same developmental and social challenges. Strangely enough, after a long history of having no students on the autistic spectrum, Sacred Heart now had two—both in sixth-grade writing.

"There was another kid in my class who was a little different, a girl," Clay recalls. "She was like me—really into one thing, her one gift—but she was a lot different around people than me. She didn't have *any* friends."

"Yes, we had the girl Clay mentioned. She *was* like a young Temple Grandin," Enriquez says, referring to the scientist who may be the world's foremost writer on autism—and is autistic herself. "My other autistic student was so in-your-face, and it was just fascinating! Clay was the reserved one. He would just shut down and not do anything. Sometimes being in-your-face makes you realize more, so we concluded, 'That's who she is,' and we let her go.

"Whereas with Clay I pushed, and I shouldn't have. I'm just glad I was the encouraging kind of teacher, not the grumpy kind. I was like, 'We're gonna get this, we're gonna get this,' and keeping him after school . . . I look back on it now and go, *Oh my God, beat me over the head. Don't let me do that to another kid again.*"

When Clay fell behind early in his writing assignments, Enriquez took quick action. Her decision to act immediately was vital: she understood that whereas most kids can right themselves from a *laissez-faire,* I-don't-like-it-and-I-don't-care attitude, such self-regulation was far more difficult for Clay. Long before she understood the neuroscience of autism, Enriquez knew that lagging students fall out of school not only because of their inability to do the work but also because of some educators' reluctance to help them overcome the difficulty.

With Clay, she modified almost every writing assignment so that he could write about surfing, tapping directly into the creative vein that had gushed with gold when Clay wrote daily in his classroom journals a couple of years prior.

As she recalls her creative approach that triggered Clay's innate writing talent, Enriquez twirls her long locks, sits back, and smiles, her bright, focused eyes beaming from a deeply tanned face. "If there was an expository essay, I'd say, 'How do you catch a wave? I've never been on a board. Tell me how you'd do it.' If it was a narrative, I'd say, 'Write a story about your best barrel.' If it had to do with parts of speech, I'd say, 'Tell me all the verbs that have to do with surfing. Give me all the adjectives.' And then the assignments would get completed.

"What was really cool about taking this approach with Clay is that surfing is so descriptive. It might be the most descriptive sport or lifestyle activity when it comes to figures of speech. The adjectives! The adverbs that support the adjectives! I could get really excited with him, because he would go into a different place. He was out on his board, on a wave. I was not there. He was completely comfortable talking to himself about what was happening. Many times, I wrote it down, handed it to him, and said, 'This is what you said. Write this down. See if I got it right.' He would transcribe what I'd written down into what he actually said, or meant to say, and that way we didn't have to worry about the conventions of writing mechanics. He could just say what he wanted to say."

She focused his assignments on one of her favorite subjects: direct relationships with the physical senses. "Taste was one, because I love eating almost as much as surfing," Clay says. "I would write something about what I eat. One time she gave me a paper plate. In the places where each part of your meal would be, she had me write how it feeds me, in what way. I just drew pictures of the kind of food I wanted on that part of the plate and what I was hungry for, and I wrote a little story about it."

"If you can articulate your relationship to your senses," Enriquez explains, "no matter the observation or situation, you're not only going to know yourself better, but also how and why you relate to your surroundings the way you do, and you're also going to gain deeper insight and knowledge into any environment you become a part of . . . which, I feel, triggers our innate desire to always learn and grow."

The impact of her teaching was not lost on her student. "She made me feel good about writing a lot on surfing and the ocean, because that is where I always want to go," Clay notes. "She liked my writing too. It was the first time since Mrs. Akiyama that a teacher told me she really liked the work I did."

The teacher's intense devotion and dedication paid off. Clay moved through sixth grade with a 3.1 grade point average, easily his highest overall mark since second grade. The GPA came with a bit of an asterisk: Enriquez convinced his other teachers to modify their course work so as to draw on his strengths while minimizing his weaknesses. For instance, rather than read in front of the class, a situation that petrified him far more than paddling out in shark-infested waters, Clay would complete an assignment by writing an essay or book report. Almost always, he threaded surfing into the work.

"I kind of took him under my wing, maybe because the other teachers saw that I got him. Or, to be more accurate, I was closer to getting him than they were," Enriquez says. "He's not a failure, and there was no way I was going to let that kid get an F on his report card. He just learns differently. That's on us, to learn how to connect with and bring out the best in these kids that learn differently. Why should he get an F? He got his three-point grade point average from me sitting with him after school, working with him, me saying,

'You can head to the beach as soon as we're done, but not until we're done'—and him doing the work."

As the serene Enriquez sips her coffee at a café not two hundred yards from the Marzo house, she closes her eyes, inhales deeply, and then reopens them. A deep focus emerges, rooted squarely in the larger picture of what Clay Marzo means to her, what she sees in him, how others can learn from his example, and how teaching him changed her approach to educating special needs students.

"He was poetic. There was a poetic quality to everything he saw, which makes sense, because he's feeling it at his cellular level," she says. "Most of us have to meditate and do deep visualization, or yoga postures and prayer, to reach the level he operates at all the time. Especially around water. It's his makeup. Being able to describe anything in nature . . . he was like on the other side of the clouds, describing it. He was able to describe so deeply.

"The lens he looks through is 360 degrees. When he wrote, you weren't going to get much punctuation, which would bother the heck out of the older, more traditional 'it has to be perfect' teachers, but he was describing everything as he felt it. He was looking through a very wide-angle lens. Art flows consistently throughout anything I teach and do, so with Clay, I got both well-chosen words and good drawings—usually of waves or ocean settings."

She recalls her favorite day in the classroom with the immediacy of watching a touching movie play out. "It was after school one day. It was only the two of us in the room. It was one of those 'tell me' assignments. I can see Clay in front of me, but he's *gone*, sitting on that board deep in his mind. He was able to describe the wave in a way where I had no idea *that's* what it was like to be on top of the water. I remember that, at that moment, I wanted what he had. I wanted to get on a surfboard and feel what he had just described to me. But to him, I wasn't there at all. He was just talking to himself.

"In class, he would rub his hands together or rub the desk, or trace surfing moves in the air with his hands. It took me a while to figure it out, but mentally, he was nowhere near the seat he was sitting in. He was gone, *surfing that wave*, being *on the wave*, while the rest of us thought we were watching a guy at his desk tracing swirls and curves in the air with his hand. When I watched this from the front of the room, I'm like, *Okay, I'm not calling on Clay now. He has* no idea *where we are.*"

She sits up straight, tucking her legs beneath the seat and folding her hands on top of the table. A broad smile fans across her face. "Do you know how amazing it must be to be that incredibly connected to what you love? Many of us never find out, not even for a minute or an hour. When it comes to surfing, he has that experience all the time."

Not every day was rosy. Enriquez and Jill held meetings — and an occasional tug of war — concerning the best ways for Clay to learn and to progress through school. "Mom was always trying to figure out how to make things easier," Clay remembers. "She felt comfortable talking with [Enriquez], who told me a lot how good I was doing."

"Jill cried — a lot. She was just trying to find out what would work," Enriquez explains. "She was just hoping *this teacher* would shed the light on 'What's wrong with my son? Why isn't he learning like everyone else?' It was painful for me to see a mom so attached that she's going to make it right for her son. She went to the end, to the Amen Clinic in California, to UCLA . . . she was going to find out what was wrong. That's why my heart goes out to her. She *did* find out.

"By the time Clay got to sixth grade, it was obvious academically and socially that he was very different. If we hadn't done all of those accommodations, he would have flunked. And the social side? It was like, 'Good morning, Bob.' Blank. 'Did you just hear me say good morning to you?' He's still looking at you. What's the normal reaction? 'God, kid, you are *so rude!*' Yes, it was that obvious.

"I just hung in there with Jill, trying to find out a way to make it work. And sometimes she would beg us to make an accommodation for him. 'Please, can you tell this social studies teacher not to make him read the chapter out loud and answer the seven questions? Could we let him do a project? Could we give him more time?'"

Not long ago, as Jill and a guest are dining at Betty's Beach Café, an old seaside eatery on Lahaina's north side known for its window views of passing sea turtles, the manatees of Hawaii—big, gentle, master-ful in water, and on-again, off-again when relating to humans—she says, "Clay really loves them." Then she hears a voice that makes her stop in mid-bite. She turns around to find Mary Anna Enriquez with several friends, all smiling at her. They greet each other, and as she finishes Jill puts her hand to her ear. "I'll call you," she mouths.

She turns to her guest, a smile on her face. "I love Mary Anna. What she did for Clay was so great, to see him for who he was and intuitively know how to work with an autistic kid, even though none of us knew. She was the one teacher in the middle of a bunch of really bad school experiences for Clay who took him in, figured out how to teach him, and positively reinforced him, again and again and again. And she did this while making him do the work. You know how hard it is to make Clay do anything he doesn't want to do? She found a way. I'll always be grateful to her for that."

Unfortunately for Clay, his father holds a different view of the entire situation. As Clay recalls, "The more Mom took me around to get me tested and find out what was different or wrong with me, the more Dad thought nothing was wrong. He always thought I was okay and always asked me, 'Why can't you just sit still in school and learn like everyone else?'"

Gino didn't ride Clay on everything. "I just wanted him to make enough effort to do okay in school. I didn't need a straight-A kid like a lot of other parents. But I didn't want one who didn't try either. I kept telling Jill that he just needed to get it together, to toughen up and focus more in school."

"Gino doesn't like anything abnormal," Jill says. "For him, it has to be normal. He liked that Clay was a surfer. 'C'mon, boy, do good in surfing, do good in school, buckle down.' That kind of guy. He probably thought I was crazy, but I was trying to figure out what to do. How do I help him help himself? How? It's still a struggle.

"I think Gino was in denial. He didn't go to any of the special ed meetings or parent-teacher conferences. He just gave Clay a lot of credit for surfing and was okay with mediocrity in school. 'I got Cs in school—just get through school and you'll be good.' He wasn't hands-on; he thought I was an enabler, making him a 'mama's boy.' Then again, a lot of people have said that about me. They still do. I'm pretty sure I am, to some degree. I don't want to be, but I don't know what else to do."

"I was so busy working, trying to make a living, that I didn't pay attention to a lot of his little struggles in school," Gino explains. "To me, he wasn't failing out. It wasn't a red flag. I thought he was like any other kid on Maui—'let's go surf and have fun and not worry about school.' I understand. I was one of those kids who played around in the classroom and made jokes and laughed instead of listened.

"Then I started hearing that my kid's got some weird difficulties in school. I had a hard time accepting the labels, the tests, and the explanations. I'm saying, 'Clay, *just pay attention!*' But everyone said he couldn't; it was difficult for him to process. I never fully accepted that. It's not like I wanted him to be an academic whiz. I was never the parent who pushed my kids to be a doctor, lawyer, or physicist. He's going to be what he's going to be. He'll figure it out. That's how I always saw Clay in school."

One of those who watched the growing crossfire was the teacher. Enriquez heard all about the conversations, arguments, and differences of opinion between Clay's parents from Jill—but never from Gino. "Gino knew I was Clay's teacher for English, but never asked me, 'How's Clay doing?' To me, as a teacher, it was bizarre that a parent wouldn't want to know if everything's okay in the class. 'Is he doing okay? What does he do?' He never wanted to know. He never asked.

"In some defense of Gino, there were teachers at our school who felt the same way: 'He's gotta grow out of it. Make him do it.' That was pretty tough. Gino had no idea what was going on with Clay, certainly no knowledge of Asperger's or autism, because none of us had made that particular correlation yet. I don't think anyone on the island even knew what to look for. But my own colleagues showing such insensitivity to a student's learning challenges? Well, it just spurred me on to pull Clay out of recess, get him back in class, and get him to finish that assignment."

· · ·

One autumn day a little more than a decade after he had last sat in Enriquez's classroom, Clay stood on the staircase at Ironwoods, part of the Kapalua Resort. He was checking out the surf for a quick session in his usual manner—silently, alone, reading the winds, tides, and swell direction, clicking off his observations against the super-computer of stored knowledge in his mind in order to answer one question: *Do I want to paddle out?*

As he scanned the sea, a benevolent face from the past approached him.

"I have another job as a wedding coordinator. Usually after school, in the evenings, I go to Ironwoods and have the wedding there," Enriquez explains. "One night I was coming up the steps, and Clay is standing there. He's standing at the steps in that quiet, Buddha stance he has, without a muscle flickering, just staring."

He broke his intense concentration to look into her eyes and move aside. "Hey, Clay," she said.

There was no discernible change in his facial expression. "But in his eyes, there was this sweet little smile," Enriquez says, her voice softening. "He gave me a head nod, but nothing from below the chin. How can such a strong smile only come out of your eyes?"

As soon as his old teacher walked past, Clay turned back to the sea. Enriquez, however, marveled over the quick exchange. "I walked up the rest of the steps thinking, *That was so cool! All's right with the world. That's how Buddha would have looked at the waves.* God, this kid is amazing!"

7

King Tide in Water, Ebb Tide on Land

I liked being home-schooled. I could get up in the morning, surf, do my schoolwork with Mom, surf, play on the floor with [the family dog] Kalani, then do more schoolwork and surf. Every day I got to surf three or four times a day. When you ask me about things that I think made me a better surfer, I'd say it was good to be surfing three or four times a day.

I got into shooting videos. I had to do something related to surfing because I missed paddling out all the time, like I could do when we lived in Puamana. Then I put hip-hop into my little soundtracks. What I like about hip-hop is the way the beat feels, like ripping a wave. There's the bum-bum-bum-bumphhh of the wave peeling or breaking hard, and the dude's words and the way he says them, which reminds me of throw-tails or off-the-tops or cutbacks or tube rides.

Mom gave me shit all the time about the [profane] lyrics [in the music over-dubs for the videos], but the music works for surf videos. So I dropped them into some of the videos I shot, because the beat is like the beat of riding sick waves, and it thumps through my head when I ride, and when I'm out of the water it gives me the feeling of being in the water. So if it has cussing, so what? I know all the words and say them to the music when I'm cruising around, but in the water it's all about the beat. That's why my friends like my video clips.

On Fridays, Clay was squirming in his classroom seat more than usual. It got worse as he grew older, because he knew what weekends meant — surfing with his friends and kicking butt in contests. He could sweep aside his schoolwork struggles and the strange looks and antagonistic approaches of other students, blow off all the testing he continued to undergo to better understand the world inside his brain, and focus on the arena where he reigned supreme.

Meanwhile, the entire Maui surfing brigade charged. Amateurs nationwide couldn't advance past the formidable assault of Dusty Payne, Granger Larsen, Wesley Larsen, Matty Schweitzer, Kai Barger, and Clay. They battled in contests, and they battled in daily surf sessions. "We surfed at all kinds of places on the island ... S-Bowls, Rainbows, the Pools, Shark Pit, Shitty's, Windmills, Honolua Bay, and Ironwoods," Clay says. He pauses for a moment, then resumes eye contact, a wry grin on his face. "Surf spots have pretty cool names, don't they? I like traveling around and trying to memorize all the names ... you can get the story of the place and the wave just by knowing its name."

There was plenty of precedent in the Marzo family. Cheyne was a strong trailblazer: he would parlay his distinguished amateur exploits into a professional career that lasted a decade. Clay watched Cheyne like a hawk because it had begun to occur to him that he could become a professional surfer too. Then he could feast on the perks of the lifestyle, most importantly the chance to travel to the most exotic locations around the world, which he only knew from magazine photos and his brothers' stories. All for a monthly salary plus bonuses for significant editorial coverage. What could possibly top that?

When the travel picked up significantly while Clay was still in sixth grade at Sacred Heart, somehow legitimate reasons had to be found for missing school, and not just for Clay but also for Dusty, Granger, and Wesley. It turned out to be no problem. "Ms. Waldrop [Enriquez] was really cool about letting us get out of school to surf in the big contests on the other islands, and when some of us went over to Cali or other places for contests," Clay says. "She figured out how good we were while winning, then turning pro and having our careers and living the dream."

Indeed, Enriquez viewed their trips as examples of what all students should be doing as they enter their middle school years — considering their futures. "I look at these four — Dusty, Clay, Granger, and Wesley — and on a much smaller scale, it's like The Beatles in their early days," she says, drawing raised eyebrows. *If you're comparing anyone to The Fabs, it had better be good.* "Four kids from the same town, a lot of the same friends, same schools, about the same age ...

they start hanging out together and surfing together, and then they all become stars on the world stage."

At first, Sacred Heart school administrators and fellow teachers dismissed her perspective. As the surfing quartet's successes grew and their notoriety spread, however, the faculty began to see the larger value of letting their students compete nationally and internationally. Whether they liked it or not, they knew that Maui is an island, one of the most beautiful in the world, and that educating children there involves paying a healthy amount of attention to the ocean. Kids stash their boards in bushes outside the classrooms, and the last hour of any school day when there's surf is the ultimate test of patience and forbearance for teachers. Attention spans? "Yeah, I always thought about the waves," Clay recalls, an opinion shared by every one of his surfing classmates. "Get me out of here, I need to surf."

Enriquez's idea that the surfing quartet was promoting cross-cultural exchange and striving for excellence began to take root — and other surf-crazed students eventually started aiming for the stars (and trips) too.

"After Clay, the Larsens, and Dusty left, we changed the rules in the parent-student-teacher handbook. Now if the kids have any major event they're going to, it's an excused absence," Enriquez explains. "I will not give a student-surfer an unexcused absence for trying to make it to Nationals, or surfing in Nationals — because they're trying to achieve personal excellence. How do you hold back a kid when he or she is trying to achieve excellence? You don't. It can spread to everything you do in your life. You look at people my age who grew up in, say, California . . . what did the teachers think of them being in contests or going surfing in the morning? 'Hey, kid, you got forty-eight cuts this semester; there's something wrong with you.'

"Now we've got all kinds of kids knowing they can become something internationally, winning contests as they come through our school, because Clay and the other boys showed them that they *can*. You should see how many fifth- and sixth-grade groms are trying to become really good, and now we support them."

. . .

Another thrilling aspect of top-flight amateur competition was meeting the sport's greats. At the 2003 NSSA Nationals, Clay met his hero, Rob Machado. One of the sport's all-time nice guys, the Southern Californian, now living in Australia, is considered among the greatest goofy-foot surfers in history. (Clay also surfs goofy-foot—his right foot forward as he faces the wave, thus moving to the spectator's right and his left.) Machado finished second in the world in 1995, fourth in 1997, and third in 2000. He's won four times at Banzai Pipeline, the most famous tube ride in the world. He also did his own voice-over in the blockbuster animated movie *Surf's Up*. "I love the way Rob surfs," Clay says, his eyes sparkling. "He pulls off great moves on huge waves, and he gets shacked all the time."

Clay will never forget what Machado said at a welcoming banquet for the NSSA Nationals competitors—or how it turned out: "You know, out of all you guys, there's going to be two who make a living at surfing." Machado was right: professional surfing is a huge leap from the amateur ranks, like jumping from A ball directly into the major leagues.

The audience at that banquet, however, included the largest group of future global stars since Kelly Slater, Machado, and the "Next Generation" had taken over the scene a dozen years before. "As it turned out, there was probably ten—because we were such a good group—but I remember thinking how much I wanted to be one of those two guys," Clay says.

Machado and Clay met again three years later, at the Summer X Games in Puerto Escondido, Mexico. Machado was a surfer-coach, and Clay was the youngest member of the West team. "He was really stoked to see me," Clay recalls, "and I was stoked to paddle out with one of my favorite surfers."

Also in 2003, Clay joined the Hawaiian contingent in South Africa for the Quiksilver ISA World Surfing Championship. While many Westerners venture to South Africa to go on safari, Clay and his fellow surfers were focused on Jeffreys Bay in the Eastern Cape province. J-Bay is legendary, a long, fast-tubing, right-hand break that's among the world's five favorite and most consistent waves during the Southern Hemisphere winter from June to September—perfect timing for school vacation. In the 1960s, J-Bay was primarily a hippie hangout, but Paul Naude and a few other wave riders turned the area into a surfing community in the 1970s. That spawned a legion of South African surfers from nearby towns who became World Tour stars and huge contributors to the industry, including 1977 world champion Shaun Tomson, his cousin Michael (the founder of Gotcha Sportswear, a premier brand in the 1980s), Marc Price, 1990 world titlist Martin Potter, and four-time women's world champion Wendy Botha. Today, perennial top-ten surfer Jordy Smith carries the banner.

Even though he was just thirteen, Clay reached the semifinals of the 2003 ISA World Surfing Championship against older competitors from a dozen nations in the under-sixteen division. "Surfing Jeffreys Bay with just a couple other guys out was really fun," Clay recalls. "You can ride Jeffreys Bay almost forever. It's like Rincon in California, but a lot gnarlier. J-Bay is one of the best waves I've ever ridden. I got a rush every time I took off, because I could just ride and rip and ride, and then the wave ends when your legs start really hurting . . . and it's like that all the time. I'd be out there getting rides and just . . ." he builds up, his chest expanding, "Yeahhhhhhhh!" This, from his living room, more than a decade later.

As Clay focused on competing, his preference for surfing in places without crowds grew more profound, which bothered both of his parents, though Jill, ever the protector of Clay's individuality, was more understanding than Gino. He was slowly withdrawing from daily sessions at places like Honolua Bay, which takes on the mien of a surf convention during big swells. "I wanted to do well so I could have the chance to surf great waves with no crowds to ruin my rides," he told *Freesurf* magazine. "I like surf contests when the waves are good, 'cause you get as many waves as you want with only a few guys. It feels so good when you know you're doing good. I like the bigger contests; you get to surf against more experienced surfers."

Years after that interview, while staring out at one of his favorite Maui spots, he says, "That's the one thing about the World Tour that I really like. You get to surf these classic spots — Teahupo'o, J-Bay, Trestles, Pipeline, Tavarua — with only three other guys out there. Or, if you make the man-on-man rounds, even better. One other guy.

Just like having that one friend. No one else to hassle you or fuck up your waves."

Meanwhile, the prevailing attitude toward school couldn't have been more diametrically opposite for mother and son. After sixth grade, Clay transferred up the road to Lahaina Intermediate, where he learned how intense, combative, and cruel middle school can be for overly sensitive students. Especially students with learning and communication issues that remained a mystery. Students like him. According to Enriquez, because of the prevailing ignorance in 2003 about how to identify and teach students on the autism spectrum, Clay never had a chance to succeed.

"If there is a program that is set up for a child at any place in the [autism] spectrum to fail, it's middle school," she says. "That's huge, because everything I've learned about an autistic child is that the sounds, movement, noise, bells, people constantly running around, the forty-five-minute class schedules, coming in with your supplies, going back and forth to your locker ... it runs these kids into the ground. So not only was Clay going through puberty, but now he's no longer in a self-contained place with one room and one teacher. Now there's all this passing back and forth; the transitions must have been hell for him. So his closing down happened then, and it was a case of him trying to manage getting from one class to the other — always with the deer-in-the-headlights look."

Clay's fear and loathing began before the opening bell. "I hated to even show up at the school," he says. "I would sit way down in the car until the bell rang, watching the clock, and then leave in just enough time to walk into class. After school, Mom had to be there to pick me up *exactly* when that bell rang."

"It was a major anxiety thing to get to school early," Jill adds. "That became more and more frequent as he got older. When he spent the night at friends' houses, I would have to get him right away the next morning — unless it was that one designated friend."

Clay's trouble involved not only struggles with academics and the classroom but with prejudice. The enmity of the local Hawaiian population toward *haoles,* or Caucasians, runs long and deep, stretching back to the early Christian missionaries in the nineteenth century. The Hawaiian population combines Japanese, Chinese, South Pacific Islanders, Portuguese, Koreans, and locals with direct ancestral ties to the Polynesians who first sailed to the Islands in their outrigger canoes more than a millennium ago. Westerners are considered the invaders, a dubious distinction. The territorial problem has spilled over to surfing, with areas such as Oahu's North Shore and Makaha, Maui's Honolua Bay, Kauai's Hanalei Bay, and most spots on the Big Island the scene of countless altercations over the years. The prevailing sentiment is, *Don't surf on my wave, and don't come to my beach.* While discrimination exists in locales around the world, it seems to be magnified in Hawaii.

One would think that a boy who has lived in Maui since he was nine months old would be considered local—especially when he's gained recognition as one of the nation's finest young surfers. Not so, as Clay found out firsthand.

"A local boy punched me out in the hallway because he thought I was giving him stink-eye, but I was only looking at his face to try to figure out what he wanted," he recalls, referencing a trademark characteristic of people with Asperger's, who find it nearly impossible to read facial expressions. "He thought I was staring at him, so when I kept looking at him, he punched me. You don't stare at local boys. They think it's their territory, and if they don't like you, they fight. The same thing happens in the water."

The hamster wheel of testing also fired up again at Lahaina Intermediate. This time some of it was Jill's doing. She had enrolled Clay in special education classes, to accommodate his slower processing speed, but concern arose that he might be removed from the program. "I sent him to see a specialist, and they didn't catch what it was," Jill says, rolling her green eyes and shaking her head. "They just said it was 'slow processing.' He said, 'You know, he's a surfer kid . . . kind of slow.' We heard that kind of idiotic stuff a lot."

After that visit, the hammer came down: Clay no longer qualified for special ed. Jill sought another opinion on his difficulties, which were growing at all levels—educational, social, and emotional. She was told that if there wasn't a measurable difference between Clay's

IQ and the accepted special ed level, he would lose the special ed designation he'd carried since first grade. "He needed special ed," Jill says. "He needed individual attention from someone a lot more patient and positive than some of the teachers he'd had. I was baffled by how they decided he didn't need it anymore."

The loss of special education status was the first of two pivotal events in Clay's life during middle school. The other was the family's move from Puamana, home to most of Clay and Cheyne's friends, readily accessible surf spots, and a familiar environment. The last factor was the most significant, since adaptability comes slowly, if at all, to people on the autism spectrum. The Marzos moved across Hanoapi'ilani Highway, the road between the coast and the mountains, to Launiupoko, where Jill's father, Clay Darrow, owned a five-acre tract on which there was nothing more than a pile of lava and scrub brush. Gino and Jill took two acres and went to work. Jill designed their house with the help of an architect, while Gino and his construction friends built it. They now lived 1,000 feet above sea level in the foothills of the rain-drenched West Maui Mountains, on a lava field with trucked-in dirt on top. Even though the new home was less than five miles from Puamana, it felt like another world.

"I was really bummed because I didn't have a ride to the beach unless Mom or Dad took me, and they were always busy," Clay says. "Cheyne had his chick and his pro career, so he wasn't around much. When he was, he always wanted to paddle out where the crowds were. When our tenant, Carl, moved into a rental we built above the garage, he liked to surf and he liked me. I got some rides to the beach from him, but it was still really hard to get to places unless I surfed there in contests.

"I liked the house at Puamana because it was on the ocean. At this new house, we had all kinds of different things. When it rained, the water flooded down the driveways, making it all muddy and puddles everywhere. I still hate to drive through puddles."

Jill and Gino noticed a deep change in Clay's moods and outlook after the move. Even though he had always been quiet, he would smile often and enjoyed the company of his surfing friends in Puamana. A sad, sullen boy appeared in Launiupoko.

"When I look back, one of the worst things that happened in Clay's life was us moving to Launiupoko," Jill admits. "He hated it up there. It was like we disconnected him from his power source, the water, where he could always be. We were only a few miles from the ocean, but it was a long few miles, up the hill where it rains a lot more than on the coast, no access to the beach unless he walked across the highway—which always scared me, knowing how spaced he can get when he sees the ocean, and only the ocean, in front of him. Even though we built a really nice house, I sometimes wished we never did it. As it was, we had to sell the place—because we were house-rich and pocket-poor—and move back to Puamana."

Soon after their move back to Puamana Jill could no longer take the way the faculty and students at Lahaina Intermediate treated Clay—or each other. After conferring with friends about home-schooling programs, she acted against the expressed wishes and perspectives of the other men in her house, Gino and Cheyne, and pulled Clay from school. "I went back to the school for a meeting, and the whole time I'm walking across the playground I hear 'fuck this' and 'fuck that' coming from seventh and eighth graders," Jill says. "I knew this just wasn't a good situation for Clay. He models people's behavior; that's how he makes it through social situations. When he heard it, he then said it, and then couldn't figure out why I got on his case. To him, it was perfectly acceptable because he'd seen others do it, and he lacked that discernment to figure out right from wrong. I couldn't have my kid in an environment like that. Since he'd lost his special ed status, they stuck him in a classroom with all the troublemakers. So he's modeling them. Plus he's traveling and trying to keep up with grades."

Back home, life quickly became a living hell. Fed up with the constant testing and professional opinions about what he perceived as his son's unwillingness to pay attention, Gino leveled one salvo after another at Jill and Clay. Right with him was Cheyne, who saved some of his fiercest enmity for Jill. The conflict spread across all quarters, causing battles between Cheyne and Clay, Jill and Gino, Cheyne and Gino, Clay and Gino, and ultimately leading to Cheyne's firm opposition to the way Jill was seeking out explanations for Clay's struggles.

Cheyne and Gino agreed on little as Cheyne began what every well-adjusted young man does in due course: emancipating himself from the home environment. One thing stepfather and stepson agreed on, however, was that Clay belonged in public school and that his problems with academics stemmed from his lackadaisical attitude as much as (or more than) any perceived learning or social disorder. "I think that's when the communication breakdown with Clay and me started, for sure," Cheyne says. "I think that's when the communication breakdown between Clay and a lot of people outside our family started . . . the outside world, pretty much.

"I'm a social person, and Clay is not naturally sociable like I am. So let's establish that. But I also believe that being social is a skill you can learn to some degree if you're willing to try, even if you have Asperger's. Would it be ten times harder for him than everyone else? Yeah, but I still wish he would've gone through school because it would've helped more than hurt in the end."

Though Cheyne's words hurt her, as did the early fracturing of the family, Jill was resolute that Clay needed a far more focused and individualized approach than Lahaina Intermediate would give him. Publicly, she often said that Clay was being home-schooled because of how often he was traveling for contests, which was an acceptable explanation since Dusty Payne and Granger Larsen were being home-schooled for the same reason. She and the other boys' parents learned about the Meyer B. Thompson program, which emphasizes targeted learning, a computer-based model aimed at self-starting kids. The Thompson team provides the required GED curriculum to parents, makes tutors available for specific subjects, and holds weekly meetings between a coordinating teacher, the primary home-schooling adult (usually a parent), and the student.

As Jill sorted out Clay's strengths and weaknesses and tried to make the drastic switch from doting parent to primary teacher, the areas of greatest academic concern popped up swiftly. Appearing like a sudden outbreak of brushfires, these deficits threatened to ignite a major conflagration that could engulf every educational benefit he'd derived to that point. "I saw the deficiencies in almost everything," she says. "I knew if we focused, we could get through it, but how do you focus a kid on so many subjects when he's always had trouble?"

She put Clay on a strict regimen of reading, penmanship, and math. She didn't worry about his creative writing skills, which were already substantial and had been further sharpened by Enriquez. After working with him for a while, she knew she needed help in all areas — and that help gave her deep insight into Clay's mind. "I got him a math tutor, and he would say to me, 'Clay jumps way ahead. He can't handle all the stuff to get the solution; he just gets there without doing all the work along the way,'" Jill recalls.

The tutor's remarks reminded her of Clay's modus operandi in the water, and then another revelation occurred to her, almost a *Beautiful Mind* moment: "I think there's a lot to say between this way of solving math problems, and the way he anticipates what a wave is going to do . . . he sees where it's going before just about anyone else does. He may not articulate it that well, but that's just because his mind is moving so fast and already visualizing what he's going to do on the wave, where he's going to position himself, things like that. He doesn't need to put it into words; he expresses himself nonverbally."

Eventually, home-schooling proved daunting and agonizing. For the first time, serious rifts developed between Jill and Clay, which she faced while simultaneously dealing with an increasingly critical husband who believed Clay should not have been removed from public school. Still, Gino wasn't Jill's biggest day-to-day concern. Getting Clay to focus was. "I couldn't get him off the floor with the dog, talking to the dog, playing around with the dog, barking with the dog," she says. "I think it's because the dog always loved him back, never questioned him, just loved him."

One project did take hold and later contributed to Clay's professional surfing fortunes: shooting video. The family video shelves were filled with home movies Jill had shot of Cheyne and Clay's surf sessions, along with family parties and trips. After dinner, the family would get together, whip up popcorn, and watch their movies, which was when Jill noticed that Clay liked to watch Cheyne's rides, and his own, over and over again.

"Sometimes I watch them to see what I was like as a little kid, as a little surfer," Clay says. "It's fun seeing your first tube ride that was filmed, or gnarly wipeouts as a grom. Back then, I watched the videos of Cheyne, over and over and over, because I wanted to succeed like him."

Clay's school project was fairly simple. Every day he would take the video camera to the ocean and shoot footage of others surfing. When Jill came along, which was often (after all, he needed a ride down the hill), she filmed Clay, who was beginning to show the cat-quick, explosive moves and knack for innovation and adjustment that would catapult him to international stardom. "I'd go down there and run the camera a lot," she says. "If I ever missed a wave, he was like, 'Mom, you missed *the best wave!*' Even if I missed one wave in a whole session, the crappiest little wave, he picked up on it. He knew every wave from every session, and the order he rode them."

Clay occasionally added effects like slo-mo, freeze-frame, and even basic graphics. While they aren't professional quality, the video clips reflect the thoughts of an adroit young filmmaker who made each one as distinctive as possible. Finally, he converted his clips into MP3 files and hit Send, emailing them to friends.

The video work was a saving grace, an avocation that demands an artist's vision and concept, an expert's eye with the camera, and a detail-obsessed technician's love of editing and postproduction. "The video project was perfect for Clay, because it was very visual, creative, and he could bring surfing into it," Jill says. "Plus, since the home-school program was Internet-based, he had the perfect project to not only do a correspondence school like this, but to become proficient on the Internet. He's been very good on the Internet since. He became a good video editor and producer; it was hard for me to believe a fourteen- or fifteen-year-old kid could shoot and produce videos this crisp, this good. They would be wonderful little thirty- to sixty-second movies. He didn't take the time to fine-tune them, but they were really good . . . and everybody thought so. They kept asking him to send more."

Clay's video work, combined with Jill's dedication to shooting new footage, came into play in a huge way two years later. While a

key member of Quiksilver's large and impressive professional surfing team, Cheyne told team manager Strider Wasilewski that they
needed to look at Clay, who was already a member of Quiksilver's
amateur team. Cheyne thought Clay was past the amateur level: he
saw Clay as a professional. "I told Cheyne to let me see something
where Clay was free surfing, not surfing in a contest," Wasilewski, a
former professional surfer, recalls.

Clay and Cheyne sent Wasilewski one of the videos Clay edited
and produced as a home-schooling project. That video contributed in
a big way to Quiksilver's decision to sign him professionally. So did
his perfect performances in the NSSA Nationals.

8

Perfection

I was getting my reverse throw-tail down. Surf photographers and video guys were starting to shoot it. I tried it in contests because I scored a lot of points, but I really liked doing it on every wave I could at home, where it was just me and the wave . . . a lot more comfortable. What you do is come up on the wave, slide out the tail of your board so it looks like you're in a stalling airplane, and then snap! snap! snap! and throw water out the back. Then you swing the board around so that you're surfing on the face of the wave again.

A lot of people say I'm the one who came up with it. I have seen other people do something similar to it, guys like Ry Craike and Julian Wilson, two of my favorite Australian surfers. I was starting to land this move every time.

He stared at the sparkling new Toyota Matrix, which sat in an unlikely spot — Lower Trestles. He could not keep his eyes off the red car. He imagined himself cruising the roads in Maui, pulling up to check out the surf, hip-hop and rock blasting from the speakers . . . always in this car. It belonged to him. He had to possess it. He could feel it. *I know I have to win it so I'll have a car to drive when I get my driver's license, and Mom and Dad won't have to buy me a car.*

The Matrix awaited the winner of the 2005 NSSA Nationals Open Men's Championship. When Clay, his family, and teammates flew to California for his fifth NSSA Nationals, no one expected the fourteen-year-old to move up one age group and seize the grand prize from the nation's greatest amateurs, several of whom would turn pro immediately following the event. It would be like a middleweight champion trying to oust the heavyweight.

However, his focus changed when he saw the Matrix. *Game on.*

• • •

Clay had already tasted victory in the NSSA Nationals. In 2004 he won the Open Juniors' Division, his first national title. He entered the event ranked number one in the Explorer Boys' Division in the NSSA, his second top seed for the tournament, and he also captured two Open Juniors' events. Then he finished second in the Hawaiian Amateur Surfing Association Championships in both the Open Boys' and Open Men's.

In the 2004 NSSA Nationals, Clay found all the right waves at Trestles, a shifty, tricky peak that can make a knowledge of how to read waves of paramount importance. On this day he read them masterfully, with a little Merlin thrown in. It seemed like the waves came to him when summoned. He ripped one after another, unleashing the moves that would practically sign his contracts down the line. Best of all, he didn't fall, even scoring a "perfect" on one. *Freesurf* magazine publisher Mike Latronic, a top big-wave pro surfer in the 1980s and 1990s, had this to say:

> *Marzo destroyed his early round heats so thoroughly that by the time the quarterfinals, semis and finals came around, he was pulling off hard tailslide snaps and making it look easy.*

After accepting his Explorer Boys' and Open Juniors' championship trophies on the awards scaffold, Clay jumped down and prepared to celebrate with his friends and parents, but his fellow surfers surprised him with questions. "They asked me what my strategy was." He responded with a laugh that as much as said, with typically blunt honesty, *Don't you know?* "Strategy? I just go out there and catch waves and throw it down and see what happens."

In the surfing world, new maneuvers are celebrated almost as much as the wave warriors who develop them. They are named, dissected, featured in magazines and videos, emulated, and then incorporated into the sport's colorful lexicon. You know you've made an impact when your moves show up in major contests for years, blasting from the boards of other surfers. Moves such as rail grabs, aerial floaters, roundhouse cutbacks, snaps, re-entries, floater re-entries, and getting slotted (tucking into a barrel) are as colorful in name as they are in practice. Iconic wave riders such as Gerry Lopez, Matt Kechele, Tom Carroll, Tom Curren, Shaun Tomson, Mark Richards, Cheyne Horan, the late Andy Irons, and Rob Machado spent years experimenting, falling off, and refining these moves to get them right. Then they raised the bar of performance surfing one rung at a time, none more so than Kelly Slater.

It is exceedingly rare for a surfer in the twenty-first century to come up with an entirely new maneuver. Especially when he's a young teenager. What permutation of style, contortion, and action on a wave hasn't been tried? For a fourteen-year-old to innovate a maneuver that catches the world by storm? Almost unheard of.

For that reason, the beach was abuzz over Clay's searing snaps — everyone talking about how his board seemed to switch directions beneath his feet at the most critical part of the wave, then how he'd recover, his reflexes quick as a cat's, his flexibility that of a longtime yoga practitioner. "I'm in my place, where I work with the wave and I don't care if anyone else is around, because it's just me and the wave and I have to have my greatest ride on every wave," he says. "When I pull it off, then I like to see people's reactions . . . I just want them to like what I did."

After the event, the sport's top two magazines, *Surfing* and *Surfer*, gave him glowing appraisals. The *Surfing* staff wrote:

> *14-year-old Clay Marzo was setting the standard with his speed, power and gouging turns. He was one of only two surfers who nailed a perfect 10 in the championships when he destroyed a Lowers beauty in Juniors round one. All week long you could hear the whispers on the beach: "That Clay kid rips!"*

Meanwhile, *Surfer* wrote:

> *Clay Marzo won . . . with a textbook approach, mixing combos like an all-time sesh at a low-key home break.*

What amazed the throng as much as Clay's reverse throw-tails was the fact that he won not one but two national titles. After Clay captured the Explorer Boys' final, as expected, no one anticipated that he would double in the Open Juniors' against older surfers — including Clay. "When they said over the PA that I won, I was so surprised that I dropped to my knees," he says. "Then I found out I was the first surfer from Maui to win an NSSA National title. I thought for sure my brother Cheyne won when he was surfing NSSAs, but he always seemed to get shut down on waves at Trestles, which happens when Trestles goes flat — but it wasn't flat for me. The waves came when I needed them."

It was a perfect week. Between the two divisions, Clay surfed in eight heats. He won all eight. Chris Cote of *Transworld Surf* noted:

> *Clay showed fluid style, a deep bag of tricks, and the stamina. Clay showed the crowd an amazing array of speed and flair on his way to domination in both divisions. Look for this kid to smash some pros on his way to the World Tour.*

Only one NSSA mountain remained to be conquered: the Open Men's.

Shortly after the Nationals, Clay and his fellow Hawaiians traveled to Huntington Beach, known as "Surf City USA" ever since Jan and Dean sang the phrase into American culture during the early 1960s, when surf music, sidewalk surfing, and the Hollywood-depicted beach scene were all the rage throughout the country. Clay and his friends turned out for the American Surfing Championships, a team competition. They dominated, and the reward was a wild card entry into the Open Juniors' event of the world's best-attended pro event, the US Open of Surfing, which draws crowds akin to the Rose Bowl.

Close to 100,000 people watched the contest from the beach and pier. Given Clay's deepening disdain for crowds of any kind — in the water, on the beach — it wouldn't have been a huge surprise if he had wilted under the floodlights of so many eyes and faces. Not this time. He relished the chance to surf Huntington Beach Pier's fabled south side with only three others in the water, about 5 percent of the wetsuit-clad masses who bobbed in the lineup on any given morning.

He didn't win, but it didn't matter. He put on a show. The crowd roared. Many pros watched him, not at all liking this glimpse into a future when they might be supplanted.

If that wasn't enough, Clay's 2004 season ended with a true "to the victors go the spoils" moment: *Surfing* magazine named him one of the "Hot 100" up-and-coming surfers in the world. What a perfect year . . .

The next year would be even better.

Clay began 2005 in Indonesia, where he joined a trip to shoot a new movie Quiksilver was producing, *Young Guns 2*. Even though Clay was still an amateur, Quiksilver invited him after seeing the home videos he produced. The biggest thrill for Clay wasn't so much the fact that a couple million people worldwide would eventually see the movie — he finds it very difficult, if not impossible, to project outcomes — but the chance to surf with some of his personal favorites and maybe get one or two rides in the new movie. "I loved surfing in Indo . . . all these different kinds of waves!" he later told his dad.

In April, he traveled to Australia for Camp Hobgood, an invitation-only adventure in which veteran ASP World Tour stars C. J. and Damien Hobgood instructed top juniors on how to succeed as professional surfers, presenting new approaches to strategy, performance, and developing a professional attitude. The identical twins organized the camp with their manager, Mitch Varnes, who would later handle Clay's endorsement deals and manage his career. *Surfing* magazine called Camp Hobgood "the pre-eminent training camp for America's most promising surfers." Clay attended with Dusty Payne, California surfers Nick Rosa, Chris Waring, and Dane Gudauskas, and Florida's Jeremy Johnston and Eric Geiselman, all of whom he had defeated in past competitions. *Surfing* and Fuel TV provided substantial media coverage.

The Hobgood brothers have been recurrent faces in and out of the world's top sixteen since 1999 — an eternity in a sport in which careers peak at ages twenty-five to twenty-eight and few win after thirty. (Although that has changed since the ASP World Tour began to focus its schedule on big-wave venues, where experience and big-wave moxie often triumph over sheer youthful athleticism.) C. J. brought home the world championship in 2001, but the 9/11 attacks, which truncated the schedule, prevented him from capping it off at the season-ending Pipeline Masters. "What I really like about C. J. and Damien is they surf goofy-foot like me, and they rip it and love big tubes. So do I," Clay said after the camp.

As the camp participants surfed great waves all week, the Hobgoods continually schooled them on the steps they needed to take to become solid pro surfers. Since the subject was surfing and the idea was to create a livelihood wrapped around his favorite sport, Clay was locked in. He absorbed the week like a six-foot-one sponge, impressing the Hobgoods. "I really wanted to be a great pro surfer, and the waves were so good that I got to do the things that bring out my best performance. The waves worked with me so much."

At the end of the camp, the Hobgoods held a contest; the winner would receive the "King of the Camp" award. For the first time, Clay found himself in an event in which more than a title and trophy were on the line. When he saw the king's crown, a sword, and an iPod shuffle in the mix, he locked into super-focus — that exalted place that sports champions and the most successful summon when it's time to win. The same place he went to when he saw the Matrix. Clay loves his swag, and if getting it requires kicking everyone's ass in the water, then so be it. "I still have the iPod shuffle, with all my songs from back in the day," he says. "I also won $1,000 in cash, but I couldn't really do anything with the money since I was still an amateur. I had to give up the cash a few times. I didn't care, because I had the iPod shuffle."

C. J. Hobgood came away with one question: how good and dominant could Clay Marzo be? "By the end of the trip, you watch Clay Marzo surf and feel without a doubt in your mind that he was the best 15-year-old surfer on the planet," he told *Surfing*.

> *He had all the moves, crazy airs, quick on the backhand, and a forehand to die for. He was so barrel-savvy frontside it was crazy. Plus, he blew the tail and pretty much caught air on every one of his off-the-tops. We actually nicknamed him "go-go gadget fin" at one*

point, because he did this thing where he'd hit the section, grab the tail and spin real quick — so fast, you'd be like, "wait a minute, does he have fins in?" — and then go down the line like it was normal again.

Two months after Camp Hobgood, Clay returned to Lower Trestles for the 2005 NSSA National Championships, where expectations were now very different than in any previous event he'd ever surfed. He was the defending champion in two divisions, and the other surfers and the magazines continually asked him how it felt. Predictably, he shut down. The colorful descriptions that machine-gunned off his lips when only a few friends were watching him lacerate two hours of waves turned into one-word answers. "Get him one-on-one, no matter the interviewer, and he sometimes doesn't shut up," his manager Mitch Varnes says. "He's great. Put him and a reporter in a big crowd and . . ."

As Clay recalls the moment, his shiny eyes try to bury themselves in the ground. His smile vanishes. "All I wanted to do was see my friends again and surf with only a couple more people out at Trestles."

The surf was cranking — five to six feet, with a bit of morning offshore wind and midday onshore breeze, the waves peeling both right and left. It was an ideal week at Lower Trestles. Perfection.

Then he noticed the Toyota Matrix on the beach. "When he saw that car, he turned to me and said, 'I have to have that car. If I win, that's my car! I wanna get the car,'" Gino remembers.

Every year Gino accompanied Clay to the NSSA Nationals, which they turned into father-and-son time, surfer style — catching waves on their own and eating junk food at places like Surfing Donuts and Pedro's Tacos. Jill helped out on the planning side. She organized plane tickets, made sure Clay stayed healthy, and kept his mounting victories and successes in perspective — that is, when she wasn't clipping every article, photo, and advertisement tear sheet to put in what became one of the more comprehensive scrapbook collections possessed by a professional surfer.

In the Open Men's final, Clay threw down his magic full-force. He opened with a perfect 10-point ride, his third such score in a 2005 NSSA event. Earlier in the year, at Pinetrees in Kauai, he had planted two perfect 10s in the Open Juniors' final of Regionals.

It is exceedingly difficult to post a perfect 10. Competitors are subjectively scored by five judges, all highly knowledgeable and experienced watermen, who use a variety of criteria: wave selection, difficulty of maneuvers, length of ride on the best part of a wave, how well the surfer connects maneuvers, overall style, and an "X" factor — how the performance matches up against the combined potential of the conditions and the surfer. The high and low scores are thrown out, and the other three are averaged. A 10-point ride is as infrequent in a high-level surfing event as a 10 in national, international, or Olympic-level gymnastics.

Clay found that out in a hurry. On his next wave, he managed only a 6.0. While Gino was exhorting him to dig deeper, to connect his maneuvers better, Clay shrugged and turned his board around to distance himself from his father's voice. Instead, he listened to the ocean as he always did — with his hands in the water, feeling the subtlest of currents and shifts of water before paddling into the places where he felt the next good waves would break.

Everyone in the final was ripping, but none more so than Torrey Meister, against whom Clay had competed before in HASA events. Meister, who lived in Haleiwa, the entry point to Oahu's fabled North Shore, opened with a sizzling 9-point ride. Then he threw down another big score, an 8.

"You're down! You're down! You need an 8!" Gino yelled at Clay from shore.

Clay heard that one. "I didn't really think about being down, but then I remembered something: no victory, no car," he later said.

Late in the heat, a big set came. Clay turned around and dropped in late and deep, *impossibly* late, an abrupt one-way ticket to the painful rock reef for nearly every other surfer on the planet. But that was where his hands, eyes, and instinct led him, and by God that was where it was either going to happen or not. He somehow stayed on his feet, his cat-quick reflexes matched by practically unfathomable balance, and found himself far back in the barrel. Several seconds later—an amount of time so long that some surfers call it "camping in there"—he shot out at blazing speed, launched into a reverse throw-tail, nailed it, and threw his arms high into the air. "Yeahhhh-hhh!" Every person on the beach heard him. They also saw the greatest ride of his amateur career.

They went crazy.

A minute later, the judges' scores were posted: 10-10-10. Another perfect 10! The NSSA Nationals score only the two best rides, no matter how many a surfer catches during the heat, so Clay now sat on a perfect score of 20—the first in the organization's twenty-seven-year history, and still unmatched (as of 2014). There was no way mathematically that Meister could catch him.

"The car was mine!" Clay exclaims, instantly flashing back to that moment. "Everyone cheered and came up to me when I got out of the water. I usually hate it when lots of people I don't know come up to me, because you don't know who likes you or who hates you and there are a lot of hateful people out there, but this time I knew almost everybody, so it was really cool."

One of the people who cheered as he worked was Alan Gibby, whose company, DynoComm Productions, had opened the floodgates for regular surf programming on ESPN, network affiliates, and other networks worldwide in the 1980s, providing a steady stream of shows for the next twenty-five years. Gibby has seen and filmed hundreds of contests, including most NSSA Nationals and major tournaments at Lower Trestles. Even now, nearly a decade after Clay's perfect performance, the surf broadcast pioneer marvels at what he saw.

"From my view, Marzo's NSSA performance is right up there with Tom Curren's win in the Stubbies Surf Trials in 1982 and Kelly Slater's Star-Trunks win in 1990, before Quiksilver signed him," Gibby says. "As Clay came to the beach and as his buddies lifted him into the air, the crowd energy and excitement was something I will never forget. He knew he had done something special.

"Clay's surfing in that contest was so effortless, though he does have power when he wants to turn it on. I saw him pull off the first move in the final and thought to myself, *Did I really just see that? Am I seeing things?* Then he did the same maneuver again, perfectly. I knew it was history-making. I rushed back to our studio that evening and watched his final wave fifty times."

Meanwhile, Jill's amazement over Clay's accomplishment soared through the roof — and she's not one to understate either of her sons' surfing prowess. "He wasn't even supposed to be in that final, because of his age," she points out, "and the other funny thing was, he now had this car but he was too young to drive it! So it just sat in our driveway until he got his license. All these years later, despite the money he's made, he still has that car. He's still as obsessed with that car as the day he won it. It's starting to get a little banged up, but you can't tell him that. He feels like it's a waste to get rid of it."

Clay won the car, the Governor's Cup as the Open Men's champion, and an award he still cherishes: the Kalani Robb Most Inspirational Award. Robb was a world-title contender in the 1990s, part of the amazing Next Generation that also included Slater, Machado, Benji Weatherly, Conan Hayes, and Shane Dorian. "Kalani Robb is one of my favorite surfers ever — the dude rips! I even named my dog after him," Clay said while petting Robb's furry namesake.

Later the Marzos learned that Clay was only the third fifteen-year-old to win Open Men's. When they heard the news while surfing a World Tour event, C. J. and Damien Hobgood must have thought, *What else would anyone expect, after what we saw at Camp Hobgood?*

Clay not only won his title but also led a full-throttle Hawaiian onslaught at the NSSA Nationals. They won four of the six open divisions with a cast now familiar to the surfing world. The Open Girls' belonged to Carissa Moore, who later won the 2011 and 2013 ASP World Tour titles after capturing a record eleven NSSA National Division crowns. She also was named the 2013 *Glamour* Magazine Woman of the Year. Barger won the Open Juniors'; later he became pro surfing's Junior World Champion. John John Florence beat Kolohe Andino in the Open Boys'; today they are among the world's top-ranked surfers. Mason Ho, who finished fourth in the Open Men's, won the 2013 Hawaiian Island Creations Pro. His father, Michael, was a top-five surfer in the World Tour's early years.

One other performer set the motivational and inspirational tone for Clay and the Hawaiians. Their fellow competitor and good friend

Bethany Hamilton finished fourth in the Open Women's, her first NSSA Nationals since losing her left arm to a tiger shark. Her resulting memoir, *Soul Surfer: A True Story of Faith, Family, and Fighting to Get Back on the Board,* was a bestseller. In addition, her NSSA performance was depicted (somewhat accurately) in the 2011 biopic *Soul Surfer,* which starred Dennis Quaid, Helen Hunt, and Carrie Underwood. Hamilton served as a consultant.

A few months later, the Hawaiians returned to California for the Quiksilver ISA World Junior Surfing Championships at Huntington Beach. They kept their feet pinned to the accelerator. Clay relished every moment, joining his friends and unleashing his best surfing while feeling pressure-free in the twenty-seven-nation competition. He finished second to Tonino Benson in the Under-Sixteen Boys' Division, Carissa Moore took third in the Under-Eighteen Girls', and Payne and Granger Larsen both made their finals. Hawaii captured the world team title by a wide margin over Brazil and the United States. (In surfing, Hawaii is considered separate from the US mainland.) One of the coaches told the *Honolulu Advertiser,* "Those two guys [Tonino and Clay] carried us to the team win because we were the only team to get a first and a second in any division — that's a lot of points."

After reminiscing and viewing scrapbooks and videos from his remarkable 2005 season, Clay grows silent. He locks into his distant glare, then returns his concentration to the room a minute later. "I don't like looking back," he says. "Right after it happens, I'm over it. I move on. But at the 2005 Nationals, it was like winning the Olympics. My life changed forever."

9

New Sensation

My dream was coming true. People thought I was a different person, like a freak, and my style was totally different. I kept getting more and more movie and photo trips because everyone liked the way I surfed. I always go for it on every wave, give everything I have to every moment in the water. People see that as being different, because in contests they hold back a lot of times so they can connect certain moves and turns and score points. When I can go for it in a contest and not fall off, I score a lot of points and do really well. Like getting two perfect 10s in Nationals. Sometimes I blow it and fall off, but not towards the end of my amateur career. That's why I turned pro when I was at the top of my game and still getting better.

It happened fast. Lightning fast. Surf manufacturers flush with cash stumbled over each other to sign Clay. The benefits were too good to resist. As one of the world's most dynamic, creative, and physically striking surfers, Clay would be the focal point of photo shoots, leading to vast editorial coverage in magazines and videos. In the surf media business, if you show up in magazines, your sponsors receive free exposure and you get paid incentives. Clay would draw photographers and video producers from Indonesia to France, from the US mainland and Hawaii to Australia, and from all points in between. He was the boy who had it all. Not since eventual eleven-time world champion Kelly Slater turned pro in 1990 had a wave rider offered a company so much potential exposure or stirred up such excitement.

"I didn't know much about turning pro or everything you have to do as a pro," he recalls. "I just wanted to take trips and surf contests all over the world with my Maui crew, and also surf with some of my heroes, like Kelly Slater."

The fight for Clay's services began on the *Young Guns 2* trip. The "talent," young and veteran surfers from the United States, Hawaii, and Australia, cruised off the Sumatran coast on the *Indies IV*, a 115-foot yacht with private cabins the size of hotel rooms. The "stars" walked around in white robes and spent their nonsurfing time watching TV and movies, listening to music, riding Jet Skis, and eating food prepared by gourmet chefs. Several times a day, a helicopter would leave the pad on the yacht's roof deck and fly along the coastlines of the Mentawais and Nias, searching for waves. It wasn't difficult. As Clay puts it, "The waves were perfect!"

His involvement in *Young Guns 2* became possible because of the DVD he sent Quiksilver at Cheyne's urging. "The video was so mind-boggling that I immediately turned it over to Quiksilver International so I could get this kid on the *Young Guns* trip," former team manager Strider Wasilewski said. "What blew me away was how difficult his moves were, and how he took chances on every part of the wave, doing stuff no one else would even try, but how natural it was for him. He never seemed to waver, even in the worst situations. He'd come out of it on his feet, like a cat."

Young Guns 2 featured global surf stars like Slater, Dane Reynolds, and Freddie Pattachia, along with up-and-coming talent such as Clay and Julian Wilson. At fifteen, Clay was the youngest rider. During the two weeks when seven videographers were filming in the Mentawais, the group discovered a thick left-handed break called Greenbush. Clay took one look at the wave, watched how it hollowed out, and thought he'd just died and gone to heaven. The skilled cameramen filmed the surfers in ways he had never dreamed of being filmed — footage was shot from helicopter angles, from Sea-Doos, and from inside the barrels, with surfers racing toward the camera and then exiting the waves. Then the cameramen would be thrashed on the reefs or hard-sand bottoms, but no matter. To paraphrase George Lucas, they did anything they had to do to get the shot.

For a Maui boy whose previous trips centered on competition and adult supervision, the experience of surfing some of the Indian Ocean's finest waves with so much freedom was overwhelming — and eye-opening. It was in Indonesia, on this trip, that Clay was first bitten by the notion of making a living by freestyle surfing.

Gino remembers an aspect of the trip that impressed Quiksilver as much as Clay's limitless talent. "The Australia Quiksilver rep had Julian Wilson as their young protégé," he says. "I heard through Strider that the rep was baiting Strider with comments like, 'Hey, let's see how good this Clay Marzo kid of yours is, wait till he gets up against Julian Wilson...' It was a bit in the spirit of 'My Aussie is better than your Yank,' part of the water sports rivalry between Oz and America that's been going on for forty years, between surfing, the America's Cup...

"Well, Clay blew Julian Wilson out of the water. His turns were far more dynamic and difficult. Julian could see what Clay was doing and made sure to learn from [Clay's moves], which made him a stronger World Tour competitor."

Clay's other highlight was surfing alone with Kelly Slater. Slater has dominated pro surfing since 1990. During that time, he has forced officials to rewrite judging criteria to favor bigger, riskier moves, while extending the limits of performance wave riding. In 2013 Slater won a record seventh Pipeline Masters title and very nearly his twelfth world title at the age of forty-two. Six of the top thirty surfers on the ASP World Tour *hadn't even been born* when Slater won his first crown in 1992. Many sports pundits have compared Slater to Michael Jordan, Tiger Woods, and other great sports champions, for the way he not only dominated his sport but increased the overall performance level.

On this day in Indonesia, the starstruck teenager surfed with his idol for an hour. "We were really quiet out there, didn't say a lot, he watched me surf, and I watched him surf. He gave me a couple of tips about turns and certain moves, but that was it. On shore, he told all of us some stories about his adventures all over the world. I listened to every word he said. I wanted to live those exciting stories in my own surfing, so I could tell other people someday."

Clay was the breakout surfer of the *Young Guns 2* trip. One magazine described him as "the technical new-school phenom." Quiksilver quickly made the phenom a household name by inserting DVDs into every subscription and newsstand copy of *Surfer, Surfing, Transworld Surf, Tracks* (Australia), and *Surfing Life* (Australia) magazines. That amounted to hundreds of thousands of free DVDs.

"Literally overnight, he became a surf star," Strider says. "You know how you might have a great product, yet if no one sees it, it's not known as a great product? It was the same thing. When that movie got into people's hands, they saw Clay. He's been a star ever since."

"When my career took off, people kept pointing to *Young Guns 2* as the movie that helped to make me," Clay says. "What I remember is how great the waves were — and how much I liked shooting video. And surfing with Kelly."

A few months later, in the fall of 2005, the Maui crew received a feature story in *Freesurf,* Hawaii's premier surfing magazine. The article, "Maui No Ka 'Oi: A Generation of Maui's Finest Comes of Age," featured interviews with seasoned hands — including Clay's on-again off-again coach Matt Kinoshita — who were asked to comment on the hot young surfers. "Clay is about the most explosive surfer I have ever seen," Kinoshita said. "He is an inventive surfer and doesn't copy the style of others. I hope he gets due credit for his innovative surfing style."

Clay also chimed in. "I like to compete. It brings up the level of surfing. We are all really competitive on Maui and we are all still really good friends."

A barrage of phone calls, sales pitches, cash and merchandise offers, travel assurances, and other promises flooded the Marzos' phone line. Managers and agents called in earnest, seeking to sign Clay before someone else swooped him up. Jill and Gino were initially joyous, then overwhelmed, and finally overmatched. How could two parents with limited direct knowledge of the surf business deal with it? Five years prior, they had experienced Cheyne's jump into the pro ranks, but Cheyne, always the independent one, handled most of his own negotiations. Besides, he remained loyal to his amateur sponsors and signed contracts with them before the others had a chance.

This was different. Clay was the star free agent in the market, the perceived future of performance surfing, the kid with the raw ability no one had seen in fifteen years. Think of it as the surfing equivalent of LeBron James in the summer of 2014. "We had to make the right decisions for him and with him," Gino says. "This was kind of a bidding war."

The Marzos looked for someone who could deftly navigate the negotiations about to take place. Friends in the business urged them to contact Mitch Varnes, a highly respected surfing manager-agent who had followed Clay after two of his clients, the Hobgood brothers, told him how the kid had supercharged their surf camp. Varnes brought a diverse combination of surf industry knowledge, media savvy, and financial acumen into his business. A longtime surfer and distance runner (he has run numerous marathons), he promotes regional and national surfing and running events. He also was the East Coast editor of *Surfing* magazine in the late 1980s, a public affairs officer for NASA (and the voice of Mission Control on several space shuttle launches), and an investment adviser. He knew most of the surf industry's key players well. He also represented a pair of world champions, C. J. Hobgood and four-time women's world champ Lisa Andersen. Varnes worked both inside and outside the industry to build solid financial and media bases for his clients.

Varnes remembers the call from the Marzos well. He could sense the excitement and anxiety that can overwhelm the parents of young athletes when promises of money and fame suddenly come knocking on their door. "Within two or three weeks of NSSA Nationals, I was contacted by his parents," he recalls. "The Marzos were essentially being stalked by agents and managers wanting to sign Clay, promising him all sorts of deals. I did some homework, and this kid had great potential, and I liked talking with his parents. I spoke to them on the phone a couple more times, then flew out to Maui to meet Clay.

"I thought Clay was a great guy. I thought that, with the exception of Kelly Slater, he had more potential than any surfer I'd seen in my life. I saw the potential for a multiple world champion."

Gino also liked Varnes instantly. "Mitch worked with some up-and-coming surfers, which we liked too. He knew what to do with the young guys," he says.

In 2006 Clay turned pro. Mitch convinced several of Clay's amateur sponsors to re-sign him to a professional contract, led by the biggest of all, Quiksilver. Then he shopped a very hot market and landed several more sponsors, basically covering every product category with sweet deals: surfboards, wetsuits, clothing, sunglasses, sandals, shoes, and more. There wasn't a hotter ticket than Clay Marzo.

Or as *Australian Surfing Life* put it: "Surfing balls-out, no care for life and limb approach, constantly in fast-forward."

"Anybody who's ever seen Clay surf knows he's a freak; he's amazing," Varnes says. "He's a natural. That alone shows great potential. Then you look at how he was brought up, how he was coached or mentored, mainly by his father, but also by others around him. And he's got Dusty Payne, Granger Larsen, Kai Barger, these kids of the same age, same area, all pushing each other. All of them became successful pro surfers. Clay has beaten these guys, and you look at it and think, *He's better than these guys.*"

Once Clay signed, the older pros started weighing in. Damien Hobgood, one of the world's top thirty surfers for the past fifteen years, predicted, "I see Clay getting it all soon; he's just gotta keep that hunger." A top Hawaiian pro and ASP World Tour contest winner from the 1980s and 1990s, John Shimooka, added, "Clay is like one of those gremlins. Add water and he turns into a completely different animal. He's very humble on land, but he's extraordinarily confident in water."

Add water. That's how it is for every surfer, right?

Varnes put together Clay's endorsements and began devising a strategy to put him into position to win a world title. First, he had to deal with expectations: Clay was surfing's newest rock star. Like all rock stars, everyone seemed to know him on a first-name basis. Rock and Roll Hall of Famer Marty Balin, one of his generation's most outstanding vocalists despite living with a lifelong social disorder, said of this phenomenon, "Everyone thinks they know you inside and out, and they're your friends, but you don't know any of them. Learn to say 'thank you' and move on."

"With all the serious athletes I work with, we lay out a plan in November and December, outlining what our goals are contest-wise, performance-wise, and media-wise for the coming year," Varnes explains. "Clay and I did this for the first two or three years. He was really interested in surfing well and becoming a world title contender. This kid had everything you need talent-wise to be a world champion, plus the mystique of being different and quirky. Clay was ready to make his move."

Varnes's phone rang early and often as magazines sought interviews or invited Clay to join them on magazine-sponsored photo or video shoots when he wasn't fulfilling trip, appearance, and contest obligations for his sponsors.

Gina Marzo recalls how intense life around the house became when her big brother's star ascended. "I was in elementary school, but I remember all the posters, the big checks. I remember feeling like, *That's my brother. Wow!*" she says. "I was in awe. I didn't get what was happening. Interviews, phone calls, traveling, more and more things kept popping up around the corner for Clay. He was a sensation."

After *Young Guns 2,* the NSSA Nationals, and the ISA World Juniors, more photographers sought him out. Clay was surfing in contests, following the road map laid out by Varnes and his father to gain valuable experience in the dog-eat-dog world of World Championship Tour qualifying. Still, shutterbugs and videographers approached him as a freestyle surfer, or "free surfer." "That's what surfing or any sport in nature is about—you and the wave. Or the cliff, or trail," Clay says. "I like it when it's just you and the wave."

One such feature came from *Australian Surfing Life,* which ran a photo spread about California freestyle surfer Dane Reynolds and Clay. It started, "Watch Out World, It's . . . The Dynamic Duo! Blowing Minds, Breaking Hearts and Busting Air, Thrill to Youth Gone Wild *in* . . . The Dane and Clay Show." The two would often be mentioned in the same sentence and compared for the next decade, for reasons that would reveal themselves in coming years.

Clay relished the surfing lifestyle, but he had to get used to doing interviews. "There were so many of them, and I didn't know what to say. I do well if it's one person at a time, but when they all ask me at once . . . that's hard. If I know you and we don't have a lot of people around, and we talk about things like surfing and fitness and the Lakers and eating and all the places I've surfed and some funny movies, like *Goonies* and *Jackass 2* and *Ace Ventura,* then I can talk a lot, yeah? But I had to figure out a way to make everyone happy, even though I sometimes didn't say much."

To illustrate his point, Clay often turns to an article from a Hawaiian regional magazine, *Heavywater,* which in this case broke out his answers to a series of typical surf-oriented questions:

> "I'm off by myself, studying the break and focusing."
> "Go big and make the maneuvers."
> "I've done a few WQS [World Qualifying Series] events, but haven't had much success yet."
> "Surfing as many important events as I can and taking a lot of trips."
> "I'm a fast swimmer. I'm like a fish."
> "I'm always watching and studying other surfers to see what I can learn."
> "I'm really pretty shy and quiet unless I'm around good friends and family."

Amid the excitement, Clay had to circle back to his old nemesis: school. He wanted to drop out so he could travel and compete, but Jill and Gino were dead-set on him getting his high school diploma, or at least a GED. They enrolled Clay in Hui Malama, a specialized school in Kahului, Maui's biggest town, located thirty miles from Lahaina.

"They worked with kids like me, who needed a different education because they were traveling a lot," Clay recalls. "Or just didn't deal with regular schools. I was still getting tested because school officials said I was different, I was a slow learner . . . the same shit we heard since kindergarten. My friends Granger Larsen and Bryce Henry graduated high school through Hui Malama, so we figured I could too."

In reality, the choice was a little more cut-and-dried: he had no other options. "I couldn't home-school him anymore; it was too hard," Jill says. "I had him tutored in math; the one-on-ones helped.

There was one tutor, Hai-Dai, who asked me, 'Why are you trying to educate Clay like any other kid?'

"'Because I want him to have a diploma,' I told him.

"'What's a kid like Clay going to do with a diploma?'

"I couldn't accept his point of view. However, the more I realized what the guy was saying, the more I knew how true it was. So I put him in the Hui Malama, which preps you for your GED. I knew he'd never have the normal high school experience, so we were just going to get his GED."

Jill drove Clay to Kahului, an hour-long drive, three days a week in his hard-won Toyota Matrix. When he walked into the classroom, he saw not twenty-five or thirty people but four or five. *Perfect.* The new setting promised the same faces every day, familiarity, and comfort. It dissolved his apprehension about crowds and unfamiliar people; plus, the teacher spelled out attainable expectations and kept them simple, a perfect approach for anyone on the autism spectrum (although he was still undiagnosed at this time). "A lot of times in school, they never told me what they wanted and then they would say all this stuff in class and I wouldn't know what they were saying or what I was supposed to do," Clay says. "This was different."

Still, his time at Hui Malama fell short. "He did good there, tried very hard and showed an effort I hadn't seen from him in years — except for his video projects — but the teacher said he didn't hold his information," Jill says. "They were going to try to test him for his GED one subject at a time, an approach they used with kids who had short attention and retention spans. But Clay was traveling a lot more. Finally, I followed what Hai-Dai said, and we stopped. He made it past eleventh grade, but he never did graduate. It wasn't going to serve him, and I realized that."

Since then, Jill has second-guessed her decision. "Yeah, that's something I think about a lot, because as he gets older and we all know you can't make it in professional surfing forever, that GED becomes more and more important."

Once he left Hui Malama, Clay embarked on a travel schedule split between media-based surf trips and contests. Then, in the summer of 2006, a year after winning the NSSA National Open Men's, he received an invitation every surfer in the world coveted: ESPN's Summer X Games XIII. After years of dealing with inconsistent surf at Huntington Beach Pier, ESPN shifted the event to the grinding barrels of Puerto Escondido, Mexico.

When Clay heard the news, and where the contest would be held—at a place renowned for its thick, mean barrels—he rubbed his hands so furiously that Gino was concerned he'd rub them raw, a self-induced road rash. "Puerto Escondido is a really thick barrel. Thick and fast," Clay recalls, transporting himself back to Puerto Escondido as he speaks, as if that's the present moment, not a day in Maui years later. "People can die there when it's really big. The town is fun too. There were the restaurants on the street along the beach, the tourist beach, but we went into town where the real Mexican food was. We ate and surfed these thick slabs. I've never been to a contest that was so much fun."

The X Games format differed from the typical surf contest. Everything was based on team results. Each participant surfed up to six heats; sometimes coaches substituted from their "bench." For the X Games, the United States team included Hawaii and both coasts. Combined scores were added up to produce the gold medal team.

Clay has always found older surfers to admire, if not idolize, so he stood in amazement in the presence of the American coaches. First of all, there was Californian Mike Parsons, known as "Snips" in the surfing world, a rail-thin former top-sixteen World Tour surfer better known for surfing sixty-foot monster waves off Cortes Bank, a subterranean reef a hundred miles west of San Diego. The other coach was Florida legend Matt Kechele, whose "Kech Air" became one of the East Coast's signature maneuvers in the 1980s. "He was blasting huge airs thirty years ago, before almost anyone else," Clay says. "I loved watching those old guys in surf movies."

The third man was Rob Machado. Machado remembered talking with Clay and his fellow Maui future stars at the NSSA Nationals, and he was thrilled that one of the kids was now the most explosive and unpredictable surfer on the West team. At sixteen, Clay was also the youngest team member.

"We surfed two or three heats every day," Clay remembers, while looking at his framed X Games contest jersey and gold medal, which hang on his bedroom wall. "Everybody surfed. I liked the format better than the World Qualifying Series, because we had a four-man team that helped each other score the best waves. Usually, you're out there on your own, fighting other people. I never liked that. I really liked the team."

The tone for the tournament was set early by Californian Chris Ward, who scored a perfect 10 in what Clay describes as "a huge shack. I'll always remember that ride. It was sick." The others excelled too: Ward, Machado, wily World Tour veteran Shane Beschen, and East Coast stars Peter Mendia and Baron Knowlton. They blitzed the field to take home gold.

"Clay doesn't like to grovel in competitions in the small stuff," Gino explains. "He was on that winning US team in Puerto Escondido, and his kind of surf, just pounding, A-frame surf, six- to eight-foot barrels. Clay can hold his own with anybody in those kind of conditions."

To this day Clay considers the X Games his greatest achievement.

10

Playing on Camera

I can watch videos of me and my friends over and over again, the same waves, and I always feel like I'm on that wave and smacking the lip and getting shacked and yeah! I just want to get back out there and do it again, so I watch it again. There's always something new I see, something about how I catch a wave, what I do, or did I get shacked long enough? I get really stoked when I watch movies [filmed] in big surf, big thick slabs — especially when it's flat in Maui. I feel like that ride is happening again right now.

I'll go out in anything and charge it, and I won't come in for a long time. I know what really lame footage looks like, where people don't even really try, and it's boring. I also edited videos when I was younger, sending around clips with music and effects, so it's fun for me to work with filmers.

I've watched videos my whole life, all the time. There were the videos my mom and dad shot of my brother, then all the surf movies, and the ones shot of me. I learned so much from watching surf videos. I think every kid should watch a lot of surf videos, watch me, watch the other guys.

Shortly after Clay turned pro, he and videographer Adam Klevin hopped on a plane to Fiji's big-wave haven, Tavarua, for what became yet another defining moment in a career quickly filling up with them.

Tavarua, a twenty-nine-acre island resort, is surrounded by a coral reef that provides perfect bottom conditions for seven breaks, all exceptional: Restaurants, Tavarua Rights, Swimming Pools, Namotu Left, Wilkes Pass, Desperations, and the most famous of all, Cloudbreak. Thousands of photos and video hours have poured out of Cloudbreak, a left-hand bomb of up to twenty feet — perfect for

Clay. "He blew everybody's mind," Klevin says. "Kelly was so blown away by him."

"Kelly" would be Kelly Slater, who, for the second time in short succession, was stunned by Clay's aquatic acrobatics. How could *anyone* blow away Kelly Slater?

Whenever Slater showed up, the performance level immediately rose. What Clay and other young upstarts marveled over most was not Kelly's staying power at the top (a truly remarkable feat, no matter the sport), but his enduring ability to push the envelope. Surfers hit their apex as young as twenty-five ... which is how many years Slater has been the standard-setter. "That's how old I am," Clay says, a glow of amazement in his eyes.

Yet Slater was the one who was blown away by the teen's raw power, creativity, cat-quick reflexes, and ability to position himself in the waves perfectly — but most of all by his hunger. "I can only wish I could stay out in the water for six, eight, ten hours like he does," Slater says. "And his last wave is just as good as his first."

They paddled out at Cloudbreak. After a couple of waves, Kelly paddled over. "How is it out there for you?"

"Oh yeah, yeah, it's fun."

"Hey, right on, man, good ripping."

"Yeah, hey, Kelly."

After the session, master and pupil sat in the Jacuzzi. Clay tried to talk with Slater, but intimidation took over, drawing the curtains on his vocal cords.

"There were some great awkward moments of them trying to communicate in the Jacuzzi and then Clay just having a blast," Klevin recalls. "It's so beautiful there, and it was so cool to be there with Clay, and he's under the waterfall in the pool and just trying to get funny clips. Kelly was amazed by how he surfed."

Adam Klevin is an intense man who, by his own admission, is obsessive-compulsive (often a positive quality for a videographer and video producer). He's used that intensity to shoot thousands of Clay's rides. Originally from Southern California, Klevin first came to Maui on vacation in 1982. He walked out to Mala Wharf on the north side of Lahaina, watched the sun set over nearby Lanai, turned east to the opaque yellow-orange light glowing on the West Maui Mountains, and never left. Like many transplants, he cobbled together a variety of jobs . . . whatever it took to stay on the island. Today he's a jujitsu master and teacher, a commercial fisherman, and a premier videographer.

One day, Klevin recalls, he heard about a quintet of Maui kids tearing up the contest ranks. He put away his surfboard, grabbed his gear, and raced to Lahaina Harbor. There he saw Kai Barger, Granger and Wesley Larsen, Dusty Payne, and Clay Marzo dominating the action. As he watched more closely, Klevin's eye was drawn to one surfer in particular, to the way his moves, his fearless risk-taking, and his knack for critical wave positioning outshone the others.

"I started focusing more on Clay," he says. "Something about him, when he'd walk up and sit down, he was real natural and soulful. His hair was always wild, and I was like, 'Man, this kid, he's got something. He's different from everybody, he's smoother than everybody, he's more consistent.' He was ten times more consistent than anybody I'd ever watched surf. In fact, the first time I paddled out at Lahaina Harbor and I saw him surfing, the kids were lipping at some older guy that got in their way, but I watched him take off and just hook into this wave, and he did this tail slide thing over the tube and landed and came around this long section and did it again. On the first one, I thought, *That was dog shit luck.* Then he did it again. *Wow.*"

Clay was fourteen, just starting to put his moves together. "He was a man-child, really built, a little like Michael Phelps," Klevin recalls, alluding to Clay's background as a state swimming champion. "He had lats that seemed to go from his shoulders to his hips. I thought to myself, *This kid's designed to surf. And he's radical.* He charged much harder than kids his age, without fear. He just threw himself into anything."

Klevin and Clay formed a team. Every time Clay wanted to surf, he either called up Klevin to drive him to the beach or told the cameraman where to meet him. They shot from the moment he paddled out until the second he returned to shore. Then they packed up the gear, headed to Klevin's house, and watched video. Some viewing sessions were all-nighters. "I can watch videos of me and my friends over and over again, the same waves, and I always feel like I'm on that wave and smacking the lip and getting shacked and *yeah!* I just want to get back out there and do it again, so I watch it again," Clay says.

"He can and does sometimes spend twelve hours watching the same long video over and over," Jill says. "And over and *over,*" she adds, rolling her eyes. "He needs something that's predictable, that he can anticipate, so when he knows what's coming next, he feels it, antici-pates it—and it's like he's there again."

As Clay elaborates on his mother's comments, he sounds like a football coach or big-league pitcher studying opponents' tendencies, their strengths and weaknesses. "There's always something new I see, something about how I catch a wave, what I do, or did I get shacked long enough?" As a large wave breaks along his bedroom wall and his image zips across it, propelled from a barrel, he begins rubbing his hands at warp speed. "I like it when Adam catches me at different angles. Sometimes I drop in and get shacked before I stand up all the way. I feel like that ride is happening again right now."

Before long, Klevin and Marzo island-hopped to Oahu, and the most famous wave of them all, Banzai Pipeline. "That's when I real-ized that this kid is in a league of his own," Klevin says. "He was pick-ing the waves that the bodyboarders were going for, farther inside the wave. He'd get one, get spit out all the way down the beach, and then he'd be back out in the lineup and I'd miss the beginning of the next wave because I thought he was still getting out there. I couldn't believe how strong of a paddler he was."

Klevin became one of the videographers on the *Young Guns 2* trip. Once Quiksilver saw his footage and, more importantly, how well he anticipated Clay's rides, they promoted him to one of the top shoot-ing positions for the sequel, *Young Guns 3.* "That was a really fun time, one of the best times I've ever had surfing," Clay says. "You'd see your friends as you flew past, and that was about the only time you saw anyone. We had the whole reef to ourselves."

The shoot required Klevin to utilize all of his skills. "I would get dropped off before they paddled out, always planning everything in my head. I have to know what's gonna happen next," he says, falling back into present-moment mode, a trait he and Clay share in common. "I ran two miles to where I could find the best angle. Then here they came on the boat, Clay and everyone else. I'd get all the footage, everyone would be stoked, Clay would be stoked, and then I started getting gigs. This was perfect, because not only could I go around shooting footage for Clay, but we were putting it directly into movies with worldwide DVD and sometimes theater distribution. So I got the first gig when Julian Wilson, Dane Reynolds, and Ry Craike came to Maui. From that moment on, they saw what I did. We made that movie, *Young Guns 3*. Then I was on retainer."

In 2007, Clay appeared in numerous professional contests and movies. He surfed in a dozen different countries, and seemed to be constantly shooting videos and photos. His surf media coverage blew up. Clay was featured in full-page magazine ads with Quiksilver, Spy, Vestal, and Future Fin, his main sponsors, which put him face-to-reader in the most important and highest-circulation surf magazines in the world. Accompanying stories ran from six to ten pages and often proclaimed him "the future of the sport." The March 2007 cover of *Transworld Surf* showed Clay at Windmills, his favorite Maui break, with the heading "15 Surfers to Watch." The US Open of Surfing featured Clay on its promotional poster. He was a household name to surfers throughout the world, and kids were trying to emulate him, even though he was still too young to vote or drink and barely old enough to drive.

Clay spent much of the year surfing on the World Qualifying Series (WQS), from which the top surfers are seeded onto the World Championship Tour. Think of the WQS as a Triple A baseball league. Clay won $2,500 for finishing third in the Hobgood Challenge, and then won the Fins Free Challenge in Micronesia, both events that focused on freestyle surfing. He struggled from the beginning, however, with the structured format and judging criteria of the WQS. "It was really hard for me to keep going to all these contests where I really didn't know anybody, and it's hard for me to surf for points instead of making everything happen I can on every wave and always going for it," he says.

Still, he electrified the surfing world. *Young Guns 3* was released and won the 2007 Surfer Poll Movie Awards. He also appeared in the highly regarded *Tomorrow Today,* along with Dane Reynolds and Bobby Martinez, two of his favorites. That was followed by *Stranger Than Fiction,* and then an episode of ESPN's *E: 60.* To cap off the year, he starred in *Burn,* which took him to Fiji, the Galápagos Islands, Mexico, Samoa, Indonesia, France, Tahiti, Hawaii, the Maldives, and Australia.

"Someone once told me how many miles we covered for [*Burn*] . . . something like 30,000," Clay says. "Maybe more. That was crazy to surf in so many different places, and it was really hard for me to get my travel shit together and get there, but once I got in the water . . . yeah!"

While Clay appeared in plenty of commercial surf films, he much preferred underground films — those made on a pauper's budget and distributed surfer-to-surfer and by word-of-mouth. This love of underground movies makes perfect sense: his quietness has always given him a mysterious aura, more so today than ever before. His penchant for off-the-grid shooting jumped a few pegs in 2008 when he and one of his favorite fellow riders, Dane Reynolds, co-starred in *The Collection.* "We are featured in different parts of the movie; we never surf together in it," Clay explains. "My part was shot by Adam in Maui. We shot a lot of my sequences at the Mill [Windmills]. It's a really nice wave; probably my favorite in Maui. Some was shot at Scorpions. Dane shot his sequences at home in Ventura [California], and Rincon and the Ranch [famous California places], with some Mexico footage in there. We switch back and forth through the whole movie. It's a good underground film, just showing us at home. He surfs in his home breaks; I surf in mine."

Beyond his greatness and public appeal, there was another reason why videographers and photographers flocked to Clay, a reason Klevin kept secret for as long as possible: Clay's intrinsic knowledge of the process, combined with his willingness to surf any wave that formed. "I'll charge it, and I won't come in for a long time," he says. "I know what really lame footage looks like, where people don't even really try, and it's boring. I also edited videos when I was younger, sending around clips with music and effects, so it's fun for me to work with filmers.

"I've watched videos my whole life, all the time. There were the videos my mom and dad shot of my brother, then all the surf movies, and the ones shot of me. I learned so much from watching surf videos. I think every kid should watch a lot of surf videos, watch me, watch the other guys."

Clay has a contingent of fans among videographers, led by his biggest fans of all, Klevin and the director of *Just Add Water* and *What Happened to Clay Marzo?*—Jamie Tierney, who first noticed his natural ability in front of a camera in 2008. "That's the thing—Clay really understands what a good shot is and what a good surfing sequence is," Tierney says. "A lot of guys don't. They get out there and don't hit the critical parts of the wave, or they half-ass it, and the footage is boring. Clay is never boring. He's always charging in fifth gear. I don't even think he's capable of backing off. When he focuses on a wave, that's all that exists on the face of the earth—that wave. That's the gift of Asperger's, right there. He's great to work with."

Clay tries to remember every wave he surfs—in sequence. This uncanny knack for mental cataloging, sometimes from many sessions before, astonishes those who don't know him and still draws raised eyebrows from his closest friends and associates. "I can watch a clip with Adam when we're editing and—*boom!*—it all comes back: 'Okay, three waves from now, I did *this*. Okay, no, not this one, go, fast-forward.' I play them and feel them and feel myself coming out of the shack or snapping off the lip over and over and over . . . yeah, brah! Every single clip. I replay them at least three to four times, five times the really good ones," he says.

Klevin recalls a viewing session when they squabbled over the waves filmed that day. "Clay and I were arguing over his best waves, and one popped up on the screen. 'Not that one . . .' Clay said to me.

"'Wait a minute, let's just look,' I told him.

"'Yeah, dude . . . watch . . . see? I fell.'

"'How did you know that?' I asked him. 'I don't even know that, and I watched it all and I filmed it all.'"

When Clay hears the story, he laughs. "Happens all the time. I remember my waves."

"That's one thing about Clay that's really interesting, kind of like *Rain Man*," Klevin says, invoking Dustin Hoffman's 1986 Academy Award–winning autistic character. (Interestingly, the Academy Award–winning writer of *Rain Man*, Ron Bass, has taken an interest in Clay's story as well.) "It's the same thing with travel. He'll remember the gates, the airport, what the plane's like: 'I don't like that plane, that plane has this on it.' He remembers little subtleties that you'll never remember like, 'That's right, oh, you're right.'"

Most of all, Clay enjoys surfing in front of the camera. One would think all professional surfers do, but often they can't take the drudgery of shooting take after take. (It's not that different from Hollywood, except for the exquisite settings.) Given Clay's aversion to live social situations, he enjoys being viewed by thousands or even millions on their DVD players instead of in person; being watched on video provides the all-important degree of separation that the vast majority of those living with Asperger's syndrome covet.

"He definitely knows how to surf in the camera," Tierney says. "He knows what's a clip and what's not. And he always goes full tilt; he never freezes. Some of the very best guys sometimes go out there, play around, kind of half-ass it. Clay only knows one way to surf. He's going to go straight off the bottom, he's going to hit the lip like a cannon, and either throw it into a layback or slide his tail or get air. It's going to be full velocity and full effort. That's what appeals to me and appeals to other people. Some guys go hard and look ugly doing it, but Clay's got that style that shows up, even in the middle of situations where you think, *Oh my God, he's never going to make that*, and his body is as graceful and flowing as ever.

"There aren't three or four surfers in the world more electric than him."

· · ·

Clay has built an equally solid relationship with surf photographers. Like their video counterparts, surf photographers form close alliances with surfers, working hand-in-hand with them to deliver the stunning shots envied the world over. Some, like Clay's personal favorites Erik Aeder, Jeff Hornbaker, and Bob Barbour, have been at it for four decades. The relationship is truly reciprocal: the photographer gets paid for the shot, and the surfer picks up an incentive check for being the subject.

While Clay certainly appreciates getting paid, the rapport he shares with photographers goes deeper, into the subtle levels shared by artists. "I like the water photographers a lot, because they will take chances and wipe out in waves, sometimes getting hurt, to get the great shots," he says. "I like the way they take photos like they're art. They know how to make the photo about both you and the wave coming together, dancing as much as riding. They get into a lot more than just the move you're doing. I like a lot of the newer guys, but it's the older photographers who are artists. I like artists."

The other requirement for shooting videos and photos is getting there. As Clay readily admits, travel has caused more problems in his career than anything else, and he has sometimes missed photo shoots, contest entries, and promotional opportunities. "There have been quite a few misses," manager Mitch Varnes says, an assessment seconded by Wasilewski. Jill Marzo disputes the notion of "quite a few," but she concurs that getting Clay out of the house and onto a plane is as tough as moving a 1,000-pound man through the front door.

Even though Clay lives midway between the US mainland and the South Pacific, getting to almost any surfing destination still requires many hours of flying, then connecting from the arrival airport to the spot itself. Surf trips to remote destinations are not one- or two-stop connections through airport hubs. Some of those perfect waves that people see in magazines, travel brochures, or DVDs are located on islands that resemble Tom Hanks's home in *Castaway*. They feel just as remote too. It often takes a combination of cars, boats, barges, motorcycles, and other local transportation to get surfers to their destinations. It's a trying process for even the hardiest travelers; you won't hear any pro surfers extolling the virtues of sitting in airports for ten-hour stretches or waiting hours for their local ride to arrive. Many pros have retired from the competition arena long before they turned thirty to avoid further travel.

"Now multiply that by fifty for someone dealing with Asperger's syndrome," says behavioral counselor Carolyn Jackson.

"I don't like airports, the crowds in airports, sitting on planes, or having to deal with customs, shipping my boards and all the other stuff," Clay says. "No one thinks about how much we travel and how much time we spend in airplanes and airports, or taking boats to all the islands, some of the boats really small and gnarly. My mom and I figured out that I spent something like $80,000 in travel one year.

"I have trouble finding gates. I have a hard time focusing when there are all these randoms [people] I've never seen before and all this noise and people running around in a hurry. I'm never really sure what they think, or what they want, or what they say about me."

His indoctrination into solo international travel didn't help either. During his explosion onto the world stage, he flew to Australia and then Bali to try to meet up with Dane Reynolds and Bruce Irons, the Hawaiian freestyle star. Everything was fine until a huge storm made it impossible for Clay to get across the water. "The local islanders couldn't get me out to the island where the boat was. They couldn't speak English, and I was stuck on this weird island with them. It was kinda scary, like a freaky movie or something," he recalls, a shudder passing through his eyes.

"Those were four of the longest days of my life," Jill recalls, "just trying to keep him calm on the phone and trying to figure out how to get him home at the same time."

At the behest of Jill and Varnes, Clay hired Klevin to accompany him on his travels, which served the dual purpose of adding to their video library. He also started wearing a document pouch around his neck, which held his itinerary, boarding passes, passport, and other travel documents. After Jill booked flights and organized itineraries, Klevin helped Clay navigate airports and make connecting flights on time, which is stressful enough for someone not dealing with high anxiety, aversion to loud noises, and corresponding tunnel vision, all Asperger's characteristics. "I was like a production guy/road manager/cinematographer/personal assistant," Klevin explains. "Just getting him there and taking care of little comfort things. If he had that to look forward to, he'd be all right."

Sometimes their exchanges bordered on the comical. Klevin recalls one instance at the Los Angeles International Airport baggage claim. "I'll go get the rental car," he said.

"Oh, get it quick, yeah? I'm gonna wait here." Clay didn't like seeing the swirl of unfamiliar faces at LAX.

A few minutes later, Klevin returned. "All right, I got it, let's go. Load it up."

Clay hit him with the first question he often asks when clear of the airport hubbub. "Yeah, brah, where we eating?"

"We're going to In-N-Out."

Clay threw on his headphones, listened to his music, and finally relaxed, leaving Klevin temporarily befuddled. Then it hit Klevin: "The little things make him real happy. Best Foods mayonnaise, candies, always having a bottle of water. He always needs to have his bottle of water with him. That's how it was — on just about every trip."

Klevin smiles and sighs as he takes in a Lahaina sunset. "We've been through a lot. I'd coordinate the trips with Jill or Mitch [Varnes], go here, go there, make sure the stickers were on the boards, get rental cars, put gas in the car, be at events and promotions on time . . . He only surfed and ate and laughed. I don't think he understood what it really took to be a professional athlete. Not that he really had to — he was probably the most famous surfer in the world except for Slater and (the late three-time world champion) Andy Irons. No cross-training, no stretching, nothing. Just a natural phenom. That's Clay."

Slowly, Klevin saw a change, a more relaxed person. "He actually became a great traveler," Klevin says. "At first it was really challenging, people doubted him, but he can overcome things and make it — he closes off the world, he's got noise-canceling headphones, his hoodie, cap, and sunglasses. I started taking notes from him and being more like Clay and trying to relax like he can."

Then there were the blowups. Everyone who knows both men agrees that you don't want to piss off either of them. Imagine them firing on each other. "He thinks I'm bossy," Clay says, "but I just want to get to where we're going, and get in the water. Plus, I think he talks too much, and it's really hard for me when anyone talks too much to me . . . the dude's intense."

Two fights stand out for Klevin. The first happened at his home in Maui, a simple house surrounded by the lush foliage, streams, and coconut palms one might see on the Discovery Channel. As has happened several times in Clay's life, it started with a misread of a social cue and instantly mushroomed from there.

"We were in my house, and everybody's there," Klevin recalls, "and out of the blue, no prompting whatsoever, Clay says to me, 'You're a kook.'

"'What?' Well, nobody talks to me like that. Nobody . . . on this whole island. Clay sometimes takes things people say wrong, even little jokes, and you don't realize he's taken it the wrong way. And then he can say inappropriate things. Like this time."

Klevin exercised the restraint befitting a black belt who knows his capabilities. He walked over to Clay and dumped him out of the chair in which he sat. "Get the hell out of my house!" he yelled.

Thus banished, Clay sat on the outside curb. *What's wrong with this kook?* he wondered.

Klevin turned to the others, all of whom knew and/or surfed with Clay on a regular basis. "Yeah, that's Clay," several in the group said, without offering further explanation.

After that, Klevin walked outside. "Hey look, dude. I love filming, I love doing this, but you've gotta show respect for me in there," he told Clay. "You can't talk down to me like that. I'm doing a service here."

Clay got the message and never again patronized Klevin in front of others. That's not to say it didn't happen privately . . . such as a moment in Spain, while en route to the Quiksilver Pro France. "I just got sick of him when we were driving up the road," Clay recalls. "I told him, 'Let's pull over. We're gonna fight.'"

"'Dude, I don't think you want to go there,'" Klevin remembers saying, chuckling at the memory. "I'm actually trained and you're not eighteen yet, so I think we just better wait on that one." He paused, and then switched into tough love mode: "You do this, you do that, you do that, and you know, in life, those are pussy characteristics. That's spineless shit."

Whatever, dude, Clay thought.

Then Klevin turned the situation around. "But look, you see this anger you're feeling right now? I want you to go out in this heat, and I want you to take those waves apart and win. We're here for a reason. I don't want to fight with you, but I'm not gonna take this crap."

Clay proceeded to easily win the heat, which is not always possible in the dog-eat-dog World Qualifying Series arena. After filming the performance, Klevin ran toward the water to congratulate Clay. They gave each other a hug. "I just needed to get in the water and rip, get away from him for a minute," Clay says, a wry grin on his face. "When I'm in the water, everything else in the world goes away. It makes a lot of things better for me."

It wasn't over yet. Clay had been telling Klevin repeatedly that he was finished with Spain — and with Klevin. Eventually, Clay's anger reached a boiling point. "There was something fun I wanted to do. I don't remember what, but it was like the one fun thing," Clay recalls. "Adam was always grinding on business stuff, so he's like, 'Can we just wait until we go somewhere else? I don't know if that's a good idea.'"

Sparks flew from Clay's eyes. "I could feel myself going red. 'I don't like your face. You look like Freddy Krueger when you're mad.' I started laughing."

Klevin started to chuckle as well, in part to diffuse what he quickly recognized as Clay's anger beginning to redline. "That's right," he said.

"I'm gonna throw a rock at it," Clay told him.

Klevin's smile vanished. "Go ahead. Throw it. It'll be the last move you make."

"Adam's been really good for Clay," Varnes says. "You look around, and many of the top pro surfers have their own videographers. [Three-time world champion] Mick Fanning's had one for years,

Dane Reynolds has had his guy on the payroll for years. Adam is a great cinematographer. No question that Adam is obsessed with getting good quality, but more importantly, he's obsessed with doing the best for Clay. That's the part that came out whenever they traveled."

While Clay traveled throughout 2007 and 2008, his struggles worried Varnes and his sponsors, who'd invested six figures annually in him. They couldn't figure out why he handled simple situations so awkwardly or became so uncomfortable when meeting people at promotions, events, and sponsor get-togethers. As Clay started to perceive the worry around him, an old tape played in his head — the testing he underwent in school, testing that had added up to a fat "zero."

Little did he know that another, more decisive round was about to happen.

11

Storm Clouds

A bunch of kids surrounded me out of nowhere and told me how great I was and wanted to touch my board and that I was their favorite surfer and could I give them my autograph? That really surprised me. It was kind of a trip. I'm like, "Dude, I'm just like you. We all surf." But they saw me as this star.

I know people think it's pretty cool, and I like to help when I can, like with the autistic kids in Surfers Healing camps, but it's hard when you don't know any of them. They're all faces you haven't seen before. That makes me nervous. So does surfing in contests where I don't know anybody, which is totally different than when I was a kid and I had all my friends there all the time. You just don't know who has hate in them and who doesn't.

What made Clay so "different" from others? His biggest sponsor, Quiksilver, wanted to find out — and the sooner the better.

School administrators, friends, and even family members had asked the same question since Clay was six. Trying one test after another, they'd come up with an alphabet soup of diagnoses — ADD, ADHD, OCD, SAD, GAD — that proved to be nothing more than guesstimates. When you're dealing with the life of a kid trying to cope with a world that completely confuses him, the damage of a missed diagnosis cannot be underestimated. His life was filled with them. Neither Clay nor his parents wanted to endure another battery of tests, especially when his surfing career was taking off.

However, Quiksilver paid the largest salary of any of his sponsors, a six-figure annual investment. They sent him on surf trips as one of their two most photographed and sought-after surfers (Slater being the other), so they decided to dictate how their relationship with Clay would proceed.

With good reason. After Clay signed his first big contract, the billion-dollar clothing manufacturer set up a dinner meeting in Australia with international officers, directors, and managers. Clay knew a few of the management-level staff members, so it seemed like a somewhat comfortable situation, though even the smoothest socialite might have found it a bit daunting to join the company brass for an introductory dinner halfway around the world.

When dinner was served, everything changed. A cloud settled over Clay's brain, abject fear and trepidation replacing his initial curiosity, and he curled into his fortress-thick wall. He ate quickly, eyes constantly looking at his plate and never meeting another person's. When asked questions, he responded with single-word answers. Or no answers at all. Then, to the astonishment of everyone else in the room, Clay finished his meal, stood up, and walked to a corner of the restaurant. He broke out his ear buds and the iPod he'd won at Camp Hobgood, lay down on a bench, and listened to music.

"He was with people he liked, Strider and a bunch of other guys. He didn't talk to anybody the whole time," Tierney recalls. "When we finished dinner, he walked away. I'm thinking, *What's this kid doing?* Like everybody else, I thought maybe he didn't like dinner, was in a bad mood . . . I didn't know what was going on."

As it turned out, Clay thought the same thing. His mind morphed into a dangerous bombing range — the by-product of too much sudden, unfamiliar stimulation — dropping internal questions on him: *Didn't I surf well enough for them? Didn't I get them enough photos and spreads and good footage in the videos? Why are they looking at me like this? Why do they want to know all these things about me?* "I was wondering why all these people were looking at me the way they did, with faces like I was rude and there was something wrong with me," he later said.

Everyone was shaken, Clay by the harrowing experience of having all eyes trained on him, and the Quiksilver officials over his behavior and the reasons why they signed him in the first place.

The next morning Clay showed up for a quick surf and saw Tierney in the water. He paddled over, smiling slightly. "Hey, Jamie, how's it going?"

Pure surprise registered across Tierney's face. After the troublesome dinner, Tierney couldn't believe Clay was acting as if it never happened. "I could see there was something a little different, not just a matter of being rude, but he had an issue in social situations," he notes.

Wasilewski had seen Clay's apprehension in other Quiksilver meetings and wasn't as surprised as the others. "I noticed right away that he was a different person. We used to look at each other while at a table of people in a work atmosphere, and I could see the discomfort not only with him but with people higher up in the company. They'd look at me like, *What's wrong with this kid?* At the same time they'd be exchanging these looks with me, Clay and I would also be having nonverbal communication. He would tell me things silently, and I would respond to him with body language or facial cues, then we'd talk about it later," he says.

While Clay brushed past the Quiksilver pow-wow, one of the company's top executives did not. One executive expressed a strong objection to Clay's behavior and openly questioned the company's decision to sign him. He pulled Wasilewski aside, after which Clay realized two things: some people at Quiksilver didn't like him, and Wasilewski was a true friend.

"There was obvious concern from guys that didn't understand him, guys high up," Wasilewski recalls. "The one executive told me, 'I don't want to deal with him.'

"I said, 'Look, the guy's different. He's got something else going on.'

"'Well, it looks to me like he's an asshole, stoned, or whatever. I just don't see why he's around.' He wanted to get rid of Clay."

Years later, Wasilewski shakes his head as he talks about it, the memory both fresh and unpleasant. "At that point, I just looked at this guy and said, 'You don't want to help this kid? He obviously needs help. You don't want to take the time to look into something we can do for him?'

"'Then tell me, Strider, what is it? Tell me what's going on.'

"For him, it was a numbers thing, a time thing—and he had no time for Clay. He needed a name, a label, something to call whatever was going on with Clay . . . or else."

Clay had two very strong allies at Quiksilver—CEO Bob Mc-

Knight, who co-founded the company, and Tierney. As Tierney continued to observe Clay's mannerisms and awkwardness in social situations, along with his superhuman focus on one specific activity — surfing — his psychology schooling and acquired knowledge kicked in.

"After a few days, I said to Strider, 'Have you ever heard of this thing called Asperger's syndrome?'" Tierney says. "I asked a few other people at Quiksilver, and no one had ever heard of it. My mom's a psychologist, and works with kids with learning disabilities, including autism and Asperger's, and I've taken some classes. I'm definitely an amateur, but I do know some things, and this kid seemed to me to have characteristics of Asperger's. I knew he didn't have a learning disability per se, because kids with learning disabilities aren't capable of vividly remembering every wave they rode for the last five or six sessions . . . or, in Clay's case, the best waves he's ridden at every place he's ever surfed. He's incredibly smart.

"Once they took a look at that, they said, 'Wow, this sounds a lot like Clay.' And once I described Clay to my mom, she said, 'Yeah, take a look at Asperger's.'"

Clay's career moved forward with a growing frequency of mind-boggling events, both good and bad. In January 2008, he entered the O'Neill Sebastian Inlet Pro, a World Qualifying Series tournament. The event, held an hour south of Cape Canaveral at one of Florida's premier surf spots and contest venues, was organized and produced by Mitch Varnes, Clay's manager. It was the first of many planned WQS competitions for Clay, per the strategy he and Varnes had developed to qualify for the World Tour. Within the O'Neill Sebastian Inlet Pro was a second, independent contest, the Red Bull Tow-At. In that event, the surfer who launched into the biggest aerials and blasted the most radical maneuvers would win a Sea-Doo personal watercraft vehicle. A freestyle surfing competition . . . a vehicle as the top prize . . .

Suddenly, Clay's laissez-faire attitude about the WQS event vanished. "I already had my car from winning the NSSA Nationals, and I really wanted the Sea-Doo," he recalls.

He just missed, finishing second to Josh Kerr, another phenomenal talent. "In the main contest, he was eliminated in his first or second heat, which really disappointed me," Varnes says. "In the tow-at, he knew there was a Sea-Doo on the beach, with keys in the ignition. With Clay, a money prize never mattered. But a vehicle, like a car or Sea-Doo? It's a tangible prize; he can see it on the beach. We handed the keys to Josh on the spot, and Sea-Doo shipped it to him. Clay really wanted that Sea-Doo shipped to Maui."

While the tow-at event marked the highlight of Clay's trip to Florida, a seemingly complimentary and flattering incident on the beach rattled the eighteen-year-old star — when he was asked to sign autographs, he froze. When they heard about Clay's reaction — a situation that would repeat almost everywhere he went — his parents shook their heads but were not surprised. "He wasn't that much part of the group," Gino says. "I don't think he felt as comfortable. He likes the one-on-one. That went for contests and hanging on the beach too."

When asked to look back on the day, Varnes thinks about it for a moment. "Florida might have been a defining moment. I've done signings with him at the US Open of Surfing and in New York City and New Jersey, and it's the same thing. He's always been totally withdrawn when he's swamped with these kids, but it goes with the territory. If you're a pro athlete or Olympian in any sport, of course people want to be near you and talk to you and touch you and get your autograph. Sure, that could be a defining moment, but he's had many similar moments at other large venues.

"When I saw this happening, what I considered something new, I wasn't sure what to make of it. I'd already spoken with Jill many times about his other difficulties, so I knew he had some troubles with school, a hard time studying, things like that. I thought it was a learning disorder more than anything. It didn't bother me as much, because he was being paid a lot of money to travel around and surf, and not a single sponsor complained about it. They did want him to surf contests, but they didn't make it a priority, as long as he was traveling, surfing, and being prominent in the media."

● ● ●

That autumn Clay joined a dozen other riders on a Quiksilver promotional boat trip to Fiji. As the boat steamed to an outlying island,
Clay moved around constantly, rubbing his hands, talking much
more than usual. He visualized himself unloading on the waves with
the purest fury and might, dropping in from seemingly impossible
positions to uncork reverse throw-tails, tube rides, and deep cutbacks
and re-entries. Approaching the situation for which he lived, the experience that made his life on land more tolerable, he couldn't have
been more thrilled.

Suddenly, a massive tropical disturbance rushed out of nowhere
and smacked them with furious winds and high seas. "We got hit by
some thirty-foot seas," Wasilewski recalls. "We headed right into it.
We were taking on water, and huge diesel drums were flying all over
the deck. It was not a good situation. The Indian captain asked me,
'Do we keep going? Do we turn around?'

"'What are we looking at?' I asked.

"'About a fifty-fifty chance.'

"'Of making it through the storm?'

"'Of living.'"

Wasilewski, no stranger to close calls as a big-wave surfer, found
himself staring at his own mortality face-to-face — as well as that
of the others. While the crew huddled in the galley and underneath
chairs, rocking back and forth and praying fervently, Wasilewski put
the matter to a group vote: Do we ride out the storm? Or try to head
back?

The surfers decided to ride out the storm, but pure fear registered
in the eyes of everyone on board. He felt the same fear.

One passenger, however, exhibited a calmness bordering on the
absurd: Clay. While the boat continued to bounce up and down,
with rain squalls and wave tops washing across the deck, Clay asked
Strider, "You're not going to let me die, are you?" He was as mellow as
if he'd just emerged from a daylong meditation.

"No, Clay, you'll be fine," Wasilewski told him.

Clay grabbed his surfboards to protect them, just as concerned
about his equipment as he was about his own physical safety. "Good.
I don't want to die today," he said.

"All these guys were going crazy, hiding and making their peace with God, but Clay got really quiet, with no emotion in his face, no raised voice, just, 'Good,'" Wasilewski recalls. "If I'd ever had any question that this kid was different from the rest of us, it was answered right there."

Clay walked away. A couple of minutes later, Wasilewski staggered past, struggling to keep his balance on the rocky boat. "What's happening now? We're gonna die, aren't we?" Clay asked, his anxiety finally rising.

"No, Clay, we're not going to die. I won't let you die."

"I'm not gonna die?"

"No."

"I just sat and looked down at the deck and let everyone else freak out," Clay later said.

Wasilewski returned his focus to the task at hand: escaping the storm. "We made the turn, a very technical thing with a 140-foot boat, and rode right up the face of these waves," he recalls. "The lip pushed the bow, and we rode straight down, the swells breaking on the helm of the boat. The boat's like forty feet out of the water, waves breaking on it—all of this during the middle of the night. And Clay never once screamed, yelled, or panicked. Just about everyone else on the boat did."

During the aborted trip, Clay mentioned to Wasilewski that doctors in Southern California "X-rayed my brain." The MRI confirmed for Wasilewski that Quiksilver's mandate to the Marzos to continue testing Clay had been followed.

A week later, Wasilewski would call Jill. "I don't know what's going on, but Clay's different. He said something about you guys X-raying his brain. Did you?"

"We did a brain scan, yes."

Even though Quiksilver pressed for the tests, Jill had tried to keep the information from them, because she was afraid they would drop Clay from the team—a costly, six-figure hit on his present and future. Her own high anxiety was redlining. "I constantly worried about that," Jill says. "What else did Clay know how to do but surf? How else would he make money?"

Now Quiksilver knew. "Have you found out anything from those brain scans?" Wasilewski asked.

Jill's stomach beelined toward her throat. *Is this it?* "No, no, we're still working on it. Why?"

"Because on this trip, all these guys are panicking in the storm we hit, and I have never seen anyone in that critical of a situation who acted that calmly."

Wasilewski paused for a moment, then laid down the heavy lumber: "Jill, we need to know what to call what is going on with Clay. We need some sort of diagnosis, or explanation. They [Quiksilver directors] want a label. They're all over me about it. They want an answer as to what's going on. We may never get that answer, but let's try to find out what it is."

After they hung up, Jill sat silently for an hour, perplexed. How did Clay manage to act so calmly in such a life-threatening situation? Was it because he was on the ocean, where he felt comfortable, even in the middle of a ferocious storm? Why would his calm demeanor during a storm concern Quiksilver as much as the more legitimate concerns they'd already voiced?

"At first, I thought this was weird, because he panics about things like throwing up," she says. "But as I watch Clay more and more and see how totally unafraid [he is with] things he feels comfortable in — like oceans, hiking, being around nature — I realize that if there was an emergency, I'd want Clay next to me. His reaction is almost a primal thing — handle it now, panic later. I've never seen him panic when it's related to the ocean."

That was when a realization came to her: she and Quiksilver weren't on a collision course at all — they were on the same page. She'd wanted answers for a dozen years, and now Quiksilver was forcing her hand. Maybe that wasn't a bad thing.

She and Clay flew to Newport Beach to visit the Amen Clinic. The research and therapeutic center works with kids and teens living at all levels of the spectrum, from nonfunctional autism to Asperger's syndrome, as well as with other learning and social disorders. Jill, already exhausted and frustrated from trying to understand how her son ticked, had to deal with Clay getting surly. He spent the trip either in silence or asking her, "Why more tests? *I'm over it!*"

Gino and Cheyne took a much dimmer view of the matter. "When I decided to take Clay for the brain scan, Gino didn't understand why I was going," Jill says. "He didn't understand, or want to understand, much about Clay's situation at all. He thought it was a cop-out. So I didn't tell anyone, and we went. I was still trying to figure out ways I could help him."

Jill knew that Gino would either accept the situation in his own time or continue to deny it, but she had experienced enough recently to press forward, not to mention Quiksilver's veiled threats to drop Clay. One of the more famous incidents pertained to a TV commercial shoot for Quiksilver, featuring Clay talking on camera about the virtues of the new board shorts he was wearing. While the camera rolled, Clay looked down and described what he saw, absent the filters and censors that normally wired people utilize. "They should be a little longer. Maybe with better material too," he said. "And I don't like the color."

Then he remembered he was on camera. "Why, do you want me to like them?"

Quiksilver didn't air the commercial, but later inserted it into *Just Add Water* to illustrate the direct line Aspies take when asked for their opinion. That clip eventually went viral on YouTube. "How could I say something good if I didn't like them?" Clay recalls. "I just made a couple of suggestions."

Some among the Quiksilver brass clamored anew to release Clay from his contract. However, McKnight, one of the most likable and caring executives in the surfing industry (not to mention one of its finest businessmen), saw matters another way.

When Jill heard about the shoot, her anxiety increased. "I was seeing more and more signs that worried and concerned me, and I was trying to keep his career going and balancing out . . . I was feeling like, 'Who's going to sponsor him if he can't even shake someone's hand or talk to them . . . or even care?' I knew I had to do something — not only for my son but for me. I could see the innocence in him, he knew vegetables were good for him, so when he'd eat them, he'd say, 'These are for my brain, Mom,' or, 'I'm going to take the blue-green algae and I'm thinking better now.'"

She shook her head as tears formed in her eyes. "That's not normal."

The Amen Clinic nearly became a disaster when Clay walked in the door and sat in the waiting room. "All of these little autistic kids five or six years old were running around the waiting room before going into these tubes, and I'm sitting there, like, *What the fuck?* I didn't want to do this," he recalls, his voice rising. Years later, the memories of his testing experiences still mass together whenever provoked, leaving him visibly distressed and ready to stop talking for the rest of the day.

Finally, a nurse led Clay to "the tube." He entered the hyperbaric chamber for an MRI, a harrowing, claustrophobic struggle for most people. The effect on Clay was the diametric opposite: he relaxed completely, comforted by the absence of noise and strange faces. He listened to music and occasionally waved to Jill, who waited with tears streaming down her face. He reacted the same way to all ten MRI exams, feeling just as comfortable on his last pass as on his first.

"I was thinking, *This is so sad*," Jill recalls, "but he was fine with it. It made me realize, *whatever is different about the way his brain is wired, this is a real thing.* It didn't faze him."

Jill and Clay remained at the Amen Clinic for two days of MRIs and additional tests. When doctors returned to discuss the results, they couldn't offer anything conclusive. *What else is new?* Jill thought. They mentioned the so-called Ring of Fire, in which an excessive number of brain neurons from the frontal lobe fire at once to create sensory overload. They talked about OCD and a variety of anxiety and stress disorders, but there was not a single mention of autism or Asperger's. "They just told me what kinds of supplements to use with him, what kind of learner he might be—he might not ever be able to learn like most people. I didn't get any real answers," Jill says.

Clay adds, whimsically, "Why did I have to leave Maui and give up all this surfing time to be there?"

The results, or lack thereof, did not sit well at Quiksilver. They ramped up the pressure on Wasilewski and the Marzos to deliver quantifiable medical results and a diagnosis, or they would drop Clay. Part of their concern was that they'd started to move forward on the *Just Add Water* documentary. Having just enjoyed success with a film featuring Dane Reynolds (*First Chapter*), Quiksilver had decided that another freestyle surfing movie about a popular team rider would find a ready audience. "Clay was the next guy up," Tierney says.

Then, following Wasilewski's suggestion, which Tierney wholeheartedly embraced, they changed the conceptual direction to delve into the reasons behind Clay's eccentricities, socially awkward ways, and entombing quietness.

"I got really upset with Quiksilver's attitude," Wasilewski says. "If they would've let Clay go, I would've left too. I couldn't believe they didn't want to help someone in that situation. For some things, there just isn't an easy answer, and that's true with Clay. But they wanted one.

"That's when Bob McKnight got into the conversation. He said, 'I love this. Let's do something for him. Let's find out what's going on.' That's when I turned the planned movie around and pitched it as a documentary."

Wasilewski and Tierney had their movie angle, but Quiksilver still wanted a diagnosis before investing another ounce of time, energy, or money. They floated the idea of Varnes and company representatives flying to Maui to sit down with the Marzos. "They recommended to me, then the Marzos, that Clay fly to California for more medical evaluations," Varnes recalls. "Jamie was fairly sure Clay had Asperger's, which, like everyone else, I knew nothing about. But there was something about how he said it that made me think, 'I wonder if . . .'"

In Maui, Varnes and Wasilewski had a pleasant and conversant evening with Gino, Jill, and Clay. They discussed the next step: one more series of tests, this time with Dr. Chitra Bhakta, an autism expert in Orange County, California, known to Quiksilver.

That was when Jill reached the end of her rope. "She freaked out," Clay recalls. "Quiksilver knew that I was different, and she was afraid I would lose my sponsorship. I was eighteen and had nothing in my life that I cared about or did really well except surfing. I still don't."

While Wasilewski and Jill knew the status of Clay's relationship with Quiksilver, they never told him. Why add more anxiety and stress to a situation already packed with tension? "I never got into the conversation with Clay because of how sensitive he was," Wasilewski explains. "He was at that place where he was already borderline overwhelmed, an eighteen-year-old trying to keep up with a crazy year where he was now a major star. Anyone would be overwhelmed. I wasn't going to add this."

The next day Wasilewski invited Jill and Clay to lunch. He got right to the point. "Have you heard of Asperger's syndrome?" he asked.

After a lifetime of never knowing about the disorder, they'd just heard it mentioned twice in a ten-minute span. Call it synchronicity. On the way to lunch, Jill's mother, Joanna Darrow, had called and brought up the same question, based on research she'd been doing on her home computer to help her grandson. "It was very ironic these two people mentioned the word 'Asperger's' to me in the same day," Jill says.

However, after a dozen years of riding the diagnostic seesaw, her staying power had vanished. "I'd become anti-label," she says. "I decided that Clay's Clay, he's his own person, and we're going to do the best with what we've got. I didn't want any more testing. He's been tested for ADD, ADHD, and OCD, different anxiety disorders, tested for special ed three times, then the Amen Clinic, which was really embarrassing and humiliating, sitting him in a place with all those little kids. Really? I was tired of testing. I felt like I was making him feel dumb for needing to be tested so much."

Those were not the words Wasilewski wanted to hear. "Can you get him tested one more time?" he asked.

Shortly afterward, Clay and Jill flew to Oahu so Clay could sign a multi-year contract with Super Brand Surfboards. The Super Brand staff buffed out their visitors with spacious rooms and all the food Clay could eat, which is to say, enough for two or three people. He has a ravenous appetite, especially after surfing. "They made me feel really special and told me a bunch of times how much they loved my surfing and the kids loved my surfing and how they could see more kids riding Super Brand Surfboards and they would pay me well . . . and they did," Clay says.

Jill knew her next words to Clay would be make-or-break, not only pertaining to his Quiksilver relationship but possibly for their own relationship as well. When Clay has listened to a perspective or directive enough, he often tunes out the directive — and the person. That daunting fear ate at her psyche.

To console and comfort herself, and Clay, she started massaging his back. Clay thrives on sports massages; he still keeps weekly massage therapy appointments when he's on Maui. While it later surprised many to learn that Clay enjoyed massage (normally, physical touch from another is anathema to those on the autism spectrum), it had been an acquired taste for him: Jill was a longtime massage therapist.

As she worked out the knots in his shoulder muscles, she took the leap. "Clay, I have to ask you something, and I want you to really hear me," she said. "They want to do one more round of testing to figure out . . . why you surf so good. What is it about you that makes you surf so good? How are you so amazing at surfing?"

Clay rolled away and looked up at her with a face as cold as an ice cap. *I don't even want to hear it.*

"I promise it will be the last time. I promise you we will never test you for anything again," she said.

"The last time?"

"Yes."

"Ever?"

"Yes."

He stared directly into her eyes. "Okay."

Clay is in his element with waves of any size, whether getting airborne on mid-sized waves (top) or paying homage to giant twenty-foot Hawaiian peaks (bottom).

DoomaPhotos

Clay toddling along the beach, already feeling at home.

Marzo family

Clay in his best environment. In the water, his social awkwardness and difficulties with day-to-day living end, and his world-renowned wave-riding magic begins.

Marzo family

An early effort at drawing surfing, wave, and ocean scenes, one of Clay's enduring passions.

Marzo family

Jill and Clay spent seventeen years not knowing the source of his on-land difficulties. Now, they work together, along with Clay's girlfriend, Jade Barton, to optimize his life with Asperger's.

Marzo family

One of Clay's many gifts is a gymnast's flexibility and acrobatic skill. Here, at one of his Maui home spots, he snaps off a powerful re-entry (top) and his signature reverse throw-tail aerial (below). *DoomaPhotos*

The young maestro, heading backside at one of his choice Maui surf spots.

Marzo family

Before he became a famous surfer, Clay was a national age-group champion swimmer. He often competed in a half dozen events per meet for his Puamana Swim Club team.

Marzo family

Jill and Gino Marzo raised their family on the beach. Clay (right) as a young competitor, with friend and fellow competitor Granger Larsen.

Marzo family

Clay is famous for two surfing maneuvers: his reverse throw-tail aerials and rail grabs (top); and his tube or barrel rides, or what he calls "slabs" (bottom). Tube riding is the ultimate surfing experience, and few surfers ride as deeply as Clay; none delivers a higher quality ride, say his friends and peers. Plenty of onlookers worldwide have hooted and hollered watching Clay shoot out of a barrel.

DoomaPhotos

Clay (left) and his older brother, Cheyne Magnusson, were Hawaiian amateur superstars who became multiple national champions. Each drew considerable press coverage before turning sixteen.

The Maui News/Matthew Thayer

Brothers Clay Marzo (left) and Cheyne Magnusson of Lahaina share a common love for surfing and are usually at the top of their divisions when competing

Brotherly love

The full Marzo family around 2006. The Marzos spent their lives at the ocean, helping create a pair of champions. Bottom row, left to right: Cheyne, Gina, and Clay. Top row: Jill and Gino.

The Marzo Family

When Clay saw the 2005 NSSA National Championships first-place prize, he told his father, "I want that car. I have to have that car." A few days later, after becoming the first and only surfer to record two perfect 10s in the same championship heat, he posed with his prize.

DoomaPhotos

What does it feel like to ride beneath and inside a breaking wave? Every surfer knows that feeling, but none gets there better or more often than Clay.

DoomaPhotos

Clay first learned to surf with his back to the wave; his "backhand" talent remains among the greatest in the world.

DoomaPhotos

The clan at Christmas 2012 (left to right): Jade Barton, Clay's girlfriend; Clay; Jill; Gina Marzo, Clay's baby sister; and Clay's half brother, Cheyne Magnusson.

Marzo family

Clay lights up when it is just him and the ocean.

DoomaPhotos

12

Diagnosis:
Asperger's Syndrome

"You have difficulties relating to others in crowds and social situations, right, Clay?"

"Yeah, that's me."

"And you have trouble figuring out what people mean by just looking at their facial expressions and body language, right?"

"Yeah."

"You're really sensitive to things you touch, hear, taste, and smell — like you love food more than anything except surfing and you can't stand sudden loud noises."

"Yeah."

"And surfing is the only thing you focus on, and you're intense . . ."

"Yeah."

" . . . and you're into having the one friend at a time, but just the one friend . . ."

Are we done? "Yeah."

Clay and Jill returned from the North Shore, heavyhearted and full of uncertainty. She knew that if their next trip to California didn't produce answers, she might never know what accounted for Clay's struggles. He certainly wasn't going to make it possible. "That's the thing I really like about my life now," he says today. "No more testing." She also realized that Quiksilver was likely to drop him despite the vociferous objections of Wasilewski and Tierney. They had to find something.

As she had done so often in the past, Jill seized the initiative. She logged on to her computer, Googled "Asperger's Syndrome," and found a self-test. She read the questions and answers. *That's Clay to a tee,* she told herself.

She called Clay into her home office and decided to run some of the questions by him. "As he kept answering, I realized over and over again, *that's Clay,*" Jill recalls. "I started crying. After all the tests, all the misdiagnoses, all these years, here was something that made sense and described Clay's behaviors and why he's so clumsy with normal things like eating and losing things and dealing with people, but yet he goes near the water and he becomes the most graceful and masterful person you'll ever see."

They returned to Southern California to meet with Michael Linden and Chitra Bhakta, the medical specialists Quiksilver recommended, at the Orange County Integrative Medical Center (OCIMC), where Bhakta is an autism specialist. After completing her residency at Harbor/King Medical Center near Los Angeles, the native of India found her calling: working with socially and developmentally disabled adults and children. Her expertise covered everything from diagnosing to offering treatments across the board, while providing wise, compassionate counsel to families.

Clay was in a sour mood throughout the trip, but Bhakta connected with him, which was never easy with Clay on the first pass, but guaranteed to soothe his anxieties if it happened. It did. "She was really nice," he says. "The only other person that nice who worked with me was Carolyn Jackson. I had a lot of uncool doctors, all the way back to school. It was nice to work with someone who cared about me. She understood. She gets a lot of people who have been through the same thing as me, being told you have all these things for years but then no one knows what it really is."

"By the time an adult is properly diagnosed with a behavior, social or mood disorder, or anything on the autism spectrum, they have been misdiagnosed an average of four times, over an average span of ten years—in the case of this young man, an entire childhood a adolescence," Dr. Jane Tanaka, a Southern California psychiatrist, points out. "One can only imagine how much suffering for both the person and family would have been avoided with a prompt diagnosis."

For the next three days, Bhakta and Linden ran Clay through a series of tests that were very different from MRIs and the testing crapshoot at the Amen Clinic. They asked written questions, conducted a face-to-face interview (dialing into not only his responses but also his vocal tone and body language), and did an exhaustive family history workup, an MRI, and a QEEG (quantitative electroencephalogram). Recently introduced to the diagnosing of disorders on the autism spectrum, the QEEG is commonly known as a "brain map." It works on the premise that individual brains are like fingerprints—each is unique. The QEEG measures general brain activity and then breaks into more specific data that indicate the areas of the brain that are over-aroused, overused, or underused. Finally, the machine delivers a detailed one-hundred-page report to the doctors. That report provided the critical information on Clay's brain function—information no one had yet seen in the twelve years since Jill started getting Clay tested.

Interestingly, Bhakta and Linden ran Clay through a battery of tests more commonly used to diagnose autism than Asperger's. For example, family and patient histories are typically not factored into an Asperger's diagnosis so much as the patient's behaviors that exist at the time of evaluation. Bhakta and Linden looked at the whole picture, as if they already knew he fell on the spectrum but were trying to pinpoint the severity of his disorder. As they moved through the process, Clay and Jill looked at each other several times, astonished by the complexity and thoroughness of the process.

What happened next shocked the Marzos, who had grown accustomed to waiting long periods of time for results . . . if they received any at all. "It didn't take my doctors long to say I had Asperger's," Clay recalls. "They also said I had signs of ADD and OCD."

"Dr. Bhakta gave him the Asperger's label, but more along the lines of autism, because of his difficulty in communicating," Wasilewski says. "What prevented her from diagnosing him as full-blown autistic was his athletic ability. You don't see that level of athleticism very often in autistic kids or teens."

They had their diagnosis. Clay broke into a warm smile that lit up his green eyes, while Jill burst into tears, letting fly a pool of repressed and disappointed hopes that had welled up inside her for eighteen years. The combined sense of release and relief brought home the reality that finally, after so many false diagnoses and dashed hopes, they could wake up the next day with a name for the way Clay's brain was wired and his particular relationship with the world. Not only that, but it was a disorder that had identifiable characteristics, ones that could be quantifiably tested and measured, and one that might have been the most intensely researched medical condition in the world during the past decade, short of cancer. Subsequently, in 2012, the Centers for Disease Control and Prevention (CDC) estimated autism prevalence in the United States at one in eighty-eight children (and one in fifty-four boys)—a 78 percent increase over its 2007 estimate. Autism affected more children than diabetes, AIDS, cancer, cerebral palsy, cystic fibrosis, muscular dystrophy, and Down syndrome—*combined*. Clay wasn't the only person in America receiving a long-awaited answer. In his case, receiving it enabled him and his mother to turn their focus to the ever-growing mountain of material on autism and Asperger's syndrome.

Asperger's syndrome is named after Dr. Hans Asperger, an Austrian pediatrician who observed the trouble that four children in his practice experienced in social situations. According to the National Institute of Neurological Disorders and Stroke, Dr. Asperger called the condition "autistic psychopathy," which he first identified in 1943 as a personality disorder that exhibited a strong tendency to isolate socially. In 1981, long after Asperger's death, British psychiatrist Lorna Wing renamed the disorder "Asperger's syndrome" in writings published worldwide. A decade later, it was officially designated as the highest—or most functional—end of the autism spectrum.

That designation was modified in May 2013 in the American Psychiatric Association's newest edition of the *Diagnostic and Statistical*

Manual of Mental Disorders (DSM-5). The *DSM-5* eliminates some familiar autism spectrum diagnoses, including an entire subset of names that had delineated degrees of functionality, and Asperger's syndrome has been dropped as well. This decision has affected millions of children in matters from special education assessment to medical insurance coverage. Asperger's syndrome has been lumped in with a single omnibus diagnosis of "autism spectrum disorder"; in other words, if you have Asperger's, you are autistic. When the *DSM-5* revisions were announced, Stuart Newman of Mind Matters PC in Oregon said that the new criteria would "create a common language we can use when we talk with school systems, parents and other doctors, and it will mean the same thing for everyone, which will be really helpful."

Many did not agree with the decision, however, and cited the findings of a team from the Autism Research Center in New York, which identified fourteen genes possibly associated with Asperger's that didn't pertain to the rest of the spectrum. In a 2012 study of 540 Australian health and education professionals, 93 percent felt that there was a concrete difference between autism and Asperger's syndrome.

Nevertheless, the Marzos had a definitive diagnosis in hand. One by one, the characteristics made complete sense: Clay's monotonous speaking voice, flat and with little facial expression. His difficulty in knowing whether to raise or lower his voice when in public, as well as his lack of ability to determine whether talking loudly was rude or inappropriate. His very few interests, but his hyper-focus on the interests he did have. His tendency to withdraw socially if confronted with unfamiliar faces, crowds, loud noises, or anything unsettling.

Clay took it from there. "I remember everything about the things I focus on the most. Like waves. I remember how I took off and pulled into a barrel or got air so I can do it again and again. I watch the same video all night long and replay certain waves and *feel* what it felt like, every time. I love that feeling, so I keep watching. I like taking pictures of every good meal I eat at a restaurant. I have thousands of pictures of meals."

Bhakta viewed Clay's behaviors and mannerisms as textbook high-end autism. "They're able to sort of function in society, and seem normal, but have enormous problems with social interaction," she says in the *Just Add Water* documentary. "They tend to have certain idiosyncrasies that are very pronounced. If you see people slapping or rubbing their hands, that in itself isn't an abnormality, what we would consider an abnormality, but for them, it's something they do to de-stress themselves.

"That one activity they have, that one thing they're expert at, they can devote exceptionally long hours and concentration [to it] that I don't think a typical person could bring."

Clay brings those long hours and concentration to surfing, which initially threw off his doctors. The hand-eye and physical coordination of a world-class athlete is not indicative of an autistic person, who is more likely to be clumsy and to lack the skills to play sports. "He is very much an athlete," behavioral therapist Carolyn Jackson says. "That's where he is very unique. He likes to play Ping-Pong, which sounds normal enough. But not for an autistic person. In my field, we call Ping-Pong 'chess on steroids,' because you use your right brain, and you use it really fast. The fact he played Ping-Pong was, to me, very different, because it requires a great deal of balance. He has the physical balance because he's a surfer, but it requires other things. I've seen him play, and I've seen him laugh."

Clay and Jill flew home, and Clay headed straight for the North Shore of Oahu, where the prestigious Triple Crown of Surfing was taking place. They had their diagnosis, and Quiksilver had its answer. They acted quickly on it, signing Clay to a lucrative four-year contract in 2008 that made him the latest professional surfer to command a six-figure salary. For Jill, it was a long-awaited Christmas present, "one of the best Christmas presents I've ever had," she says.

That was when Tierney and Wasilewski switched gears on the *Just Add Water* documentary and focused on Clay's diagnosis, hoping to share his story with the world. Tierney made contact with Dr. Tony Attwood, considered the world's leading expert on Asperger's and the author of the highly regarded guidebook *Asperger's Syndrome.* The Australian psychologist's explanation fits Clay in every detail:

The best description is that the brain is wired differently. Some things are processed so superbly, that the person has areas of excellence. There's a tendency to have a special interest. When the person with Asperger's chooses to do something, he will become an expert at it. Probably the best in the world at it.

When they become so dedicated, when they allow their minds to focus on aspects and connections no one had even thought of, they become intuitive. That's when they excel.

"I don't think of Asperger's syndrome as a disorder," Attwood continues. "It's a difference. If you're going to excel at something, you switch off the social parade, and the other parts take over."

This also explains Clay's eccentricities when he becomes excited—clapping loudly, rubbing his hands for minutes at a time, making strange sounds, his voice rising from complete flatness to an exclamatory thrill ride within the same sentence. All it takes to see it is to get into a room with him when surf video footage is rolling hot and heavy. "He gets so excited, it's infectious," Tierney says. "Most of the guys I film downplay their emotions; even when it's really good, they don't want to act like they're excited. Everyone's trying to play it cool. Clay has no interest in doing that. When he gets excited, it's fun to watch, and it gets everyone else hyped up too. The way he rubs his hands, claps them, his energy rises, the smile comes to his eyes and face, how his excitement pours out through his voice. Just the way he gets jazzed up for it . . . that's the childlike thing most people lose as they get older. I don't think it will ever go away for him."

"You can see the passion that he feels for doing what he's doing," Bhakta adds. "He's so passionate about it that it's almost like, that's what he's living for."

The realization that Clay was not alone in the autistic world helped Clay, Jill, Jackson, and, to a lesser extent, Gino unravel the twelve years of incomplete or inaccurate evaluations and assessments they had endured. Chitra Bhakta saw to that by focusing on previous incidents during Clay's growing-up years—the anxiety, the panic attacks and their triggers (big crowds, others vomiting)—and the tests that led to diagnoses of ADHD, OCD, and the leaky stomach syndrome that doctors at the Amen Clinic had mentioned. Rather than characterize leaky stomach syndrome as its own condition, Bhakta emphasized that it often accompanies the high anxiety experienced with Asperger's. Its symptoms ring familiar to many who have suffered from anxiety disorders: cramps, excessive flatulence, sensitivity to certain foods, and regular stomachaches.

The diagnosis brought everything under a big umbrella. "Jill and Gino kept being told he had ADHD, or OCD, but Asperger's is ten steps above those," Jackson says.

One other subject came up during the diagnosis: How did Clay wind up with this disorder? "Was he predisposed to it? Did he hit his head? Was it the time he got hit while on his bike? The lack of oxygen before he was born?" Jill wonders.

No one knows for sure. Current research points to structural and functional differences in certain areas of the brain. Some experts think that Asperger's syndrome may develop before birth and then subsequently affect a child's neurological wiring. At some point, it progresses and further influences the child's thought, behavior, and social interaction. For example, Clay was much more sociable as an elementary school student than he is today.

Other experts trace Asperger's to environmental or genetic factors, both of which are graphically illustrated by the Marzo family history. Jill has been diagnosed with ADHD since childhood, when she was initially treated for it, and she suffers from constant high anxiety. Gino is both ADD and ADHD. In addition to the influence of these genetic factors, Clay's environment growing up was one in which two very different personalities manifested emotionally in the home: Jill's heart and feelings are an open book, while Gino rarely displays his emotions.

"Maybe it adds up. I don't know. No one really knows for sure," Clay says. "At least we had something to call it. At least I knew why I focused the way I do on surfing. Quiksilver had their answer and I could be over it."

"We were so relieved and happy to know what it was, to have a condition we could learn more about, so that we could give Clay the best possible chances and advantages to lead his life," Jill says. "We also knew he would never have a 'normal' life as we think of it — in some ways yes, in some ways no — but I was so relieved that someone finally saw him for who he was."

Two family members didn't buy in at first: Gino and Cheyne, who had spent the past half-dozen years chastising Clay for being antisocial and underachieving in school and criticizing Jill for enabling all of it while pulling Clay out of the public school system. "I disagreed with Clay having Asperger's when I heard about it," Cheyne says. "It sounded like a convenient, miraculous diagnosis Quiksilver had come up with to justify moving forward with the movie the way they wanted to do it. I'm a trust-but-verify guy, so I went online, read up on it, and yeah — that was my brother."

Gino was a harder sell, made more so by the direct connection he made between the impending failure of his marriage and the long ordeal with Clay. "To me, everybody's different. You can't lump people into, 'They've got this Asperger's syndrome,' or whatever. I mean, to what extent? When is it a condition? And when is it a matter of tuning things out because you're thinking about something else? I think that's an important question. Learning in a class and sitting in a classroom is for people who can sit still and focus and want to learn. They say it's a hard thing for someone with Asperger's to do, the way I understand it — which I really don't. I was always the dad who said, 'Clay, pay attention. You're not stupid; you're just not focusing on your ABCs. You're thinking about the next turn you're gonna do when you get home and paddle out.'"

"I think in the end," Wasilewski says, "it helped everyone — Jill, Gino, and most of all, Clay himself — to finally know what was going on with him."

It helped the baby in the family too. Suddenly, Gina felt emboldened to talk with the older brother she treasured but with whom she felt she'd lost meaningful contact. For a deep, articulate communicator like Gina, that meant everything. She started noticing how Jill, Gino, and Cheyne were coming to clearer realizations and understandings about past events — whether or not they would admit it.

"A lot made sense to our family," she says. "Things came to light, and we were filled with happiness, since we finally understood what he was struggling with. We always knew he was different and special, so we didn't talk about it as much. It wasn't a big discussion topic; we just waited for the results. But once I found out he had Asperger's, everything changed for me. I felt like, 'No wonder!' It answered my big question about why he was so obsessed with surfing. That's all he does.

"When I watched the autism part of the movie, that also answered questions for me. I really liked the way my mom said in the beginning of the movie, 'He *has* to be in the water. You can't take that away from him.' That was the answer, to me: this is my brother, and who he is."

Even Jackson, a lifelong skeptic about labeling patterns of behavior, applauded the diagnosis. "The big picture of Clay is that sometimes, when we don't know, is it better? Or not better? I ask myself that question a lot," she says. "When I was working with him the first time, before he was diagnosed, someone would say, 'What do you think he is?' I would say, 'I don't know. I don't like to define what he is.' But within myself, I wanted to know something for sure too."

By the summer of 2008, the whole world knew.

13
Learning About Asperger's

The hard part for me is that people don't like what I say a lot of times, or how I say it. People tell me I don't talk enough, but when I do talk, they freak out over what I said. I just want to say the right thing, but it doesn't always come out the way they like it. All of a sudden, since I was this surf star who deals with filmers and writers and photographers, I had to learn when to say something, and when not to. When I did say something, I had to stop worrying about what people thought. I *always* worry what people think about me, even though they think I don't give a shit with the way I sometimes look away. I always want to say the right thing.

Carolyn would show me ways to shake people's hands when I meet them, or wait until it was my turn to eat at a group dinner, when to talk and not talk at meetings, how to handle crowds when I had to handle them, things like that. She did this over and over, and I would copy her. Just like I copied Cheyne's surfing style so that I could surf like him.

Once Clay finished with the 2007 Triple Crown of Surfing, he flew home and started his new life as a diagnosed Aspie. Jill bought him a book, *All Cats Have Asperger's*. Simply written and illustrated by Kathy Hoopman, the book focuses on fifty-five characteristics of Asperger's syndrome that are also common to house cats — an interesting correlation, since many people have noted the feline dexterity of Clay's acrobatics in the water. However, when Hoopman adds up her list of cat traits — dislikes loud noises, tendency to be aloof, extreme awareness of surroundings, need to move to the beat of their own drum — the similarities to Asperger's take shape and color.

Clay started reading the book and slowly absorbed the explanation of each characteristic. As he did, his self-awareness grew. He realized the ways in which Asperger's syndrome can be seen as a gift — a major revelation after a lifetime spent being ostracized, bullied, and chided for his way of seeing and maneuvering in a strange world that was totally out of his control. To this day, when he's in Maui and feels confused or uncertain about a life situation, he picks up the book, which sits on the family coffee table.

"Some people would say I'm an expert at surfing. So that's my gift," Clay says. "We all have a gift. I don't know how I would live without surfing. I don't want to know. I feel like I'll die if I don't surf. I have to surf. Because of that, I try to know as much as I can about boards, waves, riding waves, and the ocean."

The next step was to find bridges between the more challenging Asperger's traits and the ability to live comfortably and peacefully in a world that felt alien half the time. "When it's known someone has Asperger's when they're young, you have them with a behavior specialist that teaches them social skills, such as sticking out their hand and saying, 'Pleased to meet you,'" Jackson explains. "It becomes an automatic response in that situation. They will continue to do that if they learn that young. You can teach them to say things like, 'You look nice.' Generally, they won't go so far as to say, 'How was your day?' because they're not going to listen to the answer."

The first time Clay met with Jackson, he was constantly traveling, which is always a harrowing experience for someone who doesn't consider paying attention to details like boarding times and gate numbers a priority — if he considers them at all. "Can you imagine Clay, when he's sixteen, seventeen, or eighteen, leaving here and going to Tahiti, going to all these airports on his own, and getting somewhere, jumping on these boats, going to islands?" she asks, her eyebrows rising. "With Asperger's, one of the primary characteristics is high anxiety. He's trying to keep it in, but his anxiety is right there, he's overwhelmed, he's going to this place . . . to me, it's just incredible."

Carolyn focused on Clay's interpersonal communication skills, always a challenge with Aspies. "She asked me a bunch of questions," Clay recalls. "I did the same thing to her that I do to other people that ask me too many questions: I just went to another place. It's hard to know what to do when all these questions come at me. If someone has these questions that are really stupid, like, 'What's it like to have Asperger's?' I just think they're barneys and tune them out."

When Clay said essentially the same thing to Jackson, she objected. "No, you have to give them a response," she told him.

"We practiced over and over," Clay says. "I said what she told me to say—'Let me think about this a while'—and then 'a while' would be like a minute. Or forever. Or I would totally forget about it, move on."

"With Asperger's, they have delayed responses," Jackson says. "You and I can have a conversation, but you cannot have this kind of conversation with Clay. Because he does certain things, people have this expectation that he's not going to need external prompts to help carry a conversation, but he does need them."

Another session dealt with Clay's reactions and responses when something angered him. Despite his inner anxiety, he comes across as mellow and laid-back, a guy with the *aloha* spirit that travelers covet when they fly to Hawaii. However, when he gets angry, he simmers. One of three things then happens: he surfs the anger out of his system; he figures out what angered him, calms down, and carries on; or he "sees red." It doesn't take long for him to hit the boiling point.

"I know I am not very good dealing when I'm pissed," he says. "When I travel, or have to run around doing things I don't usually do, I need to chill. I need to go into my room, put on my headphones, and chill. Or surf. Sometimes I can't."

"It's like the cork in the wine bottle: sometimes it's going to pop," Jackson adds.

What happens when it pops? "I see red, I melt down, I lose it—and then I'm over it," he says.

"He doesn't have a filter, so if he becomes overstimulated, or there's a lot of people, or if he doesn't want to be there for his sponsor, he's going to say 'Fuck you' to those people," Jackson explains. "If someone passing by wants his autograph and he doesn't want to give one, he'll just look at them. He's not a mean guy, but this is an immediate response as a coping mechanism to get his space. That's all he wants—to have some space."

The increased attention from media and fans created a different challenge: how to deal with a blunt, unfiltered honesty that causes him to sometimes blurt out exactly how he feels. When running on his natural rhythms, he doesn't stop to concern himself about

others' feelings, the situation, whether or not his comments are po-
litically correct, or the consequences that might come down the line.
The reason? Those behavior checks and balances, natural responses
for the general population, are not wired into his brain. He has to
acquire those behaviors the only way that can possibly work for
Aspies — through exhaustive repetition.

"People don't like what I say a lot of times, or how I say it," Clay
explains. "People tell me I don't talk enough, but when I do talk, they
freak out over what I said. I just want to say the right thing, but it
doesn't always come out the way they like it. Since I was this surf
star who deals with filmers and writers and photographers, I had to
learn when to say something, and when not to. I had to stop worrying about what people thought. I *always* worry what people think
about me, even though they think I don't give a shit sometimes. I
always want to say the right thing, and I always want to do the right
thing."

"He will always tell the truth," Jackson says. "When you ask him a
question, if he answers it, it's going to be the truth. Sometimes people don't really want the truth."

Asperger's syndrome also presented a challenge for Clay when it
came to storytelling, or "talking story," as they say in Hawaii. While
most people can present concepts, share experiences, and even work
through personal difficulties by using story as an illustration or metaphor, Clay cannot. He can't make the connections. "Clay will listen,
and he laughs, but a lot of times he won't get the story. That's what
a lot of people don't realize: he doesn't fully understand the story,"
Jackson says. "But he'll see other people laugh, and he will laugh. If
he has something on his mind, what he'll do is say, 'Yeah, that's what
it was like for me . . . right? Is that right?' He's looking for validation
of what he says, because he can't give himself that validation."

Clay's self-awareness sessions with Jackson covered the simplest
gestures and expressions that most people typically learn and master as children — but not those with Asperger's or autism. "Carolyn
would show me ways to shake people's hands when I meet them, or
wait until it was my turn to eat at a group dinner, when to talk and

not talk at meetings, how to handle crowds when I had to handle them, things like that," Clay recalls. "She did this over and over, and I would copy her. Just like the way I copied Cheyne's surfing style so that I could surf like him."

"It goes for when he tries to read someone's face too," Jill says. "He's masterful at modeling facial expressions. He has to be; that's how he tries to understand what you mean when you raise your eyebrows, blink a lot, or smile in the middle of a serious discussion. After he talks with someone and gets an expression that puzzles him, he'll ask me or a friend, 'What does he mean when his face does this?' Then he makes the face, usually a spot-on imitation, and I tell him something like, 'That's the face of someone who is open, honest, and really respects you.'"

"I find it continually fascinating how Clay, and others in the spectrum, model facial and body expressions," Mary Anna Waldrop Enriquez says. "That's their way of trying to figure out the social cues — what your intentions are, if you're a kind person or not, how they can best relate to you. It's like, when you raise your eyebrows, you'd better stop and consider what you're going to say.

"People in the spectrum don't operate like that, and our mistake is that we expect them to. That's fascinating. Where is the disconnect in synapses in the brain? And how do they push it over to the other side of the brain, to what's important and non-important?"

Clay's sessions with Jackson, his study of *All Cats Have Asperger's*, and his closer adherence to the nutritional and fitness suggestions laid out by Drs. Bhakta and Linden began to show. Clay grew more conscientious when he communicated with others, and more knowledgeable about his gifts and challenges. Sometimes the learned behaviors and changed habits would stick. However, because they were not automatic responses or didn't embed in his brain to become second nature, he had to work at them constantly. Talk about a profound case of "practice, practice, and practice."

"Clay became more interested in eating healthier, watching diet, lifting weights, working out, more interested in his health," Varnes says. "I think the weight of the world came off his shoulders, and his mom's, when they got the diagnosis, and now he just wanted to focus on the goals we were setting out.

"Clay will do anything you want him to do. If you get him one-on-one, and you take care of all the logistical things that he has trouble handling—that a lot of people have trouble handling, for that matter—he's great. He'll turn it on. But you gotta get him there."

Another challenge faced Clay post-diagnosis: how to better relate to his girlfriend at the time, Alicia Yamada. They met while surfing, when Clay was fifteen and she was seventeen. When people asked him questions or wanted to talk extensively with him, she would answer and take care of business. They were constantly together. Jill liked Alicia right away, but Gino's skepticism, from the very beginning, would hurt his relationship with Clay. "They both thought she was a little too old for me, but she was nice, and she loved surfing, and that's really all I cared about. If you're nice and you like surfing, I'm stoked," Clay remembers. "But when it comes to knowing what chicks like or how they do things . . ."

"Clay had no idea," Jill says. "None at all. Kids with Asperger's are always in their own worlds, and these are worlds other people can't get into all the way. Especially girls. He knew nothing about how to relate to girls, as a boyfriend, and the girl needed to understand that she would always come second to surfing. That's not what you want if you're a girl. To this day, I believe that he can have relationships only because the two girls he's been with, Alicia and Jade [Barton], are so into surfing. And he's a really good-looking kid, tall, dark, green eyes, one of the world's best surfers . . . what girl *wouldn't* like that? But without surfing, I don't know that he'd ever have a relationship. They are hard enough for the rest of us"—she pauses and chuckles—"but really, really hard for people on the spectrum."

When Jackson worked with Clay, Alicia didn't join him—at first. However, as their fights grew, Jill insisted that they visit Jackson together. "He did not have the skills to make her feel important to him," Jackson explains. "She *was* important to him, but he couldn't show it. Luckily, Alicia didn't have a lot of needs; most girls do. She accepted Clay for who he was."

One day Jackson asked him, "Is Alicia going to pick you up today?"
"Yeah."

"So when she does, I want you to say, 'You look nice today, Alicia.'"
"Okay."

"And then tell her another nice thing or two . . . some sort of compliment."

"Okay."

They walked out of Jackson's house. Alicia was there to pick up Clay, who smiled as he walked toward the truck. "You look nice Alicia today," he said, transposing the last two words. He added something about possibly going out on a date.

Alicia grew excited. "Where did *that* come from?"

"'Wow, that felt really good,' Alicia told me," Jackson says. "And she told Clay that too. But it wasn't something he was going to follow up on. His brain isn't wired to do so.

"So I was teaching him ways to have empathy with others. How do you think someone else felt? Can you understand why they feel the way they do? Can you be there with their feelings, regardless of your own? He won't go that far. That's a very common by-product of Asperger's."

About fifteen months after Clay's diagnosis, a new set of issues arose that reached beyond the purview of Jill and Carolyn Jackson: his growing protests over having to travel for surf contests and video shoots, a necessity of any professional surfer's livelihood. Besides surfing itself, making videos was what he loved to do more than any other thing in the professional surfing world — not to mention that videos had made him a global star — but he hated the travel involved.

Jill and Jackson turned to Dr. Tony Attwood. They sent the results of Clay's PET scans, QEEG and other tests, the diagnosis from Dr. Bhakta, and Jackson's notes to Attwood's Australia office. He wrote back, in part:

> *I had an opportunity to discuss Clay's current situation and diagnosis of Asperger's syndrome with his mother, Jill, and Carolyn, his behavioral specialist, on 27 March 2009. It appears that Clay has cut*

back on his professional or competitive surfing and I am concerned
if he should stop all competitive surfing. I think his experience over
the last year or so has indicated the maximum amount of travel
and competitions that he can cope with, but I do not think that the
alternative of no competitions would be appropriate, as surfing is an
essential part of Clay's life and self-identity and he enjoys some of
the aspects of competitions.

His mother described Clay as having significant sleep problems
and it may be worthwhile to refer Clay to a sleep clinic to see if this
has significant effect on his mood and abilities. He may also benefit
from strategies to encourage relaxation such as meditation, and it
would also be valuable to incorporate his girlfriend in the support
network that he has to reduce stress.

Professor Tony Attwood

Jill and Clay began to treat Attwood's words as gospel when it came to the future direction of his surfing career. Furthermore, his Quiksilver contract emphasized not only contests but free surfing. Since it was easily Clay's largest endorsement deal—and one of the largest contracts for any surfer—he began gravitating toward free surfing, which would prove to be a pivotal turn in his life.

The difference between the two styles? Freedom, as Clay sees it. "With contest surfing, you have to show up on a schedule, surf twenty- or thirty-minute heats, and score as many points as you can," he explains. "You have to catch enough waves to get your scores and do the moves judges want to see. You have to watch your opponents, who are always playing head games. I hate that. People are haters when they do that. Sometimes I even paddle away from them, out of the contest zone, catch some waves on my own.

"Free surfing is part of my gift from Asperger's. I paddle out, catch all the waves I want, and no one keeps score. A lot of times no one even sees what I do, because I'm alone. It's just me and the ocean. And maybe a sea turtle."

The world was about to be reminded of Clay's free-surfing prowess in the water—and learn about his difficulties out of it.

14

Just Add Water: The Movie

I think everyone would love it if someone made a movie about them. Surf movies are a big part of every surfer's life growing up. Like every other kid, I dreamed of having a surf movie made about me. Every time I saw my favorite surfers, I thought about myself on-screen. I wanted everyone to watch me surf. I wanted to surf so perfectly because I wanted Adam [Klevin] and the other filmers to feel like they got the best footage ever.

I was really happy when Quiksilver told me they were making a movie about me. I wanted it to be the best movie ever, and I wanted people to hoot and holler when they saw me on the screen. Something I could watch over and over again and never get sick of. Will they think I rip? Will they like the way I surf? What about all the things the other dudes say about me? What if they don't like it?

I wanted *Just Add Water* to be sick . . . really sick.

Hundreds of people stood outside the Maui Arts and Cultural Center's Castle Theater on a typically warm, buttery summer evening to see one of their own star in a surf movie, but this wasn't just another surf flick. The buzz behind the fifty-minute documentary—which had drawn a standing-room-only crowd—had been growing for months. It would not be an ordinary night of mindless hooting and hollering, although plenty of cheers would cascade throughout the theater once the lights went down.

Inside, Clay fidgeted uncomfortably, twirling his curly hair and almost pulling some of it out. He was excited to see the movie on which he'd spent so much time in the past year, filming and advising directors, producers, and cinematographers. However, the large crowd induced the edginess and anxiety that had always caused him to shy away, walk off by himself, or otherwise shut down. The ever-nagging questions ripped through his psyche like a serrated knife: *Will they think I rip? Will they like the way I surf? What about all the things the other dudes say about me? What if they don't like it?*

At least there were no surprises on-screen. He knew what to anticipate: the sight of himself flying through the air, racing across faces of waves two to three times as high as his six-foot-one size and sinking deeply into barrels. Yet he didn't care that the night would be focused on his brilliance in the water so much as he cared about how it would be presented.

Surf films have been part of the culture since Tom Blake, Doc Ball, Pete Peterson, Bud Browne, and Leroy Grannis, all iconic figures in the surfing world, started shooting photographs and home movies many decades ago. They grew in stature in the 1950s, when fledgling moviemakers Bruce Brown, Walt Phillips, John Severson, and Grant Rohloff ran story lines through their footage. They produced films with telltale titles like *Barefoot Adventure, Waterlogged, Surfing Hollow Days, Have Board Will Travel, Too Hot to Handle, Once Upon a Wave, Sunset Surf Craze,* and *Big Wednesday* (the 1961 original; it was remade by Warner Brothers in 1978). Hollywood's superficial surf culture blitzkrieg, depicted in the Frankie Avalon and Annette Funicello *Beach Party* flicks and the Gidget franchise, prompted surf filmmakers to dig deeper to present the authentic California and Hawaii surfing worlds. It also gave them an opportunity to broaden their audience. Surf cinema broke onto the world stage in 1965 when Brown took Robert August and Mike Hynson around the world, filmed them, and presented *The Endless Summer,* the most-watched surf movie of all time. A half-century later, it still makes commemorative runs through old beach town theaters. Seven years after *The Endless Summer,* the second most celebrated movie, *Five Summer Stories,* came along. In 1977, the first film to chronicle pro surfing, *Free Ride,* thrilled worldwide audiences.

A young Gino Marzo spent the 1970s watching these movies in Southern California high school gyms, local theaters, and community centers. He was no different than any other scruffy-haired, surf-stoked kid in the audience, except for something he didn't yet know: a generation later, his son would be the subject of the most original surf documentary since the genre's halcyon days. "I hadn't really thought of it that way," he says, "but it has always been a *big deal* to be in a surf film. Some of that is lost on kids now, because everything goes straight to DVD, you buy it in a surf shop, and then go watch it at home. Back in the day, you appear in a surf movie that goes to theaters and gyms, and you're a very big deal. That's what I think about *Just Add Water.* It's a *very big deal* type of movie."

Like his dad, Clay watched everything that came out, including his personal favorites: *Thicker Than Water, Step into Liquid, Occy: The Occumentary,* and *Riding Giants.* He visualized himself catching that wave, making that turn, slotting deeply into that barrel. "Every time I saw my favorite surfers, I thought about myself on-screen. I wanted everyone to watch me surf. I wanted them to be happy with me," he says.

One of the first to consider a Clay Marzo–focused movie was Adam Klevin. While others pondered the idea and talked about it among themselves, Adam approached Clay. "Hey, let's try to get a movie done on you."

"We did that *Transworld Surfing* movie, *Tomorrow and Today,* and a couple other things," Klevin recalls. "When Metal Storm [the original production company that Quiksilver hired to make *Just Add Water*] put me on retainer, I pitched them and said, 'Hey, Clay is like the James Dean of the surfing world. He is *way* different than everybody else.' And I can bring to the table a little glimpse into his mind; you guys have never seen anything like it. He's brutally honest but quiet all the time, and interesting, and twirling his hair, and there's just something raw about him, like nobody else."

That conversation started the ball rolling. Wasilewski, along with Tierney, had already formed a set of ideas. They would become the primary decision-making team, with Wasilewski serving as executive producer and Tierney as director. They collaborated to not only obtain the money from Quiksilver to move forward but to make sure the Quiksilver brand was an intrinsic part of the film. With the mightiest brand platform in the surfing industry, they were assured of good reach. They had no idea how much that reach would expand.

They started shooting in Fiji in August 2007, three months before Clay's Asperger's syndrome diagnosis. Three videographers were on hand, but Klevin was the primary shooter because he knew Clay's tendencies inside and out. He could anticipate next moves better than anyone, even though he, too, was sometimes blindsided by Clay's sudden switches in direction or aerial blasts that stretched the tentacles of gravity. "I wanted to surf so perfectly because I wanted Adam and the other filmers to feel like they got the best footage ever," Clay recalls.

Wasilewski listened to Klevin's pleas about looking at the bigger picture about Clay: *What makes him do the things he does?* He studied Clay from that angle, thought about Quiksilver's pressure to obtain a diagnosis, and decided that Clay's unique relationship with the world was just as important as the surfing.

"Everyone knew there was something different about Clay, something unique about him. Let's focus on that," he says. "We conceived the movie before the diagnosis. A lot of people thought he was a kook, or a jerk, the way he'd talk to them. Or not talk at all. But really, he was this amazing guy whose brain works completely differently than anyone else's, and I was lucky enough to be able to see it when I hung out with him."

Wasilewski found Tierney, and they agreed to the approach. Clay wasn't so enthusiastic. "They thought that because people didn't know me, they would get more into a *story* about me, my story, instead of just an hour of surf action," he says. "I wanted a pure surf film, but that's what they decided."

"Surfing has a tradition as a great storytelling culture, people telling stories of their successes, and building an aura and mystique around it," Tierney says. "These personalities, these surfers, become larger than life, truly unique characters. Those are the guys who were around when I was getting into surfing—Tom Curren, Martin Potter, and Mark Occhilupo, and older guys like Mark Richards, Shaun Tomson, and Peter Townend. All were world champions, but more than that, *personalities* with mystique.

"Surf films had a lot to do with that. You see that in all the older surf films. But today it seems like 99 percent of all surf movies lack a story. It's just clips put together. *Just Add Water* really hit home because it was a human-interest story about a great surfer. People are hungry for good stories."

The team spent almost a year working on the movie. Klevin shot early footage in Maui, Fiji, Australia, France, and Tahiti. It included a return visit to Teahupo'o, where Clay had wowed everyone as a sixteen-year-old by challenging a monster of a wave, then receiving personal first aid from big-wave maestro Laird Hamilton for his painful effort.

The only way to reach Teahupo'o is by boat. Once in the lineup, a thick wave lip pitches directly ahead, and the rider looks directly at the reef below, where plenty of boards, broken bones, and scraped flesh have collected over the years. The barrels are wide enough to drive through with a small car, but they close out fast. Teahupo'o can reach twenty feet, not an uncommon sight for Hawaiian surfers any given winter, but as Clay points out, it's "a *sick* twenty feet. People get hurt badly all the time. A few have even died there."

When Clay, Tierney, and Klevin reached the airport in Papeete, Tahiti, they learned that Teahupo'o was maxing out, breaking so fast that surfers couldn't paddle into the wave without tow-in help. Clay grew noticeably frightened, a rare sight. "He was freaking out because it was going to be the biggest swell of the year, a tow-in swell at Teahupo'o, and he was in the trials [of the Quiksilver Pro]," Tierney says.

"I'm going to die! I'm going to die! I'm going to die! I'm going to die!" Clay repeated rhythmically, like an apocalyptic mantra.

"No, no, you're going to be fine," Tierney said.

"I'm going to die!"

"You know how to surf these barrels. You're going to be fine.'"

Clay shook his head. "No, I'm going to die!"

He didn't die. However, he did almost win the trials.

"It was huge," he recalls. "We had to tow in one of the days. I'm not a tow-in surfer, and really didn't know much about it, but I got a couple of big tow barrels. Huge shacks."

After the event, the group stayed for two weeks to shoot movie footage. It was there that one of Clay's friends from Western Australia, freestyle surfer Ry Craike, noticed something he found amazing, as Tierney recalls. "When the waves are good, Tahiti's a perfect place for Clay, because he loves the barrel, the clear water, the reefs, mountains, forests . . . it's a natural, mellow environment. I remember Ry saying, 'All life is for him is get up, surf, eat, sleep, surf, eat, sleep.'"

Just Add Water built on the premise that Clay's brain is wired to focus on one area of interest with absolute clarity and certainty, a trademark of Asperger's syndrome. Jill opens the movie off-camera by saying, "You ask for a label? A condition? I can just say that outside of the water, life does not come easy for Clay. He lives very much in the present, that place where most of us want to be. When the ocean's going off and he's not in it, he becomes uncomfortable in his skin. He has to feel it."

Tierney shot the open after Clay had been diagnosed. Until the diagnosis came, they sweated through every filmmaker's worst nightmare: the possibility of *getting it wrong.* "That was a big deal, finding out what was up with him," Tierney says. "The thinking was, if we're going to put this out, we've got to get him diagnosed, especially if we're going to do these interviews with the other pro surfers and experts."

"Even though his diagnosis came during the filming, the movie played right out to the original vision we were rolling on," Wasilewski adds. "We just let it unfold in front of us. We told Clay's story, and the diagnosis gave people a better idea who he was. It explained his world. It was unbelievably cool how the cards played in everyone's favor connected with this movie."

They also worked with their star beyond the live action. Occasionally, Clay would view the dailies and comment on what he liked and didn't like. When they reached editing and postproduction, his musical preferences and previous experience producing home videos came into play. Some of the song choices on the soundtrack were his. However, he knew little about the terrestrial part of the film, the scenes shot on land. This included a telltale shot in which he spins around on a street corner in a large city, baffled and discombobulated by the noise, lights, and masses — and then the shot quick-cuts to him sitting in the water, thrilled to be back "home." "They'd tell me about it, but I'd be like, 'I trust you, just do what you want with that, brah,'" Clay remembers.

Tierney believes firmly in collaboration. With *Just Add Water,* he stepped outside the surfing world following principal shooting and contacted Shaun Peterson, the director of TV reality shows such as *Rule the Mix, Electric Spoofaloo, My Date,* and *The Juice Box.* He also produced the indie film *Living in Missouri* (1999), which captured nearly a dozen awards at film festivals worldwide. "We would edit from 6:00 PM until three or four in the morning, night after night," Tierney recalls. "It was fantastic. He's an exceptional editor. This was his first surf project, but that's what we wanted, a great editor outside surf to put our documentary together."

In a nod to Clay's impact on the surfing world, Tierney interviewed many of surfing's elite over the past quarter-century: Kelly Slater, Dane Reynolds, Ry Craike, the late Andy Irons, C. J. Hobgood, Mark Occhilupo, Jake Paterson, Jeremy Flores, and many others. Some of their comments in sharing their insights were hilarious, while others were poignant and moving. One of Clay's favorites came from Irons, who won three world titles before dying suddenly in 2010. "His personality . . . he's a trip, quiet and shy and reserved," Irons says. "But when he's in the water, he's like radical Black Sabbath — he just goes for it. He's a totally different guy. The way he rubs his hands . . . I love that. Whenever he sees a left, he'll start using that one."

"I think Andy really understood me. I miss him," Clay says quietly.

Tierney also interviewed Drs. Bhakta and Attwood. During his bit, Attwood dropped a lot of jaws when he said about Clay, "What he'll do is have a schema of many waves he's ridden before, and then be able to predict what to do in that situation. So his brain disconnects from everyday functions and just becomes one with the wave. He'll intuitively know what the wave's doing, so he'll anticipate that, and be ahead of everyone else."

Despite all the work, Tierney was unsure if Clay would like the finished product. He and Wasilewski told him it would include plenty of surfing, but they didn't offer specifics on the story line. Clay thought it would be a surfing film, with a mention of Asperger's and a few interviews. It turned out to be much, much more.

"The movie was meant to be a documentary with some insane surfing," Tierney explains. "Honestly, I was scared that I was going to show Clay this thing, and he was going to hate it and not want it to come out, because he was expecting a surf film."

Eight months after shooting began, Tierney and Wasilewski walked into a Quiksilver meeting with a trailer in hand. After they saw it, everyone in the room realized the potential impact of the film. "The first thing that surprised me was the response to the trailer. It was great," Tierney says. "After we showed it in the internal meetings, we put it on Surfline, the big surfing weather forecasting and news website. There were two hundred comments on it *that day*."

Wasilewski, Tierney, and Klevin traveled to New Jersey to show the rough cut to a select audience. Among them was Klevin's sister, Sloane Klevin, the winner of two Emmys, a Peabody Award, a Sundance Audience Award, and the 2008 Academy Award for Best Documentary for *Taxi to the Dark Side*. She also made *Real Women Have Curves* and *Freakonomics*.

"She came down and met us in New Jersey, and we were showing the roughs on tour, and she said, 'I love it, I love it, but you can't have black transitions, there's too many of this and that,'" Klevin recalls. "Jamie was there, he took notes and listened, he and Shaun Peterson changed it, and it turned out great. Jamie did what it took to make the film great, and you can't ask for more as a videographer. Or, in my case, one who personally wanted to make sure only the very best shots of Clay got in there. I love the way it came out. I can watch it a thousand times."

A couple of months prior to the premiere, Clay and a few friends watched *Just Add Water* at Klevin's house. Only Clay didn't know it beforehand. Klevin fired up the trailer, surprising everyone. Before ten seconds had passed, the "Yeah, dude!" and "You da man, brah!" and other surf lingo superlatives were blowing through the house.

"He was looking at me and seeing if everybody liked it," Klevin recalls, "and making his little sounds, rubbing his hands. He was so excited."

After the trailer finished, one of Clay's friends turned to him. "Ah yeah, Clay, that's gonna be the sickest movie."

"Wanna see the movie now?" Klevin asked.

"What?"

He played the whole film, which stunned the roomful of surfers, who were used to seeing an entirely different type of format. "To this day I get chicken skin and my eyes almost well up remembering that night, and watching that movie, because of what we put into it and because of how special he is and how it actually showed what he's made of," Klevin says.

Tierney learned of Clay's positive, excited reaction to the movie. "I was totally surprised when he watched it and liked it," he says. "I know it's not exactly what he wanted, but he liked it, learned something about himself, and liked what the other people said about him too."

Just Add Water played throughout the United States and Australia in the last four months of 2008 and was then shipped to surf shops, movie stores, and major booksellers as a DVD. It became the most talked-about surf film in years. "Clay was a star before *Just Add Water* came out," Tierney says. "After it came out, he became a star outside the surf world too."

Wasilewski agrees. "The response was amazing. People were stoked to find out what was going on, that there was an explanation. The nonsurfing world was touched by seeing someone so challenged doing so well. I had people from different parts of the world coming up and saying, 'It's so great to see this.' We saw this from community to community. People from all over love it. There's a story there for people to grab hold of. It's beyond the surfing niche."

"I saw Andy Irons a couple months after the movie came out," Tierney recalls. "He had done a couple interviews with us. He said to me, 'I'm so happy I was in that movie. I'm bipolar and I've always been afraid to tell anybody, I've been afraid for that to come out, but I'm happy Clay got his situation out there.'"

The response was followed by outreach. Varnes and Clay started receiving letters from parents of kids living with full-blown autism or Asperger's. They looked up to Clay because of the film's revelations, and because of how he happened to be a world-class athlete in the coolest sport on the planet. "I don't really know what to say to them," Clay points out, "but it was really cool that they got to see me surf, and maybe they'll want to go surfing one day. Surfing is good for everyone. I like to help kids get into the water."

Certainly, the flood of letters planted a seed that Varnes, Jill, and Clay would cultivate into a new direction for his career, one that will continue into the future.

"Most people know someone who deals with something like Asperger's or autism, or they have a kid that does, a friend, or even themselves," Tierney adds. "It's sort of everywhere in this society. These types of stories are out there, but they're very rarely told. When people put them out, you get this human connection that doesn't come with a regular surf film. Suddenly, you want to know this guy, root for this guy, and you gain interest in him as a person. It changes things."

As *Just Add Water* gained traction, its makers found themselves encountering people far outside their realm, in places where a surf movie would ordinarily be regarded as a flick from another planet. "I know a lady in New York who's gotten the movie into the New York school system," Wasilewski says. "They watch it to show there's a different world, to show people with challenges, but that just because these people have challenges doesn't mean they can't excel at something. Thousands and thousands of kids have seen it, probably millions by now. It's a very cool thing."

Only one piece remained to complete the film's remarkable journey: recognition. It didn't take long. The movie won the prestigious 2008 Surfer Poll Video Award. Furthermore, Clay won Best Video Performance by a Male over two of his personal heroes, Andy Irons and Dane Reynolds. He also placed fourth in Best (Individual) Video Maneuver.

"I don't think there's another surf company out there that would have understood what we were trying to do," Tierney says, "or had the guts to actually do it."

As *Just Add Water* continued to garner attention outside the surfing world, people seemed to catch on to the story in all corners. Even the international media, like everyone else, was fascinated by the young Maui surfer with a drop-dead handsomeness that continually drew neck-snapping looks from women, an ability in the sport of kings unlike any other in the world, and a disorder that begged the question: how can he be autistic and a world-class athlete at the same time?

What followed was a four-month descent on Maui by top-flight media outlets — networks and cable outlets, mainstream magazines and news sites, a harrowing proposition for even the best-adjusted, most camera-loving teenager. For a kid whose most difficult challenge was communicating?

"We were really stoked about them visiting me, but it was hard," Clay recalls.

"A lot of people think I just didn't want to say anything, but what scares me is that I will say the wrong thing and people won't like it. They'll think I'm rude or an asshole or something is wrong with me. I wanted everyone to be happy with what they could write or say about me. It wasn't the surf media, where I could say something and everyone would get it right away, because they know the language and waves or whatever, or just go, 'Yeah, that's Clay.' It was like they were on the beach and I really wanted to hit the wave for them."

Acting on behalf of the family, Jackson took charge and prepped Clay for the visits from people who for the most part, Clay quickly pointed out, had never paddled or stood on a surfboard. To someone both surfing-centric and autistic, that recognition means the difference between speaking to someone as a "brah," a friend, and fidgeting through non sequitur questions like, "What's it like to surf with Asperger's?"

Jackson sent him off with an ideal antidote to the challenge that would freeze him most of all: a tough question that would require some thought while a camera was staring him in the face. "They can shut off their cameras. Don't think you have to say something," she told him. "Be who you are. Let them ask you the question, and say what you think. Just accept that they're here to hear your answer."

Which was exactly what happened, as Varnes recalls. "They focused on how good he is as a surfer," he says. "People with Asperger's and highly functioning social disorders tend to focus more on the mind, things like mathematics, music, the things they collect, whatever. Athletics is not normally a strong quality, but they do have strong structures — except for the least structured sport of all, freestyle surfing. Which impressed them even more."

For Clay, two people stood out most: ESPN's Lisa Salter, who regaled Gino and Clay — both huge LA Lakers basketball fans — with tales of her always positive dealings with superstar center Shaquille O'Neal; and Paul Solataroff, whom *Rolling Stone* sent out to write a feature on the mysterious wunderkind — but who received quite a revelation of his own, as Clay recalls.

While poring over memorabilia, Solataroff noticed a photograph of Clay sitting on his board, his arms raised to an approaching twenty-foot wave in pure supplication, as if to say, *Sweep me away, my love.* "It was taken while the wave was coming at me," Clay explains. "I remember everything about sessions like this."

"What do you think when you look at the picture now?" Solataroff asked.

"Besides wanting to be on the wave right now?"

"Yeah? What else?"

"When I was out there, even though that wave in front of me was blowing up, I knew there was a bigger one right after it."

Earlier, while they were checking out the surf at Windmills, Clay's favorite daily winter spot on Maui, Clay had told Solataroff, "Waves are like toys from God." Later, he added that surfing saved him.

"What from?" Solataroff asked.

"I see things different, from the back of my brain, while other people see them from the front. It's not good or bad, just how I am. Sort of makes it harder, you know?"

Solataroff then asked Clay how his perception made matters harder. "I need help to get some things done and to get to places on time," he said.

It was a telling comment on the other side of Clay's world: his life struggles outside the water.

15

Cheyne and Me

We got right back into it. In the first session, at maxed-out Scorps, four to five feet Hawaiian [eight- to ten-foot faces], it was like "Who's getting the biggest waves? Who's getting the deepest barrels?" It makes me surf better, and I'm sure it makes him surf better.

I looked up to Cheyne. I wanted to surf like him, be like him, show up at the beach and win contests like him. I wanted the same career. He was my brother, the best surfer on Maui, and a pro surfer. I wanted to be just like my brother.

Cheyne did some things I still don't really get. He thought I was slow and stupid when I was still in school, like I was just making excuses or being lazy. Mom would talk to him, but they'd just fight a lot about it. Then thinking I kept him out of the film [*Just Add Water*] on purpose . . . I didn't even know until it came out!

So yeah, I'm stoked he came over and we surfed and everything was cool again . . . but he still hardly ever comes around. He's always working or in Cali with his girl or something.

In the winter of 2012, Cheyne Magnusson and Clay Marzo paddled out, as they had done hundreds of times before. However, this session differed from the others: it was their first in the four years since they had last seen each other. It speaks to one of the most interesting, heartbreaking, and ultimately redeeming brotherly relationships in the surfing world, one in which everything from Clay's social struggles to Cheyne's strong personality would factor heavily.

Cheyne flew to Maui for Christmas after Jill strongly persuaded him to step forward and mend fences that had begun splintering a decade before, when Cheyne and Gino formed a united front against Jill and Clay when it came to Clay's growing withdrawal from school and others and his growing inability to focus on anything but surfing. The rift came to a most unpleasant head a half-decade later, when the biopic documentary *Just Add Water* came out — minus any participation from or footage with Cheyne.

Now, four years after they'd last spent time together, Cheyne was reaching out to mend a completely broken fence with his younger brother, the kid who once idolized and emulated him. Jill had facilitated the meeting, but she departed from her normal umbrella-like protection mode whenever Clay is faced with an unpleasant situation — she told her two adult sons to figure it out for themselves. She took off to spend Christmas with her parents in California, leaving Cheyne and Clay to share a house for a week.

The rift between Cheyne and Clay went beyond one problem, or two. It had grown from misperceptions and misunderstandings, differing personalities and expectations, and was exacerbated by the fact that Cheyne lived 2,500 miles away, in the Southern California beach community of Hermosa Beach.

Yet, there they were, after all the "dysfunctionality and fractures," as Cheyne puts it. Catching waves. Being brothers.

"What do we do when I don't have much to say and he doesn't have much to say? Go surfing!" Clay recalls. "We surfed at our favorite places — Scorps, Windmills, and a couple other breaks. We took turns on waves, paddled to try to catch the same waves, and surfed until we had to come in because we were too tired. It was really nice to be in the water with just my brother most of the time.

"We got right back into it. In the first session, at maxed-out Scorps, four to five feet Hawaiian [eight- to ten-foot faces], it was like 'Who's getting the biggest waves? Who's getting the deepest barrels?' It makes me surf better, and I'm sure it makes him surf better."

Cheyne carried more than his surfboard from Southern California, where he represents Body Glove Wetsuits as both a professional surfer and a marketing consultant. He brought along both his strong, gregarious, and articulate personality and a special surprise: a video camera, to shoot Clay and himself together for a Body Glove–funded movie.

"We shot a bunch of footage, and we have a whole section of Maui clips in there from Scorps and Windmills, over a three- or four-day period," Cheyne explains. "Three of the waves are just me and Clay in the water. We've got some really good shots of us sitting in the water. It had been a long time since we were seen together on a video. It definitely put a smile on my face."

As the brothers spoke, they could feel the healing energy and the opportunity to forge a new friendship. "It felt really good," Cheyne says, a bubbling excitement in his voice. "I'd be excited to see the waves, and he'd be excited to surf with me, and we'd surf all these different waves. We pushed each other, really hard. He was so good that it would push me to get better. For all those years when we were younger and he tried to keep up with me, I found out now that I was trying to keep up with him."

After all the family friction and infighting, one situation had made the kettle boil over, spilling well into the future: Quiksilver's decision in 2008 to leave Cheyne out of the *Just Add Water* documentary. The insult was so devastating to Cheyne, and the misunderstandings between all parties so profound, that it took him and Clay two years to speak to one another again — and two more years before Cheyne would fly over to surf with his brother again. Which is how it came to pass that they spent Christmas 2012 together.

Their lives didn't begin that way. "When we were kids, Cheyne took me into the water and showed me all sorts of maneuvers, which parts of the wave to ride, and which waves to catch," Clay says. "We would surf together on weekends with my dad. We [Clay and his friends] looked up to Cheyne and his generation, because they always competed and did really well."

Early on, Cheyne always had Clay's back. After all, he was the older brother by six years. He also faced the challenge of being the odd person out in a blended family, one in which a strong father figure (Gino) had assumed primary parental duties rather than his biological father. Cheyne is the son of Jill and her first husband, Tony Magnusson, a great skateboarder in the late 1970s and 1980s. Part of the superb Southern California crew that redefined performance skateboarding and made it wildly popular, Tony was among the first riders to start his own company, the H-Street Brand (which still exists). He also created a popular skateboard shoe brand, Osiris Shoes. In the 1980s, Tony made two groundbreaking skateboarding videos, *Shackle Me Not* and *Hokus Pokus*. He also changed the way skateboards were built with the "Hell Concave," which delivered more speed and flex. His skateboarding skills remained solid well into his forties, when he won the Legends of Skateboard World Championships in Germany five straight times (2001 through 2005).

Jill and Tony divorced before Cheyne reached kindergarten age, and after Jill and Gino were married, Gino took full parental responsibility. After moving to Hawaii, Cheyne spent summers in California visiting Tony and then returned to Maui. The half-brothers barely resembled each other, then and now: Clay is six-foot-one with dark blond hair, while Cheyne is five-foot-ten with fiery, strawberry-blond locks. Cheyne did catch a break in the height department: Jill is five-foot-ten, but Tony Magnusson is only five-foot-two.

By the time Clay first stood on a surfboard, Cheyne had been surfing with Gino for several years. "He skated first, because of Tony, so he knew how to do little skate things on surfboards that the other kids in his generation didn't know," Clay says. "Then Cheyne and my dad started taking me surfing. Then Cheyne did the big brother thing of showing me around."

"We had a lot of sessions at Puamana. That was always really fun," Cheyne recalls. "Gino was a good surfer, always out there on the weekends, and if anyone was giving Clay direction in surfing . . . Gino likes to tell people what to do, so he was the most influential. He's very direct. I remember Gino telling Clay what would make him a better surfer and what wouldn't. Clay took it as being a little harsh, but it wasn't meant that way. Gino had some really good tips. He pays a lot of attention to sports, he was a good athlete, and he knows things about performance. He was able to transfer that knowledge to developing a good contest surfing mentality, doing certain turns with a style that's your own . . . his guidance with Clay certainly helped."

Cheyne started winning contests when he was eight. As Cheyne's determination to compete grew and his successes mounted, Jill would run the video camera while Clay played on the beach, collecting shells but always looking up when Cheyne caught a wave.

When the surfing bug bit Clay, he decided that the one and only way to ride a wave was to get inside the barrel. Cheyne quickly corrected him, the first of many adjustments and decisions the older brother made that advanced Clay's surfing. Cheyne laughs as he recalls that first conversation: "If there was one thing that was hardest to teach him, it was that you don't have to get barreled on every wave! When we were little, all he tried to do was get barreled, even on waves that had no openings. Obviously, the barrel is the best part of surfing, but we had to yell out, 'Clay, you have to turn on this one! There's no barrel!'"

Clay nods and smiles as he hears the story. "I had a hard time listening to what he said. That's the *tube* he's talking about, the shack, the part of the wave everyone looks for! To me, the tube is sacred. I have to tuck inside every barrel I see out there. If I don't, I might miss the all-time greatest barrel. That's why I paddle out.

"He used to tell me all these other moves you pull off on waves, and I'd do them, but I'm looking to get shacked, to find a sick wedge and get as deep inside as I can. Then maybe a throw-tail reverse."

Despite his initial hesitation to try new maneuvers, Clay picked them up almost instantly from Cheyne. The way his little brother tried to emulate his style, moves, and facial expressions seemed natural to Cheyne, but a bit excessive. Now there's a ready explanation for Clay's behavior: Aspies must model expressions and responses since they have little to no facility at comprehending social cues. Along the way, Cheyne learned what many others would later find out: Clay's ability to understand and adopt new techniques or habits was directly proportional to how interested he was in the subject. While the average person learns to accept and cope with less appetizing activities or tasks, Clay dealt in a much more black-and-white way. "If you tried to teach him something that wasn't very interesting to him . . . no way. It would go in one ear and out the other," Cheyne says. "But mostly, he was the little nerdy tagalong brother. We fought like brothers, and I definitely gave him some grom abuse, but there's nothing that was extreme. Just your run-of-the-mill older brother–younger brother stuff."

Given Clay's global popularity and his status as one of the first world-class athletes diagnosed with Asperger's syndrome, conventional thinking holds that he is the one member of his family to enjoy surfing success. Not so. Cheyne dominated amateur competitions in Hawaii and was ranked number one among amateur surfers in the United States for most of the time between 1995 and 2001. He was the first Hawaiian amateur to enter the World Surfing Games in Brazil, where he made the quarterfinals against many of the world's top pros. After that, he received a nice contract from Quiksilver.

"I looked up to Cheyne," Clay says. "I wanted to surf like him, be like him, show up at the beach and win contests like him. I wanted the same career. He was my brother, the best surfer on Maui, and a pro surfer. I wanted to be just like my brother."

When Clay started to become successful, Cheyne didn't act like a self-absorbed brother who never wants the little kid to become as good. Rather, he openly shared his secrets and strategies and dissected the videos Jill shot. "Once he started entering contests, it was really cool," Cheyne says. "I was already established and had my game going in Maui, and I was in the Junior Men's Division, so a few pegs up from him. Because of my experience, I was able to tell him where to sit, what to wait for, don't catch too many waves or go for everything. I gave him some guidance.

"I took pride in being his big brother, having the role of big brother, and showing him the ropes, introducing him to people in the industry I knew, even my friends. And the people at Quiksilver who ended up signing him."

The Marzo scrapbooks have two different sections from when Clay was thirteen and Cheyne was nineteen. On the left page of the first section, Cheyne graces the cover of *Surfer* magazine's May 2002 edition, blasting off the lip at Rocky Point on Oahu. On the right side is an article about Clay's NSSA Open Boys' and Explorer Menehune regional titles at Turtle Bay, five miles up Kamehameha Highway from Rocky Point.

The second section is equally impressive. On one side is a July 24,

2002, cover story in the *Maui News* about Cheyne embarking on international surf trips (to Indonesia, California, Mexico, France, and Spain) subsidized by Quiksilver. A month later, *Transworld Surf* magazine chronicled the Indonesia trip, and Cheyne, in a massive twenty-page photo layout.

In that article, Cheyne takes advantage of the platform to send a broadside missive to every upcoming surfer: they will have to deal with his brother, and it won't be fun. "People will think I'm saying it just because Clay's my brother, but that's not the case. I think he's the best surfer I have ever seen at his age. I think he's going to be a national champion and he's going to be much better than I am. He has some unbelievable moves in the water, and he's a competitive freak."

Among those watching the brothers ascend was their baby sister Gina. "The thing I love about both my brothers, and the way Mom and Dad were supporting them, is that they did it with passion — they didn't do it for the fame or the money, although that came later," she says. "Especially Clay. I've always been proud of them for that.

"I want to be successful like my brothers in the sports realm. I remember a time when Clay was in a really big contest on the mainland. I was maybe nine or ten. He won, and I heard my mom screaming when she was watching on the Internet, 'I've never been more proud of him! I've never been more proud of him!' I started crying. I said, 'You've never been that proud of me . . .'

"I was really jealous of them. But now I'm really proud of both of them."

As Clay and his friends served notice of their potential, Cheyne and his buddies took it upon themselves to educate the up-and-comers on the choices and expectations they would need to consider. "I used to give all those kids rides in the back of my truck, if they were hitchhiking, take them surfing, then to get something to eat," Cheyne remembers. "I tried to do that for that generation and the ones underneath them because that's what the older guys on Maui did for us. Clay's friends asked questions constantly about what I did as a pro surfer. Constantly. All of them.

"By the time that whole group was about ten or eleven, I could see who was on the path towards professional surfing success. There was my brother, of course, along with Kai Barger, Granger, Wesley, Dusty ... definitely on their way. I tried to give them advice, or give them waves when I could, take them out on a good day, take them to talk to little kids on Maui, make sure they understood that this is part of what you do as a pro surfer. I included Clay in all of that.

"When it was good, I rounded up these kids to go to the best spot, get them in bigger waves — as big as they could handle. While they were out there, it definitely pushed me to do better. You want to set a bar higher than the local competition. I definitely gave them advice about competition and working well with your sponsors. How much did they use? I do know the generation below mine was the power-house generation, the money generation. Clay and his crew were the best kids in Hawaii. They made out financially from it. That's a testament to where my generation set the bar at, as well as the fact that these guys are really talented and dedicated."

After Cheyne secured his driver's license, he began taking Clay to the big stuff on a regular basis: namely, maximum-strength Honolua Bay and Windmills. While a twelve-foot wave seems 50 percent bigger than an eight-foot wave on paper, the proportional increase in power and speed is threefold, if not more. That explains why spots like Sunset Beach, Pipeline, and other big-wave breaks teem with surfers at lower heights, but once those waves jack up, the crowds disappear and out come only the heartiest, most skillful riders.

Cheyne took Clay into "some really sick stuff," to use Clay's term, beyond his outer range at that point. "I took him out in stuff way bigger than I was surfing at his age. I knew that he could do it," Cheyne explains. "The thing about Windmills is, all those guys in Maui are great surfers, but there's only a handful who want to deal with Windmills when it's ten feet [twenty-foot faces] or bigger. Those were the best days — and the gnarliest days.

"When I was his age, I wished I had an older brother to take me out on those days. What I had was a coach, in Matt Kinoshita, but he was on the other side of the island. When I was getting into bigger stuff, Matt was the only guy who would take me out and push me. I paid that one forward, and I took Clay out in stuff that, to an outsider, would be beyond his ability level — but I never acted like it was too big for him. I didn't want to shake his confidence. Even in sticky situations, I would say, 'It's minor. You're fine.' I think that's the attitude you need to take when you're trying to push someone's limits. If they say they're scared, and you say, 'You should be scared,' then the next time they're going to be twice as scared. Or they won't paddle out at all."

Clay's dislike of crowds started in school, where local boys taunted, antagonized, and bullied him with abusive slurs like "retard," "slow," and "stupid *haole* boy." His withdrawal continued in the water, making it tough to continue surfing with Cheyne, the diametric opposite to Clay in personality. Cheyne is outgoing, engaging, and ready to join any crowd if it means better waves. "He looked for friends to surf with, and I just wanted to go in the water with him ... or no one," Clay recalls. "I had my favorite spots, like he did, but they were different spots."

"We used to get in arguments all the time about where we'd surf. He'd want to go left, and I'd say, 'I'm driving and I'm a regular footer, so you're going right,'" Cheyne recalls. "I love Honolua Bay, and I don't have that much of a problem with crowds. I don't prefer them, but to surf a wave that good? No worries, you know?"

When Clay hears Cheyne's comment, his face turns sullen. "If he wants to surf in the crowded places, like Honolua Bay, I won't paddle out with him, yeah?"

Clay's aversion to crowds is so absolute that, over the years, it has cost him photo shoots, contest appearances, and countless big-wave days in the crowned jewels of the sport, like Banzai Pipeline. It continually surfaces, no matter how ridiculous it seems. One day he and a friend pulled up at Windmills, a little oasis of trees, a small creek, and a beach strewn with coconuts, driftwood, and rocks, a few miles from Honolua Bay. The break to the right — the one that Clay made internationally known with more than a half-dozen magazine cover shots — was too small to fire. He gazed a hundred yards away, at the southern wave, but kept glancing to his side, where a teenager sat on a Vespa, a hoodie over his head and a surfboard tucked between his legs. The teen was trying to decide if he would surf. "You've gotta go out. There's no one else out, and it's the best wave we've seen in days," Clay's friend said.

"No way . . . I don't like that guy over there. He's a random. I don't want to surf if he paddles out."

They waited for almost an hour. Finally, the other surfer decided to leave. As he turned the Vespa around, Clay grabbed his surfboard and paddled out for an electrifying session in which he made perfectly substandard waves look great.

"It's extreme," Cheyne says. "I didn't know he'd gotten this bad about crowds until I moved away. But I knew he hated it when a lot of people were in the water. So when I came home for Christmas [in 2012] and we were trying to film for the movie, I intentionally looked for an empty break. I pulled up at Scorpion Bowls, and there was no one out. I called Clay and said, 'I'm paddling out. There's no one out.'"

Clay jumped in his car and drove five minutes to Scorps (the local nickname for Scorpion Bowls). What happened next borders on the ridiculous — but not if one of the parties is wired with a disorder that makes the presence of any unfamiliar faces an exercise in high anxiety and borderline paranoia. "In between me getting there and paddling out, a boogie boarder showed up," Clay says, picking up the moment and ensuing conversation from the part of his brain that remembers *everything*. "The dude caught a wave, barely anything. But it could have been my wave. 'I thought you said there was nobody out!' I yelled at Cheyne.

"'Yeah, there *was* nobody out, dude! There's just this boogie boarder, and he's hardly catching waves.'

"'I don't know. I'm gonna go in.'

"'What are you talking about? You're already catching waves!'"

Clay wanted to race home to the sanctity of the previous night's LA Lakers game, which he'd recorded on his DVR, but Cheyne talked him into staying. "I watched, and like Cheyne said, the boogie boarder wasn't any good," Clay says. "After a few minutes, I said to my brother, 'We're cool. He's not catching anything good. It's all good.'"

"I was tripping out," Cheyne says. "I didn't know he was that bad about crowds. But if you know where they aren't, and you get tons of waves . . ."

Besides the devastating impact of the family infighting over Clay's difficulties and misdiagnoses and Jill's refusal to budge from her alternative schooling approach, there was another incident that took place a few months before Clay won the 2005 NSSA Nationals. This time, the problem began with one of the most selfless, loving acts one brother could do for another — it involved Clay's surf videos and Cheyne's standing as a pro. While Cheyne felt borderline disgusted with the way Jill babied Clay, and with Clay's waning motivation to be involved in anything out of the water, he used that perception to try to bolster Clay's future in the one area he did care about.

One day Cheyne told Clay to send a homemade DVD of freestyle surfing to Quiksilver. Now a valued member of the Quiksilver team, Cheyne badly wanted the brand to sign Clay, for both business and personal reasons. If they rode for the same manufacturer, Cheyne could keep watch over Clay. "He knew I grew uncomfortable in contest scenes and trips where my friends weren't around, so he was really stoked about us being together with Quik. He could be my big brother on some of our promotions," Clay recalls.

The man in the middle was Strider Wasilewski, the team manager of the talented Quiksilver surf team. "Cheyne and I were going through negotiations, and he turned and said to me, 'You know, Strider, I don't know how it's going to work out with us, but I just want to make sure you know about my brother. I'm good, but my brother's next level. Take him on a trip. Give him a shot. Something.' I just looked at him. I was taken aback. Right in the middle of the negotiation, he puts his brother in front of himself. Never seen that before."

"That is the coolest thing my brother ever did for me," Clay says.

The unselfishness of Cheyne's generosity and degree of genuine concern for his brother became more apparent a few weeks later when Quiksilver cut a few team members in order to budget in Clay's six-figure annual salary. Among those whose heads fell on the chopping block? Cheyne.

Not surprisingly, Gino was furious. A decade later, he still is. "Whenever new kids come up and turn pro, that always happens — one of the older guys takes the fall, loses his sponsorship so they can pay the new guy," he says. "Well, Clay was the up-and-comer. Cheyne wanted a raise from Quiksilver, and rightly so, because Cheyne is a very responsible professional surfer. He'd been with them for six years, gotten lots of photographs in the magazines, made movies, been to all the promotions, done media interviews, and everything else they'd asked.

"What a slap in the face to Cheyne! They wouldn't even discuss a pay cut; they gave him nothing. That really hurt him. What do you say to a kid who's been screwed like that?"

Gino shakes his head, rubs his hands together, and looks into the distance. "Unfortunately, as we were to learn a few years later, this is how Quiksilver sometimes parts ways with their longtime team riders. They just cut them. No pay cut, no diminished role — today, they're great; tomorrow, they're gone. Without seeming to give a damn about the body of work they've done. Bush league stuff."

As damaging as Quiksilver's decision was to Cheyne's psyche, he knew that he'd done the right thing for Clay and that Quiksilver's move, though hurtful, was not mean-spirited. It was business. However, the next dustup between the brothers became their most protracted and deeply personal misunderstanding — one so filled with anger, mistrust, and hurt that they may never bounce back completely.

In 2008, when Quiksilver made the *Just Add Water* documentary about Clay's struggles with Asperger's syndrome, they left Cheyne out of the film. Completely. Not one word or frame about him. "They interviewed all these surfers and Asperger's experts, and the movie showed worldwide, but they never included my own brother!" Clay recalls. "There are a lot of stories about the reason why Cheyne was left out. Everyone has their story."

"Why did they leave my brother out of the movie?" Clay asked Jill again and again. At the time, Jill and Gino were in the end stage of their twenty-year marriage—a marriage rocked to the core by their deep opposition when it came to Clay—but they agreed on one thing: Clay was upset to the point of being inconsolable about Cheyne's omission from the film.

That's not how Cheyne saw it. He thought Jill and Clay directly or indirectly blocked him from the movie. He still has his doubts.

"One thing is for sure: neither Jill nor Clay knew he would be left out of the movie entirely," says Clay's manager, Mitch Varnes. "A decision was made higher up at Quiksilver—higher than the movie director level—that Cheyne was not going to be in the movie. Why? I have my own opinion, which I'll keep to myself, but I don't know for sure."

The ensuing destruction to Jill's relationship with her oldest son and to the brothers' rapport with each other grates on her nearly as much now as it did in 2008. "Someone with Quik told me Cheyne was not going to be in the movie. I said, 'What do you mean? That's Clay's brother! He's been there the whole time! He's a pro surfer! And he's the guy who brought Clay to you!'"

Furious, Jill called director Jamie Tierney, a staunch Clay Marzo supporter through the years (continuing right through his production of a highly acclaimed, five-part Fuel TV series on Clay's ongoing struggles with normal life and maintaining a professional career, which aired in 2014). Jamie knew the movie was complete, and he was powerless over Quiksilver's higher-up decisions. Nonetheless, in an attempt to mollify Jill and Cheyne, he told Jill, "We'll put Cheyne in at the end, in the outtakes that roll with the final credits."

When Jill called Cheyne and told him the "resolution," Cheyne was apoplectic. "Don't you dare. I'll sue them!" he yelled at her.

"I still wanted to believe Quiksilver would come to their senses and put Cheyne in there, but they didn't," Jill adds.

"When the movie came out, I found out just how mad Cheyne was. Really mad. *At me*," Clay remembers. "Quiksilver first said he would be in the movie, then he wasn't. Why say it if you don't mean it? I kept saying, 'Mom, why is Cheyne so mad at me?'"

"Because he thinks you and I made the decision to keep him out of it," Jill told him.

"He should've been in the movie. It was really stupid that they kept him out."

Cheyne broke off all communication with Jill for a year. He didn't talk again to Clay for two.

As executive producer, Strider Wasilewski was part of the group that discussed whether or not to keep Cheyne, their former longtime team rider, in the film. "He didn't accept the fact there was an Aspergian world, and Clay was part of it," Wasilewski says. "He thought we at Quiksilver were capitalizing on it for the sake of making money. That was so far from the truth. We were just trying to tell Clay's story. He didn't want to be a part of it."

After *Just Add Water* came out, the fraternal discomfort reached a physically threatening level, in Clay's eyes. He traveled to France for the Quiksilver Pro contest with Adam Klevin, who shot a fair amount of the *Just Add Water* footage. After they arrived, Klevin learned that Cheyne had also entered the Quiksilver Pro. "I heard that Cheyne told the contest director, 'I'm not going to enter if Clay does,'" Klevin says. (Cheyne denies it.)

Meanwhile, Clay was contractually obligated to enter, because Quiksilver requires their top pro riders to surf in their sponsored contests. He competed without incident.

The brothers didn't run into each other at Seignosse, Capbreton, or Hossegor, the three beaches where the contest was held. Later in the week, however, they saw each other at a party. "When I saw Cheyne, I ran," Clay says.

As time went on, Cheyne began a reassessment period that combined his strong feeling about the importance of family with the calendar's reminder that he had just turned thirty. After attending a Tony Robbins motivational seminar, he called Jill and informed her that he wanted to mend fences and fly to Maui to spend time with Clay. "That's why it was so cool when Cheyne came over and wanted to surf with me again," Clay says.

One lingering issue continued to nip at Cheyne's otherwise forgiving mind. "Whenever we have communicated, it's always been me reaching out, not Clay," he says. "Even when we were kids, when we got into fights, my grandparents and parents always said, 'Cheyne, it's up to you to apologize to Clay, to make things right. You're the oldest . . .' I always assumed that role.

"Once the movie came out and I wasn't included . . . it was very hurtful to me. I'm pretty good at keeping things in perspective, but that one really hurt. I made the mental decision not to talk to Clay until he acknowledged that that was fucked up, and apologized and made the effort to bridge that gap with me. I waited for almost two years, and I never got that phone call, or email . . . nothing.

"Looking back, I now realize it was his Asperger's, that he just didn't know what to do with the whole situation. Time heals everything, and I made the decision to reach out. Whatever happened, he's my brother, he's family, and if I have to always be the guy who's reaching out, well, I'll do it again."

Cheyne's maturity came to the forefront when he walked into the family home. "Hey, man, you're my brother, I love you, and I don't want to be not speaking to you. I want my friend back," he said, wrapping Clay in his arms.

"I love you too. I want the same thing. I'm really sorry about the movie," Clay told him.

They moved on. They would never return to the close-knit big brother–little brother rapport of their growing-up years, but how many brotherly relationships regain the closeness of childhood?

"It was so awesome. It felt good to get back to our roots and appreciate Clay for who he is, and how far he's come in his surfing, and look at it from that perspective," Cheyne says. "It gave me a new appreciation for him as a person, and our relationship, as minimal as it is right now. It makes me appreciate those moments I get with him much more than when we lived together and he was part of my daily life.

"You don't realize how precious something is until it's gone. Those days of 'Get up, Clay, get your board shorts on, jump in my truck, we're going here, and we're going to surf,' are over. It's sad. It makes surfing with him now a million times better. It seems like we didn't miss a beat. We picked up where we left off as far as having sessions together. We surfed some really fun, rippable, high-performance Maui surf, which is my favorite type of surf. I think Clay would say the same.

"I couldn't be more proud of my little brother. Look what he's accomplished, and how much of an impact he's made on all these surfers around the world."

16
Why Contests Stopped Being Fun

Contests are the hardest and most uncomfortable part of surfing for me. I don't like the games people play with each other in the water. It confuses me. It's not like when I was a kid, when Kai, Granger, Wesley, Dusty, and I always surfed the same contests and hung out and beat each other and then went home and went surfing. I loved contests then. Now no one really hangs out with each other. You fly to an airport, surf in the contest, then go to the airport and fly again. Why can't we just catch our waves, ride them as good as we can, and whoever surfs the best wins? Then go hang out?

My dad thinks that Mom and I used the Asperger's diagnosis to pull away more from contests, but even when he talks about it, you can tell that he kind of gets it. I started getting more into free surfing a long time ago. For me, competition surfing is black-and-white, and free surfing is color. I can surf all day in front of a camera, and try to get my best ride ever on every wave so that the camera guy gets it and I make the kids watching at home really stoked. But I'm over the whole thing about wearing a contest jersey.

Following the release of *Just Add Water* and the resulting hoopla, Clay rode atop the surfing world. One magazine after another heralded him not only for being the next great superstar but also for pursuing a bullet of a career despite the Asperger's diagnosis. Now when he went to contests or showed up for video shoots, people didn't give him as many fixed, quizzical stares. Their bemusement over his idiosyncrasies and antisocial tendencies were replaced by admiration for not only his ability but his courage. Surfing is a very image-conscious, social sport. What you say and do goes a long way toward defining your legacy — especially when you're a competitor closely followed by kids and teens around the globe.

Beneath all of this, however, loomed a growing problem, the shadow in the room that threatened to swallow everything whole: Clay's deepening discomfort and growing withdrawal from social situations, and his continued difficulty — sometimes bordering on inability — to take care of even the most routine tasks or responsibilities that are second nature to young adults whose brains are conventionally wired. His greatest challenge, living daily life away from the water, was about to manifest for the world to see.

Surfer and shadow collided in the 2010 World Junior Championships in what had all the glitter and gold of a crowning moment. Not only had Clay traveled to Australia for the tournament during a performance peak, but his head seemed completely in the game. He fought off his demons, his fear about surfing against hungry, opportunistic opponents. He wanted to win. He wanted to become officially recognized as the hottest "Under 21" surfer in the world, even though photographers, surfers, and fans worldwide already considered him exactly that.

The World Junior Championships has been the largest tournament in the world for young upstart pros since the mid-1970s, when it began in Sydney as the Pro Juniors. Not only did a victory bolster a surfer's reputation, but it also served as a springboard to competing for the ASP World Championship Tour crown. "If you win, you get seeded into every single World Qualifying Series event the following year," Mitch Varnes says. "It really gives you a jump-start. If you just make it through a couple of heats in some of those big, six-star events, you could be on the World Championship Tour."

If Clay won the World Juniors, his competitive career would rocket into the stratosphere from its already elevated place. "Once I made it there, maybe I had a chance to win the world title," he says. "I wanted to win that event for everyone who cared about me."

Clay surfed like a man possessed. He reached the semifinals without losing a heat, battering his opponents with his jaw-dropping maneuvers and ability to stay on his feet, no matter the degree of difficulty. He stalked waves like a cheetah and finished them off with hoots and hollers, his body supercharged with adrenaline and excitement. How much more fun could any athlete have? It was a showcase performance with all the dynamics that surf fans had come to expect from all the video releases and magazine photos. "It was awesome. I pulled off every sick maneuver I tried," Clay says.

So electrifying was Clay's early-round performance that his Maui friend Kai Barger, the 2009 World Junior champ, would declare, "He's the best surfer in the world in our age group right now. Hands down."

Victory seemed inevitable. Clay needed to show up for the semifinal heat, come in first or second, and move into the finals. No one wanted to face him, which created an immediate psychological advantage. Head games? Clay's opponents were playing them on themselves. Once in the finals, Clay felt supremely confident he would take it all. He had the perfect arsenal for championship round surfing, no matter the contest, and he relished the chance to show it off. "Clay was on a roll," Varnes says. "He was on fire. He should've been World Junior Champion."

There was only one problem: Clay never reached the finals. Or the semis. In fact, he never even paddled out.

He showed up at the beach twenty minutes after the semifinals started. Shea Perkins, who coordinated Clay's Australian schedule and shepherded him through the World Juniors and assorted promotions, apparently forgot to wake up Clay, a notoriously late sleeper. "Shea's main function was to fly with Clay from Hawaii to Australia, drive him to a good place to stay, and drive him to the contest," says Varnes, who is frustrated to this day. "That's it. And Clay misses his heat. It was because Shea let him sleep.

"Clay should've gotten himself up, but remember: this is Clay, we all knew what the Asperger's diagnosis meant, and part of it is, he has little sense of time or urgency. And he likes to sleep. I mean, Shea Perkins . . . the guy's getting paid to fly to Australia and hand-hold this guy, and can't get him to his heat on time?"

The significance of the gaffe was huge. Varnes, Wasilewski, and Clay's parents would find it more difficult to motivate him for competition, for slugging it out on the World Tour grind — which, given Clay's challenges, felt many times more cumbersome to him than it did to other competitors. What would it take to win? Why was it so hard to dominate like he used to? *Why do I care anymore?* "I didn't really like contests, but if I won or did really well, and I could get on the World Tour and give that a try, then yeah! But after the [World] Juniors, I didn't really care anymore. I was over contests."

Normally, when you're twenty and a star, you let the attitude pass and refocus on the larger goal. Instead, Clay *relaxed,* thanks to a recently negotiated four-year deal with Quiksilver that paid him six figures per year. He decided to settle for the letter of the contract — free surfing wherever he wanted and taking photographers and videographers along to shoot for magazines and surf films.

Clay had experienced an "I'm over it" moment. "Clay's right. That's another defining moment in his career," Varnes notes. "He was surfing better than anyone else down there. A lot better. And from there, it may have given him another taste of winning, like the NSSA Nationals. I think it may have launched him towards the ASP world title. Now we'll never know."

The writing had been on the wall for more than a year. When Varnes, Gino, and Clay negotiated his four-year contract with Quiksilver in 2008, shortly after the Asperger's diagnosis, Clay told Varnes, "That's what I want to be — a free surfer. Can you get me on boat trips and media trips?"

"There were still a lot of guys being paid enormous amounts of money, $300,000 to $400,000 per year, to be free surfers," Varnes says. "They just traveled around the world to surf. That was it. They didn't have to surf contests. The reason was that a lot of real surfing purists, guys who grew up during the height of soul surfing in the 1960s and 1970s, now ran the companies. In 2008 some of the companies were being publicly traded, so they had to answer to boards and shareholders. I think they looked at free surfing as their last bastion of freedom, rather than just selling out to everything. You had guys like Ry Craike, Dane Reynolds, Bruce Irons, and Clay Marzo who justified what they earned. Every company had one or two free surfers under contract."

Varnes preferred sticking to his master competition plan, according to which Clay would soon find himself in world championship contention — if he followed it. However, he went along with what Quiksilver proposed. "His job description and duties said, 'Athlete will travel the world and surf,'" Varnes says. "There were no other obligations. He didn't have to do contests; he didn't have to do PR. It was just, 'Athlete will travel the world and surf.' Can you imagine having a job description like that? I think everybody in the world would like that one! They're paying him well into six figures to do this. I couldn't argue with it.

"That eventually became our plan, along with a handful of contests every year. I was disappointed, because in sports, and sports sponsorship, everything comes down to competition. You're the best, that's how you earn your keep, and that's how you create value for yourself. I was disappointed, but I couldn't disagree, because that's where he wanted to go. He was making a lot of money and getting a lot of attention for it."

Meanwhile, Gino traced the roots of Clay's growing aversion to competition further back, to a pair of events that happened within weeks of each other in 2006. Clay returned to defend his NSSA National Championships title, knowing it would be his seventh and final Nationals, the grand finale of his scholastic career. He initially fought the idea, but when Gino, Quiksilver, and others pointed out that no one had ever successfully defended an Open Men's title, Clay seized the challenge.

However, an entirely different experience transpired at the once-magical Lower Trestles, which had provided the milieu of his ascent to competitive greatness. "When we got to the little house [in San Clemente, the beach town nearest Trestles] people were telling me, 'You don't even need to do it again. You already won. Why would it matter if you won it again?' I listened to them, and said a couple of things, which upset my dad a bit," Clay remembers.

"I thought he was crazy," Gino recalls. "I asked him, 'What do you mean, you don't need to win it again? You could win this thing for four years in a row if you want to. Nobody's ever done it.'"

Gino had a strong point. Clay was finally as old as his chief competition, plus taller and blessed with those "Michael Phelps lats for superior paddling," as Adam Klevin famously put it. He thrived on joining his friends for what, in his mind, was an expression session: everyone fires off his best and most radical moves, high-fives or flashes shaka-brah hand gestures, and may the best man win. With Casey Brown, Kekoa Cazimero, Dusty Payne, Granger Larsen, and Tanner Gudauskas in the water, could it be any better? All but Gudauskas were Hawaiians, Larsen and Payne were his age-old friends, and Brown was fast becoming one. (They still surf together occasionally.) While they drove down the slithery dirt road along the sandstone bluff overlooking Trestles, Clay turned to Gino and said, "This is gonna be so much fun! I get to go out there and surf for half an hour with my friends."

"I knew for sure he was going to repeat," Gino says. "He was pumped, he was focused, and he had friends in the water. He was a lot better than all of them."

It didn't work out that way. Rather than trade waves and match skills, the others resorted to hard-core tactics and conspired to deprive Clay of waves. Clay was stunned by their mean-spiritedness. "My friends ganged up on me and hassled me. They didn't let me catch anything."

Gino believes the plan was hatched before the heat. He saw the others huddled on the beach and took a guess as to what they were discussing. "They must have said to each other, 'Don't you let Clay get a left out here, a four-foot left, he's gonna throw a [perfect ten-point ride], and we're all gonna lose. We can't do what he does on those lefts.' That's because Clay raised the bar with his throw-tail moves."

The resulting heat moved Gino to the point of disgust. "They didn't even care about surfing or how long they've been friends. They cared about stuffing Clay," he says. "The Cazimero kid caught a couple insiders and won the Nationals. Dusty, Casey, Gudauskas, and Granger just clamped Clay's butt. Two on one side, two on the other. The set would come, and they'd bury him. And to think these guys used to stay at our house for sleepovers!"

Two months later, they returned to Lower Trestles for the 2006 Boost Mobile Pro (now the Hurley Pro), a World Championship Tour event. Clay drew a wild-card entry by virtue of his 2005 NSSA Open Men's title and his soaring popularity. His initial excitement at competing in a World Championship Series event vanished when he and Gino arrived. It was flat as a lake, always a risk during the summer in Southern California. The area relies heavily on hurricanes off Mexico, as well as the Southern Hemisphere storms that send swells thousands of miles over open ocean. When the storm window opens, Trestles lights up like the Golden Palace at sunrise. When it slams shut, the waves diminish to three feet or less. Which was what Clay saw.

A few days later, the competition began. After sitting on the beach and waiting for the official signal that it was game-on, Gino drove back to their rental and rushed through the door. "Clay, let's go, the comp's on."

"Is it any good?" Clay asked.

"No, it's flat."

"Awww."

They drove to Trestles and left their car in the parking area, then walked past the bamboo stands on the long dirt path. The twin reactors of the San Onofre nuclear power plant peeked over their shoulders. Clay turned to Gino, his mind spinning from the fuel of frustration and trashed expectations, never a good mix. "This is flat this is flat I can't surf this it's too flat . . ."

He paddled out for his heat against a couple of unheralded rookies, neither at his performance level. One caught a tiny wave and rode it until it fizzled out, then another opponent did the same thing. Clay sat and watched, feeling cheated that the waves were less than thigh-high, his desire to even stand up waning by the moment. "Ah, Clay, catch one, you just gotta catch one. That's all you gotta do!" Gino yelled from the beach.

Clay sat on his board, nonplussed. Why bother if he couldn't unleash his moves? Why not just go home and catch a summer swell on Maui, or the Big Island? "What was there to catch? Nothing. I sat outside waiting for a good wave. I waited for the whole heat. I hated it because it was flat," he said later.

On the beach, Gino's impatience grew. "Clay, you gotta go, you gotta catch one."

He caught one wave. It took a minimum of two to win.

After the heat, Gino met Clay after he'd floated over the rock reef to shore. "Did you see yellow catchin' one? And white? Didn't you look in and see them going?"

"Yeah, Dad, but they didn't do any turns. They didn't do anything."

"But you know what? They beat your ass."

They gathered Clay's boards from the competitor racks, and then talked with several Hawaiians who were in other trial heats. Gino stood by, dejected, because their expensive getaway from Hawaii ended after Clay caught one wave in a twenty-minute heat.

"Okay, let's get on the plane. This just cost us how much, and we didn't do anything. This is lame, we've been here for four days . . . let's go home," Gino said.

Go home? Clay perked up.

As they left, one of Clay's friends noticed Gino's frustration. He turned to Clay and said, "You have to wanna grovel a little harder than the next guy."

Clay's opposition to contest surfing reached an alarming stage in 2010. Already smarting from the World Juniors, and the NSSA Nationals and Boost Mobile Pro before that, he suffered through one more ignominious contest experience at the Billabong Pro Tahiti trials in Teahupo'o. Once again, a contest turned on head games — the bane of any person who is unfiltered, openly trusting, and slow to respond.

"I was surfing well enough to win the trials and get into the main event," he recalls. "If I beat my next opponent, Reef McIntosh, I would advance — but the guy waiting for me was some dude from Spain [Aritz Aranburu] that people were rooting for. He surfed Teahupo'o all the time. He knew everything about it."

Klevin accompanied Clay on the trip. "I saw [Aranburu] sitting out there, splashing water, feeling it," he says. "Clay would have to surf his absolute best to beat the dude."

Clay noticed as well. Plus, he was homesick. He looked over at Aranburu and said to Klevin, "I go home tomorrow. I'm gonna ride it off."

"What?" Darkness settled in Klevin's eyes. "Get your ass out there and win the fucking heat!"

Promptly fired up, Clay caught a high-scoring wave to take the lead on McIntosh, a lesser competitor. He was well on his way to "doubling up" McIntosh — that is, posting a two-wave score that would require McIntosh to score higher than a mathematically impossibly perfect 10 to win.

However, McIntosh knew about the 2006 NSSA Nationals, and how vulnerable Clay had been in that contest to hassling and head games. Clay might be the best pure surfer in the world not named Kelly Slater, but he was one of the easiest surfers to beat through psychological warfare. He simply couldn't fight fire with fire. McIntosh had also heard about Clay's conversation with Klevin. He paddled next to Clay and taunted him about the great surf awaiting him back home in Maui. "Maui . . . Maui . . . Maui. He only talked about Maui. Now I *really* wanted to go home," Clay recalls.

After his monologue, McIntosh caught a small wave, not nearly enough to win the heat under normal circumstances. Clay didn't take off again, however, "because I didn't feel like catching three-footers at Teahupo'o to win heats and all I could think about was going home and catching Windmills when it was firing."

McIntosh's ploy worked. He won the heat, only to lose in the next round to Aranburu, who went on to finish third in the event, which was won by another of Clay's Hawaiian friends and contemporaries, Bobby Martinez.

The incident at Teahupo'o underscored the concern felt by new Quiksilver team manager Chad Wells, Strider Wasilewski, and Varnes: Clay could handily win any heat when his mind was in the game, *but his mind was there less and less.* How many more shots to the psyche could he take? "Chad, Strider, and I used to sit down, many times, sit there with napkins, and Chad would lay it out: 'Clay, all you need are two five-point-fives, or two sixes, every heat,'" Varnes recalls. "He had done the math and calculated what Clay needed to do on a regular basis to get through. Like Cheyne said, Clay could go out there and throw down eights or nines, easily . . . but here's the Asperger's characteristic again. It's all-or-nothing with Clay, on every wave. He's either going to get an eight, nine, or perfect ten, or he's going to get a one. Nothing in between. We saw it over and over. In numerous heats, Clay's already got a six, he just needs a two or three to get through — that's one very average maneuver and nothing else — and he takes off, goes for this huge knockout move, doesn't make it, gets a one, and that's that."

Then came what may have been the knockout punch: major knee surgery to repair his medial collateral ligament, which he ripped while rearranging the face of a medium-sized wave. Plus, Gino had left the house because he and Jill had begun divorce proceedings to end their twenty-year marriage. Clay sat at home, mourning the loss of his nuclear family unit without any comprehension of the underlying reasons. Jill and Gino had been drifting apart for years, as they failed to see eye-to-eye on many issues.

As someone who lives constantly in the moment and can't process large series of contributing events — such as those that factor into a dissolving marriage — Clay never saw it coming. He had tuned in to only two sources of parental friction: the infighting over the best way to move forward with his Asperger's diagnosis, and Gino's deep dislike for his girlfriend Alicia. Clay watched Lakers games and surf videos and continued his ravenous eating habits without exercising. The result? He gained thirty pounds, more than enough to throw off the center of gravity for his one-man surfing gymnastics exhibitions.

For pro surfers, layoffs of any kind are risky. Career half-lives are short. Instant reflexes, fast-twitch muscles, and elasticity are integral components of successful surfing, and all start to head south after age twenty-five, unless the surfer buttresses his wave riding with yoga, core workouts, or other forms of intense stretching. Not Clay's style. Those who can stave off the physiological aging process until age thirty are considered anomalies, which is why the list of thirty-something surfing and tennis champions is short. When the mental edge and desire start to wane as well, professional careers falter quickly.

Clay slipped into that mind-set, which led to further tussles between him and Gino, him and Varnes, and Gino and Jill. "I got a lot of opposition on the whole contest thing," Gino says. "My ex-wife was just trying to protect Clay, like any mother would. But as recently as (the summer of 2013), Clay told me, 'Hey, Dad, I can do this, I know I can do this.' He watches the contests on TV and his arm cuts through the air, tracing the paths of the competitors' rides, and he tells me how he can beat these guys. He's talking and waving his arms, and the strategy he lays out is perfect. My kid scares the shit out of any of them when he's on. I *know* he can beat these guys! Almost everybody knows that about Clay. But to beat them, you have to actually show up at the contests and want to win."

Varnes closed ranks with Gino to try to persuade Clay to *increase* his competitive schedule, not decrease it. "Gino comes from a competitive background, played competitive sports, and he was with Clay throughout his junior career," Varnes says. "Gino and I were always on the same page. We saw competition as the path to achieving whatever you wanted to achieve.

"Jill, on the other hand, wanted Clay to be a free surfer, rather than continuing to compete. She felt the pressure Clay felt when he competed. She'd be biting her nails on the beach. When he was surfing away from home, we'd have plenty of phone calls while [she watched] his heats on the Internet, and she'd be upset.

"Then there's the Asperger's side, which we all realized when he was diagnosed. People with Asperger's are hypersensitive to everything about other people and their surroundings—especially when they don't know the people and the surroundings are unfamiliar. This makes a very big impact on your ability to travel and to be totally focused when you're in a contest environment—especially when everyone is shooting for you, which happened more than once with Clay."

During his first media blitz Clay told one interviewer, "If I had my way, I'd be a free surfer. I'd spend all my time chasing perfect waves. That's it. No people, just waves."

"I still feel that way," he says. "I will always feel that way. I don't like contests [anymore] because it can be all strategy and paddle battles and not much surfing if the waves aren't good. I probably should do more contests. I know it will help my career, but I've done so many, it's just hard to want to do any more."

Clay's older brother, an intense competitor, offered wholehearted agreement with Clay's viewpoint that surprised everyone. "The contest scene is a very difficult thing to be a part of, unless you dedicate your entire surfing energy and adjust your style to it, just because of the way the points system works, the trials, and building your seed," Cheyne explains. "It's like a four-year university. It's pretty rare today for a young guy to come onto the scene and make it in less than two years.

"Maybe Clay's attitude toward contests is partly my fault. I did the World Qualifying Series for two years, and I had a hard time coping. I'm kind of similar to Clay in that regard. I go out there, I surf differently than normal, and I get really frustrated when the judges try to keep me in their scoring boxes. I think maybe my frustration and distaste for today's contest scene rubbed off on him. I wish it hadn't, because right now he can go out there and not hold back—or even hold back a little—and pull off two eights (out of ten), no problem. When you score eights, you win contests. You become one of the top five or ten competitive surfers in the world. That's the level my brother is at. But I understand where he's coming from. We feel the same way."

If there were any lingering doubt, Clay's dislike for competition hit home at the 2010 Triple Crown of Surfing, the sport's most prestigious event. "I was so happy he was on the North Shore, because you do need to be in contests there," Jill recalls. "That's where the photographers are in the winter, the whole exposure thing, part of being a pro surfer."

However, Clay never wanted to leave Maui, where the same winter swell was beginning to show. Within hours of arriving on the North Shore, he called Jill. "It sucks!"

Normally supportive of his free-surfing proclivities, Jill grew angry. If you were a pro surfer with any standing, you surfed the North Shore. It was more than an exposure meter. It was a long-standing ritual, especially for a Hawaiian. "What do you mean, it sucks?" she responded. "It's really big and really good. I just checked. It's *really good,* Clay! Just go out there and catch your waves. All you gotta do is go out and surf."

"I'm going to go out and I'm going to lose," he said. "I want to come home. I know it's going off at [Windmills]."

"Go out and surf," Jill reiterated. "Go catch your waves!"

Clay surfed—and lost. Immediately after hearing the results, he grabbed his boards and gear, drove to Honolulu International Airport, and caught the island express twin-engine back to Maui. He sped from Kahului to his house, dropped off his clothes, and drove twenty minutes to Windmills with a photographer. While Jill, Wasilewski, Varnes, and media people along the North Shore shook their collective heads, Clay surfed pristine, uncrowded eight-foot waves. A single tube ride on a single wave became the cover shot for six different magazines worldwide.

A few months later, after the covers hit mailboxes and newsstands, yet another exposure boom, Jill said to Clay, "You don't have to do the contests if you don't want to. Just surf."

When pressed, Clay says that he remains open to competing in the right tournaments and right environments. After surfing in just one contest in 2013 and 2014 combined—the 2014 O'Neill Coldwater Classic Invitational, for the top sixteen unsponsored surfers in the world—that's debatable.

"I know what they're saying, and everyone wants me in contests, but that's not how I surf," he says. "Maybe I'll die tomorrow and not get another wave. I want every wave out there. It doesn't matter if I eat shit or not. That's why I love surfing by myself or with a friend so much. That's why it's really hard for me to think about scoring points and building a plan and catching certain waves in contests."

Building a plan . . . in the surf, Clay is a maestro. Out of it, he was finding out just how tough life could be as he struggled to connect socially and deal with adult living at the same time. In fact, the greatest struggle of his life would play out in the apprehensive silence of his inner world—far away from the competitive arena and the pages of magazines.

17

Why Is Living the Dream So Uncomfortable?

A lot of people tell me I'm living the dream. I am living the dream: I make money as a surfer, and I travel to a lot of great spots. I can get up, eat, sleep, and surf whenever I want. I have been doing it since I was fifteen. Kids try to surf like I do. I want them to surf like I do and be better than me someday, and live their dream. That really makes me happy. When you live your dream, you get to be happy.

The hardest part of staying out there is that it's a lot more uncomfortable than just being alone. A lot of guys really like the exposure—and I like photos and videos. But I'm talking about how and why people come up to me. I'm not that way. Being famous isn't my thing. Sometimes, though, that's what gets you the big money—being famous and surfing well enough to get there.

Do I want to keep living the dream? For sure. I'll do anything to keep living it for as long as I can. But it gets harder every year. I just hope I can keep living it.

Late in 2012, while already struggling to appease sponsors who wanted him to get off Maui more, to cope with life situations that baffled him completely, and to make money decisions he was incapable of making, Clay's life took yet another sharp turn into the uncertain . . . which is every Aspie's enduring nightmare. Mitch Varnes, Jill, and Clay learned that Quiksilver would not renew his endorsement contract.

Whaaaaat? He had been a member of the Quiksilver family for more than a decade, as a professional and an amateur. Quiksilver officials had intentionally used the term "family" with Clay, understanding his deep need for and psychological *reliance* on roots, an anchor, and a presence beyond a business relationship. They had also stated that he would be treated as such, beginning with their decision to

produce *Just Add Water* in 2008. As Jill requested after their marketing and promotions team announced his diagnosis to the world, they
had assured him that they would always consider his best interests.
To wake up every day to the same sponsor, week after week, year after year, was first and foremost. Nothing makes an Aspie more comfortable than predictability and repetition.

Clay and Jill asked the same question: Why would the company release him after eleven years of working together? Jill sought answers
in a letter she wrote to Bob McKnight:

> *From the age of 12, this young man has done everything your
> company has ever asked of him and more. Not only did you expose
> Clay's personal life and PROVE to others that they can overcome
> obstacles and differences; but also that others will believe in them
> and could even make a living at it.*
>
> *Clay has been taken care of by Quicksilver since the get-go, and
> has always done right by your company. He has gotten other offers
> but has stayed loyal and never strayed. He has been true, simple,
> and amazing. He has inspired children all over the world with dis-
> abilities, why you did not take more advantage of that marketing? I
> will never know. But to just drop him . . .*
>
> *I was told by everyone that Clay would be with Quik till the end,
> I trusted you, was I wrong? The worst part is that Clay was told
> that he would be a lifer. If you know Clay and his disability, he is
> a literal thinker; he believes everything to be true. He trusts. Now
> when I sat Clay down today, he looked at me in the eyes, "Mom, I
> surf good" . . . he said confused, "I am a family with them. They said
> that!"*
>
> *This is what is needed today, for one to make a difference to an-
> other person and for that person to make a difference to the world,
> someone to acknowledge their abilities and to not focus on their
> limitations. Because of your sponsorship of Clay, he was able to
> compete and to have press that showcased both his talent and his
> diagnosis of Asperger's Syndrome. Watching his skill and artistry,
> people can see that just because someone has a hurdle others do not*

*have does not mean that they are not capable of performing feats
that are impossible for other people. Clay has taken his opportunity
of fame for his accomplishments to inspire children.*

True to form, McKnight responded quickly, promising Jill and
Clay he would set up an in-house meeting to discuss the decision
with his staff. In the meeting, sports team managers and the executive team reaffirmed their decision. Jill wrote again, but it didn't matter. Quiksilver did not renew his deal when it expired in the spring of
2013. "We had counted on the Quiksilver sponsorship for a few more
years, to spend the next three to five years budgeting him for a simple
life," Jill said. "That didn't happen."

Clay took the nonrenewal personally. He fell into a depression
that abated only during a five-month trip to the Western Australia
home of his new girlfriend, Jade Barton. "I surfed good, I took trips,
I competed in their contests, and we got my Asperger's diagnosis as
part of what Quiksilver wanted," he says. "I was in all of their other
movies. They came out with a Clay Marzo line of board shorts too.
Then they cut me. They just let me go."

Tough as it was for Clay to stomach, and as much as he and Jill
struggled to believe it, Quiksilver's decision was purely business and
nothing personal. Like many other companies in the surf industry,
Quiksilver struggled mightily during and after the Great Recession
of 2008–2009, cutting most of their endorsed athlete payroll. As Peter
Townend, the 1976 world surfing champion and owner of Active Em-
pire, a surf industry consulting firm, put it, "In the surfing industry, it
wasn't a Great Recession. It's been a bloody depression."

"There was a bubble of kids that were really, really lucky with the
contracts, the hot newcomers on the scene from 2004 to, say, 2008,"
Jill says. "Clay was one of them. They all came up in the money time
for surfing. There was a group before them, my son Cheyne among
them, but they were getting a couple hundred thousand dollars a year
below Clay's group."

Clay's fall was particularly tough. Overnight he went from a six-
figure annual salary to nothing from his chief sponsor. "A lot of us got

let go. It was never anything personal," Jamie Tierney says. "That's the hardest thing for Clay to understand, because he was family. He did surf well. The movie was made around him. Quik was family to him. But the truth is, Quiksilver dropped nearly all of their sports team, and management as well, including Strider and me. The recession almost sank them."

Tierney felt that in letting Clay go, Quiksilver relinquished one of the most distinctive personalities in surfing, a throwback to another era. "People are interested in Clay and what he's doing," he says. "He's got a mystique and an aura. Seems to me those are the kind of guys you want to help your company, the guys that stand out. You don't want fifty guys who are interchangeable. And then you hear from companies, 'I want someone who's gonna do interviews well, and I can take to trade shows, and who can do autograph signings . . .' Right, but don't you want some guy out there that kids point to and go, 'That's my favorite surfer?'"

Then Tierney turned the tables. As Clay's professional career progressed and the Asperger's diagnosis became common knowledge, many in the industry accepted it and felt that the diagnosis answered some long-pressing questions. However, Varnes and Tierney believe that others used the diagnosis as an excuse to part ways with Clay, often citing one of his behavioral characteristics — such as his awkwardness in business settings — as a strike against him rather than looking at the bigger picture. Such tactics would embitter anyone, let alone a young man somewhat dependent on and fully trusting of the adults around him.

"I feel that with Clay, people who make decisions have gotten thrown off," Tierney continues. "They're like, 'I can't even talk to this kid. I don't know if I want him on a trip, because I've heard these stories . . .' It bums me out. I've gone on a bunch of trips with him, and I've always been happy with the results. Every time he travels, it ends up on a cover or in a spread or a movie. And it's been happening for ten years. What other surfer can say that besides Slater? He always gets the job done."

Varnes's feelings are mixed. On the one hand, he now understands the need for Clay to operate in a tight, secure environment he can control. On the other, appearances are part and parcel of being a professional athlete. When Varnes described one missed photo shoot, he touched upon Clay's sensitivity to off-the-cuff, flippant remarks — another Asperger's characteristic. Clay takes in all remarks literally, while being left to wonder what any accompanying facial expressions and body language mean. Most times, he can't make any further connections.

"Right after the [2011] Japanese earthquake and tsunami that wiped out the [Fukushima] nuclear power plant, we had Clay going on a trip to Indonesia," Varnes recalls. "It was a magazine boat trip, all lined up, and he was the marquee surfer. We commanded a lot of money, $10,000 or so, for Clay to be there. It was for both magazine media and a movie.

"People started telling Clay the water in Indo was radioactive. When you tell him something, he not only assumes it's true, but it's gospel to him. That's how he's wired."

"I *knew* it was radioactive. If it's radioactive, I'm not paddling out. I called Mitch [two days] before the trip and said I wasn't going," Clay remembers.

"Of course, it wasn't radioactive," Varnes says. "Clay is very influenced by what people tell him, and it really affects him."

Clay sought refuge in the two places he calls home: Jade's house along the desolate Western Australia coast, and Maui, where he parked his car and boards until he began to extend his promotional reach again through Surfers Healing, Autism Speaks, and Little Tikes in the winter of 2013–2014. As Clay grew into adulthood, autism and Asperger's groups began reaching out to him to become involved with their groups as a spokesperson or to make appearances; Clay was slowly warming to the idea.

"The hardest part of staying out there is that it's a lot more uncomfortable than just being alone," he says. "A lot of guys really like the exposure — and I like photos and videos. But I'm talking about how and why people come up to me, just ask for my autograph or take a picture with me. I'm not that way. Being famous isn't my thing. Sometimes, though, that's what gets you the big money—being famous and surfing well enough to get there."

His comments remind Klevin of a situation in California. "One day, out of the blue, he turned to me and said, 'I'm famous,'" Klevin recalls.

"'Yeah, you are. No doubt. You're famous.'

"Clay just shook his head, like it was the most unbelievable thing in the world. 'Famous . . . huh.'

"I don't think Clay ever wanted to be recognized," Klevin continues. "We'd go to California, and he wouldn't surf any of the places where people were. I'd have to talk to him for thirty minutes just to get him to walk across the beach with his board stickered up, because he didn't want people to look at him like they thought he was Kelly Slater or something. He didn't want that. He never wanted the fame and glory, any of that. That's not his thing."

In another instance, Klevin and Clay were shooting footage for *The World According to Clay,* a series of videos for Rockstar. While Clay was surfing, the Latin American sales representative for Quiksilver stopped by. "He knew who I was, and he saw the kids looking at me, but he didn't act like I was famous," Clay recalls. "We talked for a minute, and I told Adam, 'All right, cool. Right on.'"

"There's a scene where he surfed wide," Klevin says. "The kids in the water started showing up after school, he was surfing this break, and basically he goes wide, around everybody, behind everybody, all the way around the perimeter of this park. Then he gets to where the kids are. They stare at him, and he gestures back, like, 'I'm just another surfer out here,' but they knew who he was. So they kept staring."

Tierney sees Clay's situation as symptomatic of the industry's inability to adequately endorse the majority of pro surfers (whose popularity and media attention help to sell their products), let alone a surfer who needs to be handled differently. However, he also sounds a clarion call to Clay. "To be honest, I'm bummed out," he says. "I think that Clay has made quite a few mistakes in his career, but the industry has changed a lot. I'm not sure where Clay fits in with the industry today. It's gotten so much harder for surfers to make a living, especially if they're not competing. They've got to be so proactive at promoting themselves, and that's not Clay's strength.

"There's got to be a motivation that comes from him. He's got to learn to play the game a bit more. The surfing industry's not going to change for him. He's got to change for the surf industry if he still wants to do it. I certainly hope so. He's at the prime of his career. It doesn't make any sense to me that he shouldn't be supported in doing that. His surfing's not the problem."

18

Life

I like the simple things. My friend Johnny owns a place in the hills by
Honolua Bay and grows fruit trees. [Former surf star] Shane Dorian does the
same on the Big Island. He's the baddest big-wave guy, one of my
favorite surfers . . . he lives away from town, cuts his own wood, grows
his own food, comes down when there's surf. I'd like that life.

One of the big differences between now and when I was young is that I feel
like I think too much. My mind is always going; I wish it didn't do that. I'll sit at a
surf spot and watch and think, Should I go out or not? and then I won't paddle
out because it's not just right. When I was a kid, I always paddled out. Maybe it's
because I've surfed so many great waves around the world, I know these places
here, I know what I've done on these waves, and I'm just getting pickier. That's
when I know I need to slow it down and appreciate things more. Like surfing.

If the ocean is involved, Clay masters his environment. Throw in
such terrestrial tasks as balancing checkbooks, paying bills and mort-
gages, renewing driver's licenses and registrations, remembering to
put on shoes before flying overseas — and he struggles. Friends and
family keep him on task, but the fact remains that if he doesn't focus
on something, it doesn't happen. Or it turns into a moment of frustration.

Case in point: a morning run to McDonald's to fuel up for a daylong surf excursion to the weather-worn North Shore of Maui. As he
drove up in his NSSA Nationals swag, the Toyota Matrix, Clay rolled
down his window, deferred to the non-meat-eater in the car, and ad-
dressed the microphone. "Can I get two Egg McMuffins, no meat, no
Canadian bacon, just eggs and cheese?" he asked. "Two Egg McMuffins, no meat, no bacon."

A sweet, high-pitched voice replied, "What you say?"

"Two Egg McMuffins, no meat, yeah?"

"Two Egg McMuffins . . ."

"No meat — that means no Canadian bacon, just eggs and cheese. And hash browns and a Powerade . . . no meat on those Egg McMuffins . . ."

On it went, this comedic loop between a spaced-out McDonald's employee and an Aspie. *Would it ever end?*

"Okay, I have your order. Two Egg McMuffins, one meat, one no meat . . ."

"Two Egg McMuffins *no meat no Canadian bacon on them at all,* just forget you have meat in there at all, yeah?" Clay growled.

"Okay. Total $17.18."

Finally, we lurched forward to the cashier's window. Clay shook his head. "People around here are slow."

Welcome to adult life on the autistic spectrum, particularly the high end where Clay resides. It is a daily grind that is very difficult for the rest of society to comprehend. Those with Asperger's syndrome have world-class potential in the one or two areas in which their gifts lie. As for everything else life throws in? That's a supreme challenge that feels like swimming in quicksand with a mind encased in cement — and unable to decipher the simplest social cues.

This is the other side of Clay Marzo's world, one that had its run in the sun when the *Just Add Water* documentary and attendant media coverage came out, then again on a lesser scale in the winter of 2013– 2014 with the acclaimed five-episode Fuel TV miniseries *What Happened to Clay Marzo?* By and large, however, an Aspie's life plays out quietly, day by difficult day, with loneliness and confusion as regular companions, frustration riding shotgun, and limited prospects for a financially successful life outside the gift, the area of supremacy. For all the accolades he's gathered from surfing, just getting up in the morning and pressing forward might be Clay's greatest achievement, because it is never easy and quite often depressing. As for typical responsibilities like balancing checkbooks, paying rent or mortgage, servicing the car, or keeping appointments on a calendar? They don't compute. And those challenges only scratch the surface of an even larger challenge.

"He really doesn't think about or understand consequences," Jill explains. "There are some other things that have happened with Clay, things that we know not to do, or watch, but Clay doesn't really get that. In so many ways, he's an innocent, trying to make it through his days without the same discernment we have. I wake up in the middle of the night with cold sweats. I don't know how other mothers with kids wired differently cope with it when the kids are grown adults."

Jill cites a situation that happened after one of Clay's trips, when he was about to drive away to check the surf. She noticed something strange on his car. "Clay, why is the window broken on the side?" she asked. "What did you hit? Another car?"

"Yeah."

"When?"

He shrugged his shoulders. "Last week."

"Why didn't you tell me? What happened?"

"I went to take a Jacuzzi across the street . . . and I hit another car."

"Clay, that's called hit-and-run. You cannot do that."

"I didn't hurt their car."

"First of all, he didn't report the hit-and-run. He didn't really understand those consequences," Jill says. She smiles sadly, a bittersweet smile, and shakes her head. "And how many people *drive across the street?*"

After the divorce, Jill moved just north of Kaanapali, taking Clay and Gina with her. One of their new neighbors was Dusty Payne, Clay's childhood friend, fellow competitor, and now a World Tour competitor. Dusty and Clay had grown apart over the years, partially from Payne's hassling of Clay during the 2006 NSSA National Championships, and partially because they rarely saw each other, even when living a few doors apart.

While Clay was recovering from his knee surgery in 2010, Jill asked, "Why don't you go visit Dusty?"

"No, no."

A few minutes later, Clay stood up. Jill looked over. "What are you doing?"

"I'm going to Dusty's."

An hour later, Clay returned. "Where were you?" she asked.

"At Dusty's, like I told you."

"Cool, cool. I'm so glad."

A smile broke across Clay's face. "Yeah, his house is *sick*," he said. "He's got a super-sick refrigerator, and I opened it, and inside, there's a bunch of different food . . . and he eats all the healthy things. In his closet, he's got so much sponsor stuff."

Jill returned his smile. "That's neat, Clay . . . so how is he doing?"

His next comment stopped her cold. "He wasn't there."

"Clay, what do you mean? Was anybody there?"

"No."

She shook her head. "Well, you can't just go in."

"Well, you told me to go over and hang out."

"I did, but you can't just go over if he's not in the house."

Years later, as Jill recalls the story, the same sad smile stretches across her face. "Clay has trouble remembering the rules. He lives in the moment . . . a little too much for comfort."

On top of that, Clay is getting older. He has sustained remarkably few serious injuries considering the waves he rides and his relentless, go-for-broke approach, but he's starting to feel the impact. He endured the knee surgery that ended his 2009 season, along with a bruised femur, reef cuts, reef burns, and other assorted contusions. "A lot of things can hurt you when you ride waves: bouncing off reefs, hitting rocks, wiping out, getting tangled in your board leash, getting cut by the [surfboard] fins, and the board hitting you," he says. "I just don't want to get hurt anymore, because it's starting to take too long to heal, and I miss too many days in the water."

That last statement reveals an underlying reason why his inner circle works so hard to keep him sponsored: personal health and well-being, another of those confounding life issues. When he spends more than two consecutive days out of the water, his mood sours and U-turns toward a redlined darkness. "That time he couldn't go in the water after his knee surgery? Oh my God! You didn't want to be around him," Carolyn Jackson recalls. "The first time he got back out, it was on YouTube, and you could see him champing at the bit. He jumped in the water and they couldn't get him out.

"That was an interesting part of his life, when he was unable to do the very thing he has the most passion for. He substituted with food, and his emotionality was very sketchy—a lot of frustration and anger. Miserable. There were better times in his life."

The other concern is money. Just a few years ago, Clay was well on the way to self-sufficiency and financial independence. A notorious tightwad, he pocketed almost all of his salaries and incentives from his sponsors after he paid Varnes and Klevin. Jill found a two-bedroom condo in the luxurious Kapalua resort, a perfect place to invest during the real estate heyday. Unfortunately, that bubble burst in 2008, and they had to unload the property at a substantial loss. Today, what looked like a life set in financial stone has become far less certain, especially in light of the sponsorship losses. Those fears are magnified by something that's familiar to every successful professional athlete: unfamiliar faces who come out of the woodwork, claim they're a friend or long-lost relative, and ask for something as though entitled to receive it.

"Clay thinks some people mooch off him," Jill says. "He doesn't really know who to trust, and rightly so. There are a lot of people who come over and go, 'Hey, do you have a deck pad? Do you have this, do you have that? Do you have a board for me?' A board costs $600 or more! With the way he is, so giving of his things if not his money, it's really difficult. I would say to Carolyn, 'I can't handle the pressure of Clay's money. I'm afraid it's going to get messed up, and Clay and everyone else will blame me.'"

However, his generosity also manifests in smaller, more humorous ways. "Clay's really good at bringing back presents. When he goes on trips, he always brings back something for me and Gina," Jill points out. "One time Clay came back from a trip with two kitchen magnets. He puts them on my refrigerator, then turns around and walks away. Then he looked at me. 'These are cute. Where did you get these?' I asked him.

"'In Peru.'

"One said, 'John and Connie.' 'Who's John and Connie?'

"'Well, they didn't have our names.'"

She stared at the magnets, wondering what he meant. Then it dawned on her: the first initials were J and C. Jill and Clay. "He was looking at the right first letter, but he still bought the magnets even though they weren't the same name."

Emotional aging seems to accelerate in some Aspies and autistics. Their surface emotions might be frozen, or challenging to them in everyday situations, and their physical bodies and facial features remain normal for their calendar age. But at a deeper, almost imperceptible level, they develop characteristics normally associated with later stages in life, such as Clay's burning desire to live more simply. That desire is part of his contradiction: Worldly professional surfer or solitary freestylist? Live in Maui, within striking distance of the surf industry and media, or along the desolate Western Australian coast?

Carolyn Jackson feels that Clay's preferences reflect the craving that many Aspies develop to take control of their environment. "Keeping it simple works for Clay," she says. "Give him too much information, and it's not going to happen. Keep it simple. He is a very soulful guy, and he understands life in a much deeper way than most people will give him credit for. Only when you come to know him a little bit, and then he will ask you a question, and then you go, 'Wow, where did that come from, Clay?' He'll come up with a statement, a metaphor that shows how he connects things in the world. He comes up with a visual for himself — and then wants you to validate it. Then he can breathe."

As he worked with Clay on *What Happened to Clay Marzo?* Tierney realized something that he feels others should appreciate before throwing in their two cents regarding the best course for Clay to take. "First of all, none of them have to live with Asperger's syndrome," he says. "That's important to remember. This guy surfs like none of us could ever think about, but he has trouble remembering his wallet or his shoes to go into a restaurant. He gets uncomfortable if he's in a restaurant with people he doesn't know, because he *thinks* they're looking at him and imagines they can read his mind and intentions.

"The other thing is that the reality of life, the thing we're all trying to get, is to find our happiness within the thing or things we're born to do, and stick with it, without everything else getting in the way. Much as we all want to see more of Clay, that's the space he's in now. He's happy with where he is."

Much of the time he is, thanks in large part to a young Australian woman Jill Marzo calls "an angel that dropped into his life."

19

Jade

What was there to say? I just stared at her a lot. I know it's rude, but I couldn't stop. She was really hot, and I could tell she didn't mind me looking at her.

We got more and more into each other. I could tell she cared about me, because she kept trying to figure me out. I like that she's into some of the same things I am, like surfing and music. We like different kinds of music, so she listens to mine sometimes, and I try to listen to hers. But we both like music.

It's easy for her to talk to my family and friends. She loves to hang out with them. I think she loves to hang out with everybody. That makes it nice for me, because sometimes I don't know what to say. She puts smiles on people's faces, and she's cool with me surfing all the time . . . well, most of the time.

Two months after Clay and his longtime girlfriend Alicia Yamada broke up, he traveled through Australia for promotions and photo shoots. While in Western Australia, he stopped a few times at the Black Rock Café in the small coastal town of Kalbarri, 350 miles north of Perth. As always, Clay's growling stomach sought food.

Something else caught his attention: Jade Barton, a stunning blonde waitress. Her beauty and easygoing nature mesmerized him. Her sassy, brassy Australian manner of communicating was intoxicating.

Clay had no intention of moving forward. He had no idea how to make that happen, and he was woefully shy with girls. He was afraid he would say something stupid, or give the impression he was stupid because he didn't talk much. Furthermore, he'd just spent five years with Alicia, who had always taken the lead socially. He wanted to learn more about the waitress, but couldn't find the next step.

He didn't need to. The waitress was also intrigued, mesmerized by his looks and the way he stared at her, his emerald eyes drawing her in. "That's the first thing that drew me in," Jade says. "He seemed so mysterious, and all I wanted to know was what he was thinking. He wouldn't take his eyes off me. I was so intrigued by what was going on through his head that I didn't know what to think. It was an immediate attraction, and I had never felt anything like that for anyone before."

The next night Clay joined his fellow Quiksilver team rider and good friend Ry Craike at a fiftieth birthday party for a friend of Craike's family. When Craike knocked, Jade answered. As it turned out, the party was for her mother, Janet. "Ry walked straight up to me and said, 'Hey, Jade, Clay wants to talk to you,'" she recalls. "I think that was a bit of a setup, but it worked."

Jade wanted to hang out with Clay and get to know him a bit, but concern seized her: what would he think about everyone at the party being dressed up like denizens of the night? Never before had he seen a girl suited up like a pimp, right down to her black pencil mustache. "We Australians are always having a weird party with a weird theme," Jade says. "Mum decided to make her theme 'Pimps and Hoes Cross-Dress.' I definitely wasn't aiming to impress."

Clay didn't know what to say, so he remained silent. Jade shook off the awkward moment and kicked into her confident main gear, taking Clay by the arm to a place where they could sit alone and talk. Soon, she realized she was doing all of the talking. He said only a few words the entire evening before he and Craike left. She wrote it off as shyness. Or maybe he was so smitten by her that she left him speechless. So she hoped.

Both were true. "What was there to say? I just stared at her a lot," Clay recalls. "I thought about her the whole next day, but wouldn't call her. I don't call or text people unless I know them. I got a friend to tell Casey, the girl whose number he'd gotten, to call Jade. Casey called her and said I wanted to go to dinner."

At first, Jade didn't feel the same way, compliments of a hangover. "I said no and hung up," she recalls. "Once I told my sister, she wouldn't leave me alone about it. 'What's the worst that can happen? You get a free dinner out of it.'"

At dinner, Jade sat directly across from Clay, who continued to stare at her green eyes, long blonde hair, and willowy body while saying very little. "I know it's rude, but I couldn't stop. She was really hot, and I could tell she didn't mind me looking at her," he says.

Clay and Jade spent the night together, leaving her with the conflicting and sad feeling that it was beautiful, and sunrise arrived too early. Little did she know that he would try to make this gorgeous waitress *his* gorgeous waitress. "I think she thought she'd never see me again, since I lived in Maui," he says. "I had to leave to go on a Quiksilver trip with Ry and some other team riders. I wanted to see her again. Before she got up, I hugged her and said, 'Make sure you come back and see me.'"

The next week, the surfers returned to Kalbarri. Jade and Clay picked up where they left off and spent a week together, she watching him surf, he dropping by the Black Rock Café and accompanying her when she wasn't working. As the week ended and the time for Clay to leave approached, Jade took her shot: "Will you take me back to your house in Maui?" she asked.

"Okay," Clay replied without thought or delay.

"She told me later she thought I'd laugh, but I wanted her to come back to Maui," he says.

Kalbarri is a typical Western Australian town in many ways: situated with the Indian Ocean on one side and the desert outback on the other, it has a tight-knit population of 2,000, and the mouth of the Murchison River provides action for surfers, fishermen, and feeding sharks. The town consists of three grocery stores, three eateries, and the main thoroughfare, Highway 60. The surrounding beaches and coastline combine sandbars, reefs, and point breaks—a trifecta for surfers. "River mouths that flow into oceans always produce great waves," Clay explains, "because of all the sand and rocks moving around offshore. Some of the choice spots are five minutes from her house."

Furthermore, given its Southern Hemisphere location, the waves break best from April through September—precisely the period when Maui's waves typically hibernate.

Like most Kalbarri families, and much like Gino and Jill Marzo, John and Janet Barton raised their five children in an ocean lifestyle. They wasted no time indoctrinating their four daughters and one son into that lifestyle: Jade was a week old when she first entered the ocean. Four years younger than Clay, and the middle child in her family, Jade learned the art of getting along with others, stating her feelings assertively, and practicing diplomacy. "It's easy for her to talk to my family and friends," Clay says. "She loves to hang out with them. I think she loves to hang out with everybody. That makes it nice for me, because sometimes I don't know what to say. She puts smiles on people's faces, and she's cool with me surfing all the time ... well, most of the time."

John Barton is a commercial fisherman and longtime surfer; in fact, he's considered a local surfing legend. He participated in the great Australian modern freestyle surfing tradition, which traces back to a surfer he admired, Wayne Lynch, one of the most stylish and mysterious wave riders ever. Janet handled the household duties while also popping into the ocean for long swims, walks on the beach, and reading.

She also threw down the heavy hand in the family when necessary, as seventeen-year-old Jade was reminded when she stated her intention of traveling to Maui with Clay, who had already called Jill and asked her to book another ticket.

"I mentioned it to my dad, and he was all for it," Jade recalls. "He said I'd be mad not to go. He liked and respected Clay from the moment they met."

However, Janet was furious. "No way are you going to Hawaii with a boy you've only known for a week," she said.

"I'm not stupid," Jade replied. "If it didn't feel as right as it does, I wouldn't be going."

The next day Janet headed for Perth to visit her oldest daughter, but made sure to pack Jade's passport and cash she'd saved. Jade and Clay impatiently waited for her return, Clay rescheduling his trip home to do so.

When Janet returned to Kalbarri, her scowl had not left her face. However, she had realized that she considered Jade old enough to decide for herself, so she relented. "She angrily left my passport and some cash I'd been saving up on the kitchen bench, and before I knew it I was on a plane on my way to Hawaii with this boy I'd only known for two weeks," Jade says. "I knew I couldn't live my life thinking, *What if?* so I went for it. I don't regret one second of it because we have come so far since, and I love him to death."

During the fifteen-hour flight to Maui, Clay confided in Jade about his five years with Alicia and the months of tough times that had led to their breakup. He left nothing out—including his own mistakes. "She got all worried," he recalls, "but I was over Alicia, and we had been having trouble for a long time, and I wanted to be with Jade now."

"I didn't want to upset anyone or get in the way of anything, but he had me convinced he was over it and it had been falling apart for a long time," says Jade, who called upon an empathy and wisdom well beyond her years. "I didn't want to rush him into anything serious, so I kept it as fun and casual as I could."

When they landed in Honolulu, Clay started rubbing his hands together, his excitement about two things overloading him: the swell lines he saw from the air, and the dynamic blonde on his arm, whose personality was as stunning as her looks.

"I instantly fell in love," Jade says. "I loved that he was so different to any other boy I'd met, and he didn't seem one bit afraid to show it. What other surfer our age talks about their breakups so openly and honestly? Flying over the islands to Maui really opened him up. He told me all about the other islands we flew over to get there, Molokai and Lanai. It was like having my own personal tour guide."

Jade met Jill and Gina, both of whom almost instantly took her into their hearts and considered her part of the family. Gina was especially thrilled to have a girl she now calls "my big sister" around, someone closer to her age than Alicia (six years Jade's senior), as well as an ally to help her navigate a new relationship with her brother, who had become a virtual stranger to her. "Gina loves it when Jade's here, because she says I talk to her a lot more," Clay says. "I know she hangs out with Jade a lot. They're really good friends."

Soon, Clay gave Jade a grand tour of Maui in his special way, driving the tricky roads like a Formula One racer while pointing out surf spots and landmarks. She tried to keep up her perpetual good cheer while hanging on to her seat. Bearing in mind that Jade liked to watch surfing but surfed very little herself, and knowing that she loved hiking, Clay drove along the rugged North Shore and introduced her to trails, waterfalls, and tide pools.

"One time we went on a really gnarly drive of one-lane roads and sometimes no pavement," Clay remembers. "There's a place where I surf, where getting in and out is heavy, because there's big rocks. No sand beach. Just black rocks, like this whole place probably was a long time ago, way before the Polynesians came."

They inched down a steep clay road. Then it began to rain, a real problem for driving a car out. "We're in trouble, Clay!" Jade yelled.

"Nah, nah."

Clay floored the gas pedal and barely steered the fishtailing car out of danger. "Look what you almost did to us!" she yelled.

With that, Jade was introduced to the fearless, sometimes reckless side of Clay's world, the side that makes Jill break out in cold sweats. "It was funny," he says. "But that's part of what I really like about my girl: she's into the ocean and nature."

Soon, Jill introduced Jade to the gorilla in the room: Asperger's. When Jill mentioned restaurants, something clicked for Jade: his silence in the Black Rock Café in Kalbarri. More than anything, Jill wanted Jade to understand that life with Clay would not only be interesting and fun, but also challenging.

"She was so interested in it," Jill recalls. "She asked if I had books that she could read, because she wanted to learn more about it. Jade loves to read, and she really tries very hard to understand the way Clay is wired.

"It really comes out in his relationships. He can be really possessive, even jealous and controlling, and it's really hard for him to reciprocate emotionally. He prefers everyone to do it his way. For the rest of us, unless we're coldhearted, totally shut off, or so selfish we don't even consider the other person, reciprocation is a natural thing.

Clay's brain isn't wired for it, so Carolyn and I have had to work hard with him to form behaviors so Jade, and Alicia before her, can feel like he's reciprocating their affection and love. That's a hard one. It's a constant. Sometimes I feel sorry for Jade. Thank God she is a tough girl."

Jade spent much of her first visit observing Clay's mannerisms, ways of communicating, and actions closely. She then returned to Australia focused on a mission to make a life with Clay. While thinking of all that had transpired, she remembered a night after they first met. Clay showed her some of his DVDs, a mind-blowing surfing display. While she tried to absorb the greatest surfing she'd ever seen, he replayed them . . . over and over again. "I didn't know what that was about at first," she says.

She turned to a friend, an expert on Asperger's syndrome. He gave her a man's perspective on how Asperger's could affect their relationship — not only negatively, but also positively. The bright side, he told her, was that the person forms an undying loyalty to what matters most. She did the math. *Surfing. Food. Me.* That bolstered her hopes.

As her friend talked, one more memory struck her. "I had never even heard of Clay before meeting him," she says, "only to look later in the grade ten workbook I had. I did a project on *Young Guns 3,* the movie. Clay was the star of that."

As their relationship developed, Clay and Jade began to lead two lives: one in Kalbarri, and one in Maui. As his contest schedule dribbled to almost nothing, he began spending months at a time in Australia, where the Bartons integrated him into their family. Her sister Jemima started paddling out with Clay. "Clay likes to push her and make her go out in bigger waves, which I've noticed has really boosted Jemima's confidence in the water," Jade says.

Clay fell in love with his new home away from home. Who wouldn't? He felt secure and comfortable in the long-standing nuclear family with children who loved him. He paddled into some of the world's best waves, peered out at a landscape where one sees nothing but desert and ocean for hundreds of miles, and embraced a local surfing contingent that marveled at his prowess while ignoring his fame and treating him like just another bloke. He deeply appreciated that, along with something else. "No one makes him feel stupid in Australia. A lot of people do in other places, and that really upsets him," Jade says.

"My family loves Clay. My dad is absolutely gobsmacked by his surfing ability and the way he is just so different and honest and funny. My little sister, Jaali, who's thirteen, gets in his face, does weird things, makes him watch her movies and dancing, and never leaves him alone, which freaks him out a little, but I told him it's because she loves him. I'd like to think his rapport with Jaali has brought him closer to his own sister, which I see happening every time I'm in Maui."

Jade grew more accustomed to Clay's idiosyncrasies and mannerisms and learned to pause to consider the bigger picture before reacting and to connect with him on what they had in common. "Clay has done so many strange things since I met him," she says. "Like rubbing his hands. His mouth sometimes goes into this spasm where it looks like he wants to let out his excitement and emotions but doesn't know how, so he usually ends up kind of squealing or singing or slapping my arms. It's my favorite thing about him. It makes me so happy to see how happy he gets over the small things that mean so much to him. It's his own way of expressing his feelings. It has never weirded me out once.

"I can always see when he's thinking about something too, or when he's frustrated, because he'll sit twirling his hair into little knots and ripping them out. His funny side comes out when he's checking good waves, or driving and has one of his favorite rap songs on. He starts slapping the steering wheel with the backs of his hands and bounces in his seat, rapping along to the words. It amazes me how quickly he picks up on the music and the words and remembers them all. Even with my music. I'll play a song that he's never heard before, and I'll catch him in the room later that day singing my song. It's incredible! It's like it just sinks into his brain. He has a huge connection not only with the water but with his music too."

Not all is paradise. Far from it. The combination of Clay's occasionally short fuse and sudden temper and Jade's strong character and unwillingness to be pushed around or controlled can create sparks. When asked about it, Clay is open and unapologetic. "We have problems when I want to do something my way and she doesn't like it," he says. "I like listening to my kind of music, and eating where there aren't a lot of people in the restaurant. And when the surf is up, that's what we do. I go surfing, and she hangs out on the beach or bluffs."

"If you don't like his music, that's when a huge battle starts and he gets upset," Jade adds. "I also notice when we go and eat, he gets really excited and will tell me what to order, because he already knows what's good. If I enjoy the food and tell him, he will start the rubbing of the hands and sing little bits of songs or call me 'Jade-o Alfredo.' I love that. If I want something else, he'll sometimes start mumbling about how it's not very good, not the best item on the menu, on and on . . .

"Clay is a very honest person, which is good, and I respect that. He sometimes gets in a bad mood and will start saying things about Australia or my body that really upset me, and I have to kind of explain that you can't say those things to someone you love. Also speeding in his car. I have to call him out on that one a lot, how he needs to be aware of others around him and the other life he has in the car with him! When he is on the way to the surf or has something on his mind, it's almost like everything around him disappears. I could ask him a question two or three times and have him not even hear me. I've got to snap him out of it and kind of say 'Hello?'

"I'm pretty straightforward with Clay. If he's being mean, I'll tell him. I don't let him get away with much. There are ways to loosen Clay up. I just have to be careful on his moods because sometimes it can backfire."

Jill has witnessed many arguments and fights beneath her roof — and sometimes away from it. A disagreement between Jade and Clay at a Surfers Healing event in Waikiki nearly resulted in Jade buying a one-way ticket to Perth. "That was very difficult," Jill says. "Clay saw red, and when he sees red, all hell breaks loose when he can't go off by himself and chill. Well, he was on the beach with a bunch of autistic kids and their parents, he and Jade were arguing . . . it got out of hand.

"I think we are still learning how Clay will behave in a love relationship. Since empathy is not something that comes natural to him, Jade, Carolyn, and I are having to teach him the proper cues."

The other adjustment for any partner of an Aspie is focusing on the Aspie's world over his or her own. "Thank God Jade is into surfing, and Alicia before her," Jill says. "I don't think it would be possible for Clay to be in a relationship with a girl who didn't like surfing."

Partners of Aspergians also fare better if they aren't physically or emotionally needy, since their feelings are often unrecognized or misread. Jade is a consummate Aussie, chock-full of independence and self-sufficiency. Once Jackson met and talked with Jade, she wasted no time grabbing Clay by the proverbial scruff. "Clay, you're one of the lucky ones. She doesn't have a lot of needs. She's a very independent and confident girl," Jackson told him, more than once.

"Clay is warmest to me when we do things he enjoys, like cooking breakfast, watching basketball or surfing clips, or just hanging out down the beach," Jade notes. "He backs off a little when he knows I'm in a bad mood or when I start to raise my voice, or if something I'm teaching him on the computer becomes too frustrating for him. It all depends on what mood he's in, and his moods can be pretty unpredictable at times. I've learned to read him a bit more, though, and can tell as soon as he wakes up, just by if he stays in bed for a cuddle or he gets up right away and walks off."

Still, Jill wonders if the relationship will survive the long haul. That concern stems from her own inner dogfight between her desire to see him lead a life of his own and her protective desire to shield him from the world at large. "Clay doesn't see through to the consequences a lot of the time," Jill says. "A good part of that is the Asperger's. People with Asperger's have a hard time seeing how what they do affects others.

"He does not understand like most people about feelings and what it takes to care for a relationship. Jade sees this and accepts it, and they have been working on some issues as they are growing together.

It's not always good, but when something happens, they get around to working on it."

Jade concurs. "One thing I find hard with Clay is that he is a little bit less considerate of other people's feelings. He can often say mean things without thinking before he says them, and then not quite understanding why I am upset," she says. "If he is in a bad mood or the surf's no good, he usually takes his frustrations out on me. That's where I have had to consider there is a lot going through his head and to not take everything he says to heart, because later on, when we talk things through, he apologizes and tells me he didn't mean any of it. I sometimes have a short temper, and if I'm in a bad mood and he starts doing things like that, it's hard to contain myself and not go crazy at him."

Now several years into the relationship, Clay has mulled over his next step, one that combines Jade and his desire for a simpler lifestyle. "I'm thinking about moving to Western Australia," he says. "It's a perfect place — open space, great waves all the time, not a lot of people. I can see myself going out on the fishing boats with John. One time I went on a trip with John and a few other guys. We cruised out to a secret wave, but stopped on the way to catch some fish. I caught a fifteen-pound dhuie [or dhufish, a delicious Indian Ocean species], and everybody was happy with me. Then I caught another one the next morning. When we came back a few days later, I told Jade how much I loved fishing and finding secret waves in boats."

"I think West Oz (Western Australia) would be ideal for Clay because it's a lot less crowded, the food options are limited, and the waves are just how he likes them, with hardly anyone around," Jill says. "There is a good group of guys in town that love Clay and understand him. He gets along with most of them really well. I can see how much more relaxed Clay is when he is in West Oz."

20

Connecting with a Larger Community

I paddled him out, keeping him on the nose of the board. I started to talk to him about surfing, and then he gets into this whole thing about pirates. Pirates, pirates, pirates . . . he knew all kinds of things about pirates. Pirates of the Caribbean, treasure chests . . . that was his one thing. Pirates.

I sat behind him on the board. When a wave rose up to where you paddle for it, he didn't even try to stand up, or push up his arms. He didn't move. When the next wave came, I grabbed him by his shirt and jerked him to his feet, so he could feel what it was like to ride a wave. Then we fell off the board and the board hit me in the face.

We tried a couple more before paddling in. The kid was stoked. He was really happy when his parents came up. I was happy too.

The setup reminded Clay of a hundred contests he surfed as a kid. Tents, sponsor signs, and a small scaffold sat on Malibu Surfrider Beach, the epicenter of California's surfing culture in the 1950s and 1960s. The array looked like a hybrid of summer camp and a surf competition. The contest director, Israel Paskowitz, organized parents and volunteers while their kids scrambled in all directions.

The kids weren't at Malibu for a surfing competition, however. These were first-time surf sessions. They weren't routine paddle-outs either. The participants were autistic.

Clay showed up in Malibu at the invitation of Paskowitz and Surfers Healing, an organization formed in 1998 to provide the surfing experience to kids with autism and other social disorders and developmental disabilities. "Through the transformative experience of surfing, Surfers Healing attains greater mainstream acceptance for both the families of and the kids living with autism," the Surfers Healing website states. "People seem to have a lot of pre-conceived ideas about what kids with autism can or can't do. We're here to change those notions forever. Surfers Healing has spent the last fifteen years taking children with autism surfing. Our goal is to help foster the understanding and acceptance of autism."

The creator of Surfers Healing, Paskowitz is a member of California's "First Family of Surfing." Their story is one of the more eccentric in a culture filled with eccentricities. Paskowitz grew up on San Onofre State Beach, one of nine kids of Dorian and Juliette Paskowitz. Dorian, a physician, and Juliette chose to raise their family through surfing and the beach lifestyle, so they moved the entire clan into camper vans while Juliette home-schooled them. They crisscrossed the country in search of waves — the ultimate road trip for any school-age surfer. Clay found Paskowitz's past endearing and enviable. Furthermore, Paskowitz was one of three brothers who surfed longboards professionally for several seasons.

In 2008, while filming *Just Add Water*, Clay and Klevin headed to Malibu for the Surfers Healing camp. Hundreds of kids skittered about the beach, which immediately made Clay anxious. However, he'd promised Paskowitz he'd be there, and he wanted to see what it was like to assist children in far more challenging positions on the autism spectrum than himself.

"They figured that since I was a pro surfer, just diagnosed with Asperger's, I would be a good person to help," he says. "At first, I didn't want to do it. Me, helping little kids? No way. I didn't know how to show a kid who couldn't swim and had no coordination how to surf. One of the things that's really hard for me is to be patient with other people. I always try to get better at it, but it's hard. This was hard."

Soon enough, Clay received his assignment: a moderately autistic little boy. Given Clay's penchant for quietness and the boy's difficulty in speaking, the prospects were strong for a silent fifteen-minute session that would feel like an hour. Clay pulled his hair and fidgeted, unsure of how to proceed with the kid.

What happened next was magical and revealing for instructor and participant. "I paddled him out, keeping him on the nose of the board," Clay explains. "I started to talk to him about surfing, and then he gets into this whole thing about pirates. Pirates, pirates, pirates ... he knew all kinds of things about pirates. *Pirates of the Caribbean,* treasure chests ... that was his one thing. Pirates.

"I sat behind him on the board. When a wave rose up to where you paddle for it, he didn't even try to stand up, or push up his arms. He didn't move. When the next wave came, I grabbed him by his shirt and jerked him to his feet, so he could feel what it was like to ride a wave. Then we fell off the board and the board hit me in the face.

"We tried a couple more before paddling in. The kid was stoked. He was really happy when his parents came up. I was happy too."

After Clay talked to the parents, he wiggled out of his wetsuit, toweled off, changed into his board shorts, and grabbed his cell phone. The first person he called was Jill, who had prodded him into driving to Malibu after he conveyed his typical apprehensions about trying something new that involved people he didn't know.

"Mom, I did it! I surfed with the kid on my board!" he exclaimed. "The kid is cool. He's into pirates."

"I could feel his smile beaming over the phone," Jill later said. "He was really happy to help out that kid. I think it opened his eyes to how he could use his position in the surfing world, and his own experience with Asperger's, to connect with these kids."

"I don't see that happening so much with other Asperger's kids, to go someplace and not be there for themselves," Carolyn Jackson says. "Most of what these people do is for themselves. He has worked with kids and for kids, and he has not rejected that, even though his facial expressions might say, 'Whoa, I'm so un-gung-ho for this.' I saw some videos of him with the kid in Malibu, and he just picked up this kid by the shirt, and the kid is stunned, and then his arms are flailing. But instinctually, Clay knew this is what he had to do to get the kid up to ride a wave."

Clay never envisioned his surfing career taking a broad side turn into the world of charity events, promoting toys specifically designed for kids with special needs and being the spokesman for a cause, but all of that changed after the *Just Add Water* documentary broke worldwide. Suddenly, parents and educators throughout the world were sending letters to the Marzos and to Varnes about their kids, their neighbors' kids, or the siblings of their students who lived with Asperger's syndrome or full-blown autism. They thanked Clay for demonstrating that people on the spectrum could not only become good enough at something in life but also excel at it. While normally wired people make choices from many life, career, sports, or entertainment options, those on the spectrum rarely have an array of choices. Wrote one new fan:

> *My awesome loving son Brian Heins has Autism. He is age 11. Brian's birthday just passed last week. I wanted to do something very special for him for his birthday but unfortunately this great idea just popped into my head tonight. I want to create a wall in my home dedicated to Autism Awareness and on this wall I want to hang the pictures of the most powerful and influential people in our society today affiliated with Autism.*
>
> *I was hoping you could find a moment in your heart to send a picture of yourself with a special written note on that picture dedicated to my son Brian Heins. I wanted a note that was positive and inspirational. My goal is to fill an entire wall, the biggest wall in my home with pictures of influential and powerful people that are affiliated with Autism. I am going to put my son Brian's picture in the middle of the wall with your pictures surrounding his picture, the idea is to show support and love for Autism but specifically in this case for my special baby Brian Heins.*
>
> *I am thinking of naming the wall Brian's Heroes . . . When Brian looks at this wall, he will see the Moms and Dads that love and care for their children and were kind enough to care for him, just regular people just like Brian . . . the other view will be the most important, because it will be by my extended family and friends that truly don't understand Autism but see the faces of very popular people but when they read the personal notes. It will weigh heavy on their*

hearts, the special bond that Autism creates. Hopefully spreading awareness further and further and enlightening more and more people.

Respectfully Submitted,
Christopher and Michelle Heins
Manahawkin, NJ

Clay sent Brian a personal note and a handful of pictures. He later learned that the boy put them up on his wall and became an ardent follower on Clay's busy YouTube channel and website.

"We have had so many wonderful letters, from parents, brothers, and sisters, even different autism organizations," Jill says. "Every one of them starts with basically the same thing, something about their loved one and how Clay has inspired them with his surfing and his ability to get out there and show people you can be wired differently and still excel, still make a difference in the world.

"One of the surprising subjects in these letters is athletics. You never heard people say that sports was one of the focuses of autistic kids. Most are uncoordinated. But now with Clay ... he can skate, he shoots baskets well, and he's good at tennis. He used to be a good pitcher too. He's a natural athlete. You're starting to see it more as Asperger's kids come out of the woodwork. One's a good long-distance runner; another's obsessed with trail biking—he knows every trail, every bump on the trail. We get letters from parents, all these parents, who share these stories with us."

Dear Clay:

I just learned about you today, from a friend who lives in Maui and who is visiting New York. She knows about my Asperger Profile (object to use of term "Syndrome") and told me about yours.

You are fortunate to have found out about this at such a young age, and to have parents who are not afraid to seek out a "diagnosis," when they see unusual characteristics in a child.

I only found out a few years ago, and only on the suggestion of a friend of our family ... glad to know I was not alone and it was o.k.

to be "different." [I've made] two films, have you seen them? Adam and Temple. They "got it right" (in my opinion).

I am glad you found something to do that you love so much, like surfing, which helps you with this. I found "acting" (object to use of term "acting," as I have no concept of "pretending").

"Acting" is a therapeutic pathway that helps relieve the chronic stress, anxiety, depression and anger associated with Autism and Asperger's Profile. I use bodybuilding and gymnastics in the same way, to "get out of your head," as a friend at the DBSA meetings in White Plains, New York, which I started attending in November, 2008, told me.

I have often thought of learning to surf, but cannot overcome my fear of what I cannot see (sharks). I don't mind the sharks, as long as I can SEE them. (I have gone scuba diving, and hope to do so again, when I can afford it, and will be in a place where it is available, and have no fear of this at all. As long as I can SEE what is around me.)

Well, best wishes to both of you. Liked your comment "toys from God." Agree.

Lowell Joseph Gallin

The continuing stream of letters from admiring parents and others and Clay's expanding profile in the ever-growing autism community have opened new channels for him to reach others on the spectrum. Suddenly, the man who eschews social contact is finding a new sense of enjoyment from a very unlikely source—the personal appearances he grew to dislike at surf contests. He's been asked by a number of organizations to make appearances, among them the Scott Center for Autism Treatment, operated by the Florida Tech School of Psychology, and Autism Speaks, the world's leading autism science and advocacy organization. In 2014 the marketing company for Autism Speaks contacted Varnes about Clay's availability to sit on the "Not So Bored of Directors" of Little Tikes, an organization that builds a series of toys and playgrounds nationwide to accommodate the socially and developmentally disabled. "Specifically," the invitation stated, "we are interested in having people like you who can offer advice in the areas of cognitive developmental benefits, the current playground systems, as well as on the up and coming products. The ultimate intent is to use experts such as yourself in the development of Little Tikes products and we would proudly tout our partnership with you."

During their consideration process, Little Tikes officials sent Clay a questionnaire. They queried him about his life, passion for surfing, and how he could extend himself to children through a seat on the board. His answers cast a revealing light on the way he views himself as he moves forward.

"I think kids should get outside and find their own passion," he said. "'Cause inside the house . . . no good's gonna come out of that. I think a playground company is interested in me because I'm a creator and not a follower like most people. So they'd definitely be into what I think because it's totally different. I think outside the box. I don't think inside the box. I also think getting several different opinions is a good idea, because you get more options of what to think about and what's different out there. You get to choose what's different and what's cool, and not so generic."

The next question tripped up Clay: "Do you consider yourself a role model for kids?"

This is a slippery slope for any professional athlete who, whether he or she likes it or not, is perceived by children and teens as a role model. Some embrace the idea and relish the opportunity to have a positive influence on kids; others shy away from it, or simply ignore the notion. Clay started out as the latter, no doubt handcuffed by his social difficulties, but he is now slowly embracing a phase of life in which he continues to inspire by example.

"In surfing, I think I'm a role model for other kids. And yeah, also with what I do, I do my own thing and some kids might like that," he said. "I don't really do much; I just surf permanently all day, every day. I think kids definitely look up to me because they trip out on how much I surf and how good I am at it."

If that was the most satisfying answer to the Little Tikes team, one other comment was certainly the most curious. When Clay was asked, "Do you think playgrounds should be built for all types of kids to use?" he responded, "No, I don't think they should because there are too many different types of kids these days."

"Leave it to Clay to come up with that one," Varnes says with a hearty laugh.

When Clay started connecting with families and those on the spectrum, one person in Maui flashed a knowing smile. Thinking back on how Clay touched her teaching career, Mary Anna Waldrop Enriquez expresses no surprise whatsoever at this new life direction.

"The consciousness and awareness of autism and Asperger's has exploded in the last ten years," she says. "I've learned so much about autism. I saw who Clay was, and I remember him so well. I can pinpoint a lot of learning differences and challenges in kids like that, because I remember that look of Clay's, that long stare where it just isn't clicking. It's not a question of intelligence, because he's highly intelligent; it's a question of how he's wired, how he accesses and processes.

"Since him, we've had quite a few kids, which is to be expected. Recently, we had a parent thinking of moving here, was offered a good position, but his child has autism. His dad told us he's highly functioning. To take this job, he wanted to make sure we had a quality education for his son, from fourth grade through high school. One of the things I told my principal after we met with the mother, father, and boy, was, 'Susan, for Clay, we have to take this boy.'

"I had Clay for one year, and I only had him for forty minutes a day. Still, every single day I walk into the classroom I feel Clay is with me. I've got to do it right for every other student that comes. He's made a huge impact in my consciousness about children who learn differently."

Enriquez and Jackson agree that the dynamics have changed drastically, thanks to the exploding awareness of autism and Asperger's. The Clay Marzos of the world now have a platform and an opportunity to share their lives in a motivational, inspirational way. This awareness has been fueled by the work of people such as Dr. Tony Attwood and autistic scientist-author Temple Grandin, as well as by recent revelations that everyone from Albert Einstein to British singing phenom Susan Boyle to Apple creative firebrand Steve Jobs are probably Aspies.

In thinking about Clay's opportunity to take his message to the world, Jackson asks, "In the bigger picture, are we going to look at Clay as too far outside the loop? Or are we going to look at ourselves and say, are *we* too far outside the loop? When we're looking at a society where one out of eighty-eight kids is or will be diagnosed on the spectrum, that becomes a very good question."

Clay has certainly noticed the difference. "Not as many people look at me differently," he says. "Now it's just like, 'That's Clay, that's the way the dude rolls.' [Previously], everyone tried to tell me what was wrong with me or that I would never be anything except a stoned surfer. I'm just happy that more people see that I'm not a freak or this weird dude. I have a gift and I see things differently, and I like to surf and watch videos and hang out with my girl just like any other guy. It's also really cool that a lot of people say I have helped them with their lives in some way. I like that."

21

Reading the Ocean: A Gift of Asperger's

I check out the way the waves are breaking, how good their shape is, what kind
of shape — Barrels? Peeling into long rides? — and where I can paddle out
and catch waves no one else really sees. I check out the bottom at places
I haven't seen as much. Rock reef? Coral reef? River mouth? Sand bottom?
Shallow? Deep? A point break? Every type of bottom produces a different
wave. I look at how the wind is moving the water around, what the currents are
like, if there are rocks sticking up [out of the water], and how the waves are
going to hold up once I take off. I don't really think about what I'm going to do
until I take off, but I have an idea when I'm studying the surf. Sometimes you just
have to get out there and know that you'll do the right thing when it's time.

Clay's surf sessions often begin long before he paddles out. Sometimes they start a night earlier, when he hops on his computer and
logs on to Surfline.com, Weather.com, and the official NOAA website to study wave forecasts and marine readings, particularly the
buoys positioned off Kauai, the Big Island, Maui, and Oahu. Located
miles out to sea, the buoys indicate the strength of incoming swells
by their size and interval.

Whenever he sees wide, consistent intervals on the screen, Clay's
face lights up: it is a sure sign of good waves. His energy surges, he
rubs his hands, and the pure joy of surfing and being at one with the
sea rushes through him, a joy countless people rarely feel in their
lives or occupations. It is the joy of connection, between a man, his
most primal instinct, and his element — water. All of this, with hours
left until the session itself. Can it get any better?

Clay pores over the other data like a crazed scientist to determine
direction, tidal and wind conditions, and what breaks will best receive the swell. Then he shifts into professor mode. "On Maui, you

always have to watch the easterly trades; they blow all the time. They make it choppy in a lot of places. You might get six-foot surf, but it's sketchy because of the wind," he says.

He runs the information through the virtual computer of his mind, which remembers every good wave, break, swell direction, and environmental circumstance that created all of the above. This unfettered brilliance is something that those outside Clay's tight nest of friends and associates rarely, if ever, see, but it is a brilliance to behold. "I check out the way the waves are breaking, how good their shape is, what kind of shape — Barrels? Peeling into long rides? — and where I can paddle out and catch waves no one else really sees. I check out the bottom at places I haven't seen as much. Rock reef? Coral reef? River mouth? Sand bottom? Shallow? Deep? A point break? Every type of bottom produces a different wave. I look at how the wind is moving the water around, what the currents are like, if there are rocks sticking up [out of the water], and how the waves are going to hold up. I don't really think about what I'm going to do until I take off, but I have an idea when I'm studying the surf. Sometimes you just have to get out there and know that you'll do the right thing when it's time."

"Clay has the ability to read waves like someone that has been surfing for a lifetime," notes Les Potts, a surfer since the late 1950s and a longboard legend to three generations. Adds Mitch Varnes, "I've spent many evenings at Clay's house when he'd be fixated on the Internet, and marine charts and Surfline and buoy readings and winds. He pours his brain into the ocean. Clay's as smart as or smarter than any surfer when it comes to breaks, how waves work, and how the conditions will be on any given day."

He's also as happy as any person alive when he's working it out — and even happier if he sees big surf approaching. Anyone seeing him in this space can't help but ask: *What can possibly be a better guarantor of lasting happiness than living in the moment like this, all the time? Especially when playing in the seventy-five-degree ocean?*

The next morning Clay departs from his usual habit of sleeping till midmorning and rises at daybreak. An exquisite spinal tingle courses through his body. He taps his hands on the steering wheel to blaring music as he races toward the Pacific. He talks a mile a minute, his voice rising and arcing like one of his aerials. He's amping, stoked beyond containment. *It's going to be a great day.* On days like this, his performances can change the way people view surfing, including their own abilities.

"When I see Clay surfing — and keep in mind, I've seen *a lot* of surfing, all the contests with Cheyne, with Clay, my own parents when I was growing up — I am in awe," Jill says. "Even the way he walks into the water, even walking on the rocks. It blows me away. It's not just the way he anticipates the wave, but before he gets wet; just the way he gets ready. He's probably already in the water and ripping in his head. You know how you see surfers who say, 'Oh, it's breaking over there, I'll just paddle over'? Clay processes in such a different way."

Carolyn Jackson has observed his routine plenty of times as well, and she remains as amazed as Jill. "Prior to him getting in the water, you can see the enthusiasm in his body. He's *getting ready* to be part of it. What I noticed is that Clay reads people, which is so unusual with people with Asperger's. He can go into a room, and he is taking in how you think of him. He's picking up your vibe. He has this ability to energetically feel what somebody is thinking about him. He does the exact same thing when he goes into the ocean. He's reading the ocean."

Reading the ocean. The phrase surfers commonly use is "checking out the surf," but that description is woefully inadequate when it comes to Clay's genius-level perception and encyclopedic knowledge of ocean conditions. He reads the sea with the expertise of a lifelong oceanographer, the intuition of a magician, the instinct of an athlete, and a laser-sharp eye for the slightest nuances in movement.

This became readily apparent while driving along the Maui coast one day, as Clay studied a ten-mile stretch in his search for quality waves. His approach is somewhat reminiscent of an Arctic peregrine falcon, which spends the short Arctic summer constantly hunting for hares, lemmings, and other small prey to feed its ever-hungry young. Likewise, Clay hunts for waves to feed a mind and spirit that will starve without its regular allotment.

"When it's small on Maui, I look at the wind," he explains. "I can kind of tell from the wind direction and buoy readings what it's do-ing on all the islands. If it's a north wind, then I know Ho'okipa will have something. That's the most consistent spot on the North Shore [of Maui], where I surfed a lot of contests when I was a kid. It picks up north swells. Even Hana catches a north; since it's so far southeast, it catches the north straight on. Hana catches east and south too. It doesn't get the west, because west of Hana is land . . . but we don't get the west either, and we live on the west coast! It sucks. Molokai and Lanai block it. We get all these little pop-gun waves. It has to be a hu-mongous west swell to even get in here; you have to go to Oahu. But Kauai gets everything; I think it's the best island for surf, the most consistent every day. It's bigger than anywhere else too, because it's the furthest island out [in the Hawaiian Islands chain], and it faces the open ocean. There's a lot more to choose from.

"On Maui, north is the best direction. Once swells get past Molo-kai and hit the north-facing breaks, it's good. We get good north and northeast swells. We'll get the north swells first, and sometimes the east, although the Big Island can get those first. I have a friend who lives near Hilo, on the Big Island, all rainy and green, and he calls me and tells me about these slabby waves that break into really shallow water, waves that only boogie boarders would normally ride. I like those kind of waves."

"Clay is part oceanographer, part fish, and part meteorologist. He's beyond what most people think of as wave knowledge," Adam Klevin says. "He's got it mapped out. He'll go, 'I'm going to get up at nine, and I'm going here because of the tide, then I'm eating lunch . . .' He's got it down to a science.

"I can't tell you how many times we've gone to film, and I look out and say, 'This is crap, it's all wind chop, there's nothing to shoot,' and Clay says to me, 'I see something; just start filming.' I go through the footage later, and he's gotten a half-dozen tube rides no one else would ever have seen coming. He reads the ocean better than any surfer I've ever known — and probably better than anyone *they've* ever known."

When Clay was being interviewed for the Little Tikes "Not So

Bored of Directors," he elaborated on his relationship with the ocean. "Yeah, I definitely see the ocean as a playground for me, because I read waves and that's what surfers do, we're like artists, we paint pictures on waves," he wrote. "We're artists. We read waves like a book. It's just like a book on a playground, we look at the waves and the waves are our playground but we read them like books.

"I'm probably just so comfortable because that's where my comfort zone is, in the ocean. That's when I'm having the most fun. I've been in the ocean since I was little and I'm a Cancer, which is a crab and I used to run rocks and find seashells on the beach for years before I surfed. I was always right on the ocean, so I knew one day I was gonna go out there and that would be my playground, and it truly is."

For years, many have wondered how Clay so consistently slots himself in sections of waves no one else can access, how he perceives those shelves, folds, creases, pulses, pockets, ledges, striations, and "slabs" that pop up out of nowhere. He views crappy blown-out chop as an opportunity to find a hidden nugget. These nuances are surfing's equivalent of the minutest cracks on a sheer rock face, unrecognizable to all but the most expert.

"I'd say Asperger's has something to do with it," he points out. "I focus a lot more and go off feeling. With Asperger's, you have a lot more sense of feel with the one main thing you like to do, and my thing is surfing. It has definitely helped me because I'm so critical about it.

"The waves work with me. They know I have to be out there; I can't handle it when I can't get in the water. When I get out there, we're together again. My friends look at me like I'm weird, but when I feel the ocean and the ocean feels me and we start working together, well, then the waves come to me and I ride with them."

"He's not going in there to catch a wave. He's going in there to be *part* of a wave," Jackson adds. "If you take a long look at how he approaches surfing, and how he gathers and uses his knowledge, then you will see the magical side of Asperger's open up before your eyes."

The legion of admirers continues with his girlfriend. "His connection with the ocean is beyond anything I've seen before," Jade says. "One thing me and my dad always trip out on is when he is paddling back out for another wave, and there's waves breaking past him, he tends to stop and sit on his board and get the view from the barrel. Then the wave just breaks straight over him and he goes right through. Anyone else would be getting sucked over the falls and smashed. He always knows where to be and is so fast to jump to his feet and already be standing in the barrel.

"Even in small, sloppy surf you wouldn't even think twice about going out in, he paddles out and gets five barrels. I watch him with his GoPro camera, mounted to his board or a helmet, in one-foot shorebreak. The way he sits in front of the wave, studying the face of it to see what it's going to do, he will end up nailing a shot!"

Mary Anna Waldrop Enriquez believes that Clay's superior perception of ocean and wave conditions and his interactions with them are parts of a larger gift he possesses: living completely in the present. "Clay sees the world around him in 360 degrees," she says. "When it comes to the ocean, he sees it from the other side of where we do, and he feels himself in it. When you're talking about reading the ocean, he is superior, because he sees and anticipates the subtlest things about water conditions and waves. Not only anticipates, but he knows where and how to look."

In his book *Edison Gene: ADHD and the Gift of the Hunter Child,* author Thom Hartmann describes the 360-degree mind in both primal and current terms as he seeks to dispel the prevailing notion that ADD and ADHD kids are problematic and need to be medicated to be in a classroom. "It's completely unnatural to be stuck in a classroom chair for five or six hours a day," he said in a 2002 interview with Robert Yehling. "Deep down, we're hunter-gatherers. Our ancestors had to be constantly alert and aware of everything around them. It was a matter of survival. If they thought too far ahead, or worried about what happened yesterday, they could die of starvation or be killed. Kids are naturally like that; when they play, they play with the mind-set of a hunter. When we start forcing them to sit in a classroom for four, five, six hours a day, as young as four years old, they grow fidgety and their attention wanders. Then they're diagnosed with ADD or ADHD and put on Ritalin. Truth is, they're just being true to their instinctual hunter's mind."

Clay's ability to recall every significant wave he has ridden over long stretches and utilize the lessons he learned on subsequent rides in similar conditions calls to mind the second half of Hartmann's description: *gatherers*. Attwood, Enriquez, and Jackson concurred in separate comments that the Aspie mind has a penchant for collecting and possessing items that pertain to a particular fascination or interest. Or, in Clay's case, collecting waves. "His ability to recall reminds me of *Rain Man*," Enriquez says. "It is such a powerful, powerful gift. First and foremost, we need to honor it. I think it's sacred; absolutely sacred. Clay's recall happens every second of every wave, along with the 360-degree view he uses to see and feel how everything feeds into that moment—and to *anticipate it*. Snap of the fingers. That instantly."

"He does remember almost all the waves he's ever surfed," Jackson adds. "Many surfers do that, but with him, it's a lot more detailed, and the knowledge is fully retained, like data in a computer, to be used later. He'll have people filming him, and he'll watch it over and over and over again. He's connecting with the rhythm. He doesn't think like some people, who are going to do different kinds of freestyle maneuvers. He's really getting into the motion. That's why so many people really want to watch him, because of that connection."

Another sunrise. Another day. Another surf inspection. Clay heads off to Scorps outside the south end of the Kapalua Resort, the steep, fast-breaking wave that he thoroughly enjoys surfing . . . when it's breaking.

"Scorps is kind of fun, because it's a little slab," he says. "It's kind of far out there, but it's a short little barrel wave, a steep little takeoff. It throws out and hits this shallow reef, and breaks real quick, so it's this quick little barrel. Then it kind of dies out, so you just cut back and . . ."

A smallish wave hollows out and breaks, a welcome sight during a week when Maui bore a better resemblance to the Gulf Coast. His eyes jump and gleam. "See that little right? *Spit—spit—*see that? You can cut back on that, and carve it . . . see how the next wave slabs up? Then it spits you out on the reef and you've got to watch yourself to not get cut up. It doesn't have to be very big to have fun out there."

He mentally departs from the grassy hillside on which he's standing, his entire focus situated 200 yards offshore. "There's a set! Look at the set coming! Look at the first one barreling . . . here comes one — look at this one, dude! See how you go underground when you're in there, then it throws you into the shallow? Sometimes there's a little left that goes into the bay, a re-form that happens when it gets really big — but you'd rather surf somewhere else . . . you don't want to surf out here when it's bigger than five or six feet. It gets too gnarly, closes out, and throws you on that shallow reef. This is a small wave spot. It's the steepest small wave around. It's best when it's glassy, but the wind's coming from a weird direction . . . see how the wave is balling up?"

On the daily ritual goes: stop at one location and read the waves. Study them and visualize the next ride, then study some more. When the waves prove insufficient, move on. All for a purpose. "In the water, it's all about tuning in to what the wave is giving me," Clay says. "When I get out there, the rest of the world is gone. Now I'm in my world. I feel and see the ocean in my head, everywhere inside me. I sweep it with my hands, and when I do that, I feel the push of the water. Or maybe the wind changes, new movement. Then I study the horizon and watch the bumps and look for little pockets where waves pop up."

Clay's former team manager at Quiksilver, Strider Wasilewski, is no stranger to riding waves of all shapes and sizes. He spent years as a professional surfer, surfing at hundreds of locations throughout the world and learning the ins and outs of surf conditions at a level few can approach . . . let alone exceed. Clay, he says, would "be reading waves and taking lines I'd never seen before. He does a lot of tactical surfing I've never seen anybody do. He does this no-paddle turnaround, takes off sideways, and makes it. He reads things in waves none of the rest of us can see. Sometimes he even reads these things from land."

Clay could be considered surfing's version of an expert reference librarian. He knows an entire collection on his chosen subject, from cover to cover, and can dispense insightful, helpful information whenever asked. While not the Dewey Decimal System, his mental cataloging is very proficient. Like reference librarians, he appreciates some "books" more than others and focuses even more intently on them to read between the lines. For Clay, those "books" are barrels. Tubes. Slabs. Shacks. They are the "promised land" for surfers everywhere. Since 2005, he has been regularly listed among the world's top five tube riders by magazines on four continents, and with good reason. Clay is a first-chair maestro when he slots himself inside waves, dropping into them from all points of the compass.

"I always look for barrels. When I'm in the barrel, I feel like I'm in heaven. I don't hear anything except the *whoosh* of the water. When I find a slab and get shacked, I never want to come out. Every time I do come out, I know I have to get back in there. So no matter what, I scratch around to find barrels. I have to."

"He can see a barrel like nobody," Klevin says. "He can read a barrel like nobody. And he can make a barrel—I mean, there's not a day that goes by, no matter how shitty the waves are, that he doesn't get barreled. I've seen him on one knee and one foot... he can make himself *so little* in the barrel. Clay is six-foot-one, and he squeezes into barrels that five-foot groms don't get into unless they're lucky. Clay's big, but he's got short legs. I've seen him knee-board through barrels. Unbelievable barrels. Just rising, falling, weightless, weightless, driving, driving, driving, on his knees."

Another Asperger's characteristic is his ability to focus until exhaustion sets in. He spends more time in the water than the average wave rider. *Much more.* World champions, peers, videographers, sponsors, photographers, and longtime friends all tell stories of epic Clay Marzo sessions when six, eight, or even ten hours passed without him offering any indication that he was done surfing. Three times he's been rushed to the hospital for saline solution IVs after becoming dehydrated from prolonged sessions. The others might surf, ride to shore, drink or eat, paddle out again, return to shore after tiring, fuel up, make their way back into the lineup... and there would be Clay, focused on his next ride. "I sometimes sit out there until I can't catch any more waves because I have to be out there and I can't miss any good waves."

"Clay knows where to be and when to be there," Varnes says. "You see some of his sideways takeoffs in the tube, and even for me as a longtime surfer, it's some of the craziest stuff I've ever seen. You can't even think of stuff like that. He takes off sideways, he takes off under the lip, he free-fall drops, he stands up in the barrel, he's just got this way . . . in his eyes, the waves come to him."

While in Indonesia, Clay asked Slater about his apparent communication with the open ocean, how it seemingly delivers waves to him at critical times. "Clay, you already know," Slater replied.

Klevin has seen and filmed more of Clay's rides than anyone on the planet, especially in the past ten years. As an obsessive-compulsive himself, Klevin has meticulously organized and cataloged all of the footage, all of the rides. Just when he believes he has witnessed everything, something else emerges from the way Clay reads the slightest wrinkle in an oncoming wave.

"I've probably seen 40,000 of his moves — no exaggeration — and I know when there's a really radical, full-rotation, fast, high one coming. Then he'll see something in it and surprise the hell out of me," Klevin says. "But you know what's amazing? He can *remember* those clips, no matter when they were shot, and he plays them over and over so they become part of his muscle memory. So when the next chance sets up, when his wave knowledge kicks in and he positions himself, his instinct and body take over. *Anywhere.*

"The thing that impresses me about Clay is that he's a reef warrior. He just doesn't get hurt much, which is really rare for someone who takes the risks he does. That's knowledge of the wave and the ocean bottom. I've seen him get hurt on the reef maybe three times. The kid can get dry-docked on the reef and then laugh about it. He's like Houdini. He really is. *Nobody* can go unscathed like that, throwing himself into big airs over dry reef. Nobody! You would have cuts every day. That's all the evidence you need as to how Clay has this sixth sense, how he knows when to pull in, when to get out, and *where on the reef* to bail, better than any surfer I've ever seen."

Once, after yet another ride left his jaw flat on the rocks, Klevin asked, "How do you do that, Clay? Where you get in there, and it's not even an open tube, and you're feeling your way in there, and everybody thinks you went down and all of a sudden it flaps open again and you come flying out?"

"You gotta trust the wave."

As Clay navigates through his midtwenties and he and Jade bring their lives closer together, it has become evident that his path forward again resembles the purity of a good surf session after years of confusion. There are very few road maps for how to handle global sports fame as a teenager, let alone a teenager with Asperger's syndrome. His gift took him to the top of the world, but the constant demands for his time, the travel requirements, and the pressure of remaining a hero and idol to millions of kids took a toll, primarily because Aspies are not wired with any mechanisms for coping with constant attention and outside expectations. And the higher anyone's star rises, the greater the expectations.

When Clay couldn't cope anymore, he tumbled, but out of it emerged a man who knows his talents and limitations much better, who understands what makes him happy and what doesn't, and who has found lasting love in his life, along with growing skills in expressing it and reciprocating it — a rarity for anyone on the autism spectrum. He'll always have trouble coping with some mundane functions of daily living, but that comes with the territory. Now, as he adapts to the new direction of his career, he again finds purpose in personal appearances, whether he's showing up for a four-day fashion photo shoot on a cold California beach in winter, visiting young surfers, or talking to autistic kids and their parents touched by his story.

Will Clay ever return to the competitive surfing arena on a regular basis? Probably not. When he's finished with something, he proclaims to everyone that he's over it, and that's that. *Finis.* Will he continue to dazzle the media and surfers around the world with his displays of wizardry on the waves of the world? Absolutely. He will move forward as a proud free surfer, an alluring lifestyle that copped, among others, three-time world champion and current folk rock musician

Tom Curren off the pro tour when he still had one or two more titles in his fuel tank. It's happened before.

Most of all, Clay finds happiness and contentment to be his regular companions. Sure, he "redlines" in bursts of anger sometimes, but he has also come to understand where his frustration spikes and how to deal with it. He may not talk about it — especially not with those he doesn't know, and even sometimes not with those he does — but all you have to do is watch the tall, blond figure cut his tracks on a wave to recognize what purity of joy and expression look like in the flesh. Of the many story lines that converge to form Clay Marzo's young life, that might be the greatest of them all. Most of us, whatever our age, can only hope to feel that way someday.

ACKNOWLEDGMENTS

From Clay Marzo

One of my greatest pleasures in putting together *Just Add Water* was not only discussing my journey with some of the most meaningful, helpful, and influential people in my life, but also reliving that journey with them. It is in that spirit I personally thank: my mom, Jill, for being the best ever; my dad, Gino, for being there and teaching me the goods in life; my brother, Cheyne, for the huge inspiration; my sister, Gina, for understanding me and always making me so proud; my girlfriend, Jade, for all you are and do; my nana and papa for your love and everything; my dog and best friend of fourteen years, Kalani; Johnno and the Barton family for making me a part of their family; Dooma for countless great photos, especially the ones in this book; Bob Yehling for the time, attention, and care in writing this book; Mitch Varnes for the support and many years of looking out for me and for finding my sponsors; Adam Klevin for the great times and film sessions and for taking all that sun; Jason Koons for the sick boards on usually short notice; and all my fans, supporters, and sponsors—you all are the ones keeping me amped!

I'd also like to thank John Oda, Keith Abraham, Carolyn Jackson, Lisa Hoogasian, Jamie Tierney, Strider Wasilewski, Israel Paskowitz, Doc Paskowitz, Mary Anna Waldrop, Quiksilver, Brian Robbins, Robbo and the Carve Guys, Mark Teperson and the whole crew at Super, Dave Nielsen at Kelly Slater's Kommunity, Rock Star Energy, Uncle Neil, Uncle Russell, Vince and everyone at Futures, and my Maui boys and Brent for the positive vibes and constant support.

From Robert Yehling

I would also like to thank Mitch Varnes for initially proposing the idea of this book; my literary agent, Dana Newman, for believing in the project, the story, and loving the sport and lifestyle of surfing; Jill Marzo for her unwavering focus on the goals of this book; Gino Marzo for sharing many great, insightful stories from being a devoted parent who sat at hundreds of contests while watching his son become great; my childhood friends Gary and Teresa Manguso, for inspiring me by telling me about their very talented surfing son, who lives with Asperger's; and Martha Halda, whose love and support fueled this author's efforts (not to mention a momentous trip to Maui during the project). Thank you, too, to those who moved through decades of surfing journalism and surfing promotion with me: George Salvador, Bill Missett, Allen Carrasco, Steve Scholfield, Kevin Kinnear, Ian Cairns, Jim Kempton, Paul Holmes, Dave Gilovich, *Encyclopedia of Surfing* author Matt Warshaw, Jim Watson, Mike and Val Bechelli, Debbie Beacham, Graham Cassidy, Al Hunt, Jill Wing, Alisa Schwarzstein, Randy Rarick, Fred Hemmings, Pat O'Neill, R. C. Benson, Greg Marshall, Selena Osterman, Rob McGrath, Carol Holland, Mark Hartman, and my all-time favorites to work with in surfing event promotion, 1976 world champion Peter Townend and Bob Hurley. Thank you all.

GLOSSARY OF SURFING TERMS

Surfing has some of the most colorful and expressive terms, slang, and collo-quialisms in all of sports. Since Clay Marzo is a lifelong surfer, he speaks the language, which appears throughout Just Add Water. *Here is a glossary of the terms used in the book.*

Aerial — Also known as "getting air" or "launching," a dynamic maneuver in which the surfer and his board completely break free of the wave's surface, then drop back into it. Clay Marzo has been known to bust off aerials as high as eight feet above the wave.

ASP — Association of Surfing Professionals, the sanctioning body of the World Championship Series and World Qualifying Series tours.

Backside — Surfing with one's back to the wave.

Barrel — Also known as "tube," "shack," "pipeline," "slot," "green room," or "slab," the hollow, cylindrical portion of the breaking wave. Most everyday surfers consider tube riding the most exciting and fulfilling part of surfing.

Bottom turn — A basic surfing move in which the rider takes off, stands up, rides to the bottom of the wave, then turns into the direction he or she will ride.

Cutback — A maneuver in which a surfer rides on the face of the wave, then suddenly switches gears and heads in the other direction. A variation is the "S-turn," in which the surfer cuts back and then switches again.

Dawn patrol — Early morning surf sessions, usually taking place between first light and sunrise.

Expression session — A noncompetitive surf session among friends, or contestants, in which they trade off their best moves for pure enjoyment. Also known as a "soul session."

Face — The surface of the breaking wave.

Floater — A beautiful, graceful maneuver in which the surfer rides on the foam of the breaking wave, "floating" until he or she returns to the bottom of the wave.

Frontside — Surfing while facing the wave.

Goofy foot — Surfing with the right foot forward. Clay Marzo is a goofy foot.

King tide — An unusually high tide, which typically happens during full moons and tends to increase wave size.

Layback—A surfing move in which the rider bends backward almost to a prone position while riding along the face of a wave or inside a tube.

Lineup—The spot where incoming waves form and break. The term is used to describe both specific locations and crowds in the water.

Lip—The front portion of a breaking wave. It somewhat resembles a waterfall, and can attain six feet of thickness in large surf.

Longboards—Surfboards generally exceeding eight feet in length. Longboards are typically ridden on slower-breaking waves, with a greater emphasis on stylistic riding than fast performance surfing.

Menehune—A Hawaiian term for young surfers, typically under age thirteen. Also known as "gremmies," "groms," and "grommets."

NSSA—National Scholastic Surfing Association, the most prestigious of several amateur surfing organizations in the United States. Clay Marzo surfed NSSA contests for ten years.

Offshore—The direction of wind when it blows into the breaking wave from the shore, causing the waves to hold up and improving conditions.

Off-the-top—A high-performance surfing maneuver in which the rider shoots to the top of the breaking wave and redirects by quickly snapping his board sixty degrees (or more) toward the unbroken surface.

Onshore—Wind blowing toward the shore. When an onshore wind is blustery enough, it diminishes wave quality.

Paddle out—Paddling from the shore into position to catch waves. In a far different circumstance, the term also describes a group of friends paddling into a circle to hold an in-water memorial for a fellow surfer who has died.

Pe'ahi—The Hawaiian name for a surf spot on North Maui called Jaws, which, along with Banzai Pipeline, is the most (in)famous big-wave break in the world.

Peak—The triangular point at the apex of a breaking wave.

Pocket—A term of wave positioning that means either (1) situated in the most powerful portion of a wave or (2) situated inside a barrel.

Reef break—A wave location that breaks over a rock or coral reef. Reef breaks typically produce steep, peeling waves that produce optimal rides.

Re-form—A wave that originally breaks outside, then dies down only to reshape and break again, usually on a sandbar or in very shallow water.

Regular foot—Surfing with the left foot forward.

Reverse throw-tail—A Clay Marzo signature move, and very difficult because of the coordination and torque involved. The surfer turns his or her board backward in a fast-moving wave, then snaps the tail (back) to its original position.

Secret spot—A choice location known to local surfers but rarely (if ever) publicized beyond their group (for fear of creating larger crowds in the water).

Set — A series of waves, breaking one after another at intervals of five to twenty seconds. Sets can range from three to ten waves, and more.

Shaper — The maker of surfboards. Much like golfers and their club sponsors, professional surfers form strong relationships with their board shapers to create the highest-performance, most customized boards to suit their style.

Shorebreak — Waves that break very close to shore. These waves are usually very steep and break top to bottom, or "walled off."

Short boards — Surfboards generally less than eight feet in length. The fast, sudden, acrobatic, and snappy maneuvers are usually performed on short boards.

Soul surfer — A term for a surfer more concerned with the lifestyle, travel, spirit, and culture of the sport than its competitive aspect.

Style — The combination of moves and approach to wave riding that defines individual surfers.

Swell — A distinctive increase in wave size, lasting several days and caused by storms in other parts of the ocean. Swells are usually fueled by winter storms, hurricanes, tropical storms, typhoons, or other large offshore wind disturbances.

Vertical — A dynamic maneuver in which the surfer rides up the wave face and points the nose of his or her board directly toward the sky, at a ninety-degree angle, then snaps the board back into the wave face and resumes the ride.

Wipeout — A word that speaks for itself. Generally, the bigger the wave, the more dramatic (and injury-prone) the wipeout.